Change of Seasons

Change of Seasons

A MEMOIR

JOHN OATES

with Chris Epting

St. Martin's Press
New York

www.stmartins.com

The Library of Congress Cataloging-in-Publication Data is available upon request.

ISBN 978-1-250-08265-7 (hardcover)
ISBN 978-1-250-08266-4 (e-book)
ISBN 978-1-250-13140-9 (signed edition)

Designed by Kathryn Parise

Our books may be purchased in bulk for promotional, educational, or business use. Please contact your local
bookseller or the Macmillan Corporate and Premium Sales Department
at 1-800-221-7945, extension 5442, or by e-mail
at MacmillanSpecialMarkets@macmillan.com.

First Edition: March 2017

10 9 8 7 6 5 4 3 2 1

This book is dedicated to my hometowns: New York, North Wales, Philadelphia, Woody Creek, and Nashville. Of those, Music City deserves a book of its own, but this is not it. This is a "first things first" kind of book. The story of being embraced by the music community that is the heart of Nashville will impatiently have to wait until the next volume, mostly because it means so much to me.

Contents

Say not always what you know, but always know what you say.

—TIBERIUS CLAUDIUS CAESAR AUGUSTUS GERMANICUS

Introduction

PARTNERSHIP

Over the years, I've been asked on innumerable occasions how I would describe my forty-five-year partnership and fifty-year friendship with Daryl Hall. The question invariably goes like this: "What is the secret to the longevity of your relationship with Daryl Hall?"—implying, of course, that some secret pact, some unholy all-powerful force, has forged a bond between these two physically mismatched humans that has endured, outlasting multiple marriages, love affairs, byzantine record-label contracts, Machiavellian business associations, insanely gifted bandmates, and hell-raising wackos.

It's actually extremely difficult to explain, and over my entire adult lifetime I've been prodded on a regular basis into examining the phenomenon in detail in order to distill the subtleties and complexities for journalists, fans, and musicians. Even more than with a band comprising multiple members, there has always seemed to be a more focused fascination with the dynamics of what makes a duo tick—how it works and, often, how it fails.

We are not a duo. That's the "how it works" part. We are two creative individuals with a mutual respect for each other's artistic skills and just enough intelligence to not get in each other's way. If you look at the covers of our albums, you will see a common thread that may seem rather insignificant, but in reality it is quite important. First you will see an album title, and then the names: Daryl Hall and John Oates. It has *never* been Hall & Oates. We have always insisted on being perceived as two individuals working together. "Sure," you say. "Semantics be damned." But it has always been very important for us to make that distinction, even though the world feels the need to truncate and find a convenient box to keep things nice and organized. But of course, there's a lot more to it.

As people, we share many commonalties that form the foundation of our brotherhood—and "brotherhood" is a much more accurate way to portray our relationship. First and foremost, we were both blessed to be born at the exact right time. We are both old enough to have witnessed the transition from the big band era to the birth and earliest days of rock and roll. Our parents are similar in age, and we both have one younger sister. We both grew up in small Pennsylvania towns, listened to the same radio stations, went to the same type of high schools, became band leaders at an early age, and were drawn toward the city of Philadelphia and some unforeseen greater destiny.

As for the differences—let's just say we each have our own individual life-style philosophies and peculiar strategies for maneuvering through the world, all the while focusing on one unwavering and clear goal: continue making music for the rest of our lives. If you must delve and really want to know more, just listen to our songs and read the lyrics.

We became friends before we became musical and business partners. We hung out, goofed off, played with many different bands and other musicians. Then, in late September 1970, I returned from Europe and, to my surprise, found a padlock on the apartment that I had sublet to Daryl's sister, Kathy, and her boyfriend. That's when I went knocking on the blue-painted door of the quaint, colonial era Father, Son, and Holy Ghost house situated on narrow, cobblestoned Quince Street. (Father, Son, and Holy Ghost houses, or Trinity houses, were nicknamed that due to their unique, three-story design, with one room per floor. Unique to Philly, they were originally built for slaves or indentured servants).

At the time Daryl was married to a gal named Bryna and living there with a little red dog named Jo. After four months busking my way across Europe, all I had was my guitar and backpack. I was broke, with no apartment. Daryl and his wife weren't exactly expecting me to arrive on their doorstep, but without a lot of drama, they kindly invited me to move into their tiny, third-floor room, which was crammed with a sofa bed, volumes of books on sagging wooden shelves, an ancient fireplace, and an old Wurlitzer piano.

That was when Daryl and I started writing songs.

Before I began this book project one of my biggest concerns was how I would be able to tell my personal story without it becoming the Hall and Oates story minus Daryl Hall. For there can be no story of our partnership and music without him—as there can be no John Oates story without the Hall and Oates experience that has dominated most of my adult life. So as the words herein unfold, please try to understand that any lack of details regarding Daryl Hall's massive talent and enormous contribution to our music and success is not intended to diminish his importance and personal achievement. Daryl has his own unique and powerful story. One day he may choose to share it . . . or maybe not. But until then, I can only offer my own story.

Just a Kid

t's Thursday night, May 23, 1985.

Daryl Hall and John Oates are on top of the world at this point in my life.

Six number one *Billboard* hits
Thirty-four chart hits
Seven Platinum albums
Over forty million albums sold
MTV stars
Thousands of live performances
Fame, fortune, freedom

And that's barely the half of it. My name is John Oates, and it's hard to describe the lives we now lead. How did we get here? Simple. We worked like dogs. We drove tens of thousands of miles. And we never gave up in the face of failure.

. . .

BACKSTAGE. THE AIR is thick where we sit, sunk low, like twin suns surrounded by swirling planets of friends, music-business honchos, and New York City glitterati. The concert has just ended and we are at an after-show reception backstage at the Apollo Theater in Harlem. There is no more important place for us to be at this moment. This is the church of rhythm and blues.

And now we sit in silence, floating on a hot-and-sweaty high, having just come offstage with the original and legendary lead singers of the Temptations: David Ruffin and Eddie Kendricks.

Backstage at the Apollo. Left to right: Eddie Kendricks, me, Daryl, and David Ruffin.
(Courtesy John Oates)

Daryl Hall, whom I've now known for about eighteen years, is sitting next to me. The first night we ever really hung out together, back in '67, was here at the Apollo. Daryl had arranged for us to go backstage so I could meet the Temps. He thought I'd be impressed, and he was right. Daryl's group the Temptones had been discovered by them at the Uptown Theater in Philly. As we stepped through the legendary stage door from the back alley, leaving reality behind, David Ruffin, always the outsider, was slouched in the dark stairwell, leaning against the banister, cigarette dangling from his million-dollar mouth, his eyes half closed behind his trademark black, thick-framed glasses. Inside the small dressing room, the rest of the group casually milled about until we walked in. Then Paul Williams, who had taken Daryl and the Temptones under his wing a few years earlier, greeted us warmly, as did Melvin Franklin, Otis Williams, and Eddie. For me, that moment was a dream come true.

As the lights went down for the show we were escorted to front-row seats. Bathed in deep-blue light, the Temptations appeared: Shimmering silk suits, blade sharp, steps synced around the iconic single chrome stand with four microphones, like branches extended in an arc. Professional in every way imaginable, while delivering vocally with a blend that was at once effortless and spiritual. These memories and emotions played through my mind again in 1985, as I sensed a soulful cosmic circle completing itself.

Surrounded but oblivious to the well-wishers and after-show celebrations, Daryl and I just sat quietly, looking at each other. So much had transpired since we met, that night we escaped with our lives, both our groups crammed together in the service elevator at the old Adelphi Ballroom in Philly while a gang fight raged out front, in the house. Nearly two decades have passed, we don't have to talk that much; we share emotions unspoken. We've been to hell and back more than a few times. But oh, what we have to show for it.

Amid the celebratory chaos and surrounded by all of the triumphant, joyous, and boisterous noise that follows a once-in-a-lifetime show like we just performed, a calm silence hovers in the space between us. But that's the cocoon that's formed over the years, I guess. We just looked at each other. He knows. I know.

We both sense it.

"We did it, man."

"Yeah. We did it."

"There's only one place left to go."

"Down."

In that moment, we nod knowingly at each other. Our partnership started here and, for the time being, it will end here.

No big announcements necessary. Just an intuitive understanding based on thousands of shared moments that it's time for both of us to explore new things.

The legendary pianist Arthur Rubinstein said, "The seasons are what a symphony ought to be: four perfect movements in harmony

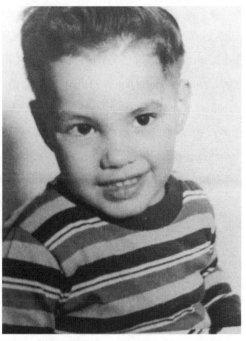

"Just a kid," early 1950s. *(Courtesy John Oates)*

with each other." Growing up on the East Coast, the change of seasons dictated your rhythm of life. That's how I grew up.

As a kid, I found the change of seasons whimsical. But now, having grown a bit older, I know the seasons go beyond just weather. They become metaphorical. We measure our lives against them. They reflect the circumstances of our existence.

And there would never be a season in my life quite like the one I was about to experience.

I DON'T CARE about fame. I've always been famous. This is not a boast, it's just a fact. Being born the first male grandchild in a matriarchal Italian family bestows one with an anointed position from birth. Being naturally blessed with musical talent ratchets up that status. And so from birth an imaginary crown was placed atop my developing personality.

I am the son of the greatest generation, the ones who won the war, who would build the next chapter of the American Dream, the progeny of turn-of-the-century immigrants from Europe. My father's father was an English military policeman stationed on the Rock of Gibraltar who married a local girl of Spanish and Moorish descent. They came to America right after World War I. Around the same time, a young couple from the Salerno area in southern Italy made that same pilgrimage across the Atlantic, through Ellis Island, settling in the growing Italian ghetto of Manhattan's Lower East Side.

Thursday April 7, 1948, Al Jolson was voted most popular singer in America by *Variety* magazine and Columbia Records introduced the new 33⅓ long-playing record album. At 1 A.M. that day, I was introduced to the world at Bellevue Hospital in New York City, starring as the first child born to Anna and Alfred Oates.

To say that I was a hit from the moment I was born would not be far from the truth. Like I said, as the first male grandson in an Italian immigrant family, my revered position was established before I could utter a sound. A few years later when I began to sing, the coronation was uncontestable.

But thirteen months later, I was back in that same hospital, rushed into the emergency room with a severe tonsil infection. The doctors informed my parents that it would be best to remove my tonsils. After the operation, in the middle of the night, with my father and mother keeping vigil by my crib, I suddenly began coughing up blood. My panic-stricken parents screamed for help. As nurses rushed

My parents, Anna and Alfred, as they are as of this writing. *(Courtesy John Oates)*

me into the operating room, they told my parents, "He's drowning in his own blood . . . we need to cut open his throat." The stiches had broken and there was no time to spare. I can only imagine the horror my mother and father, just in their early twenties, must have felt hearing those words. My mother pleaded with the doctors to not cut open my throat but was told surgeons didn't think they could operate effectively through the tiny mouth of an infant. Dr. Thoie, the man in charge, told my folks that he would try his best and somehow he managed without cutting my throat open. He saved my life and my career. I don't even know his first name, but I owe him everything.

MY MOTHER'S LARGE Italian family, who all lived within a few blocks of each other in the lower twenties between First and Third Avenues, dominated my early life. In the neighborhod I grew up in, wash was done by hand, clothes hung on the fire escapes to dry; kids escaped the summer heat by playing in the gushing water of illegally wrenched-open fire hydrants; the Catholic church said the mass in Latin and Italian. On the other side of the East River, in Queens, my father's side of the family seemed to gradually slip away. Over time they became seldom-seen shadowy relations.

At the tender age of two, perched upon my mother's knee, I made my first record: An acapella rendition of "Here Comes Peter Cottontail" etched into lacquer in a tiny Voice-O-Graph recording booth at Coney Island. For about forty cents, anyone could record their own voice direct to disc. I still have that record! A few years later I'd return to that same booth, this time on my own two feet, for an encore recording: "All Shook Up," the Otis Blackwell classic that I heard Elvis singing on the radio.

I couldn't explain it. I just knew: I was a singer.

My mother wasn't shy about encouraging my young gifts, so in no time I was glued to the little AM radio in our Lower East Side tenement apartment, learning the hits of the day—in English and, in some cases, Italian. My mom's side of the family, the Italian side, dominated over the British/Spanish back-ground of my dad's side, and so that's what I mostly identified with as a kid.

I may have been praying for a guitar. *(Courtesy John Oates)*

My first gig was a weekly residency down in my Uncle Joe's basement in Bergenfield, New Jersey. That's where our big family would gather on Sunday afternoons, the long plastic-covered table overflowing with antipasti, lasagna, or macaroni with meatballs and sausage, and Uncle Joe's sweet homemade red wine served in tiny milk glasses. Then, for dessert, it was showtime!

With my biggest fan, the loud and flamboyant Aunt Mary, front and center, I would step out onto the black-and-white-checkered linoleum floor and rip into a heart-wrenching rendition of Johnnie Ray's 1952 torch ballad, "Cry," tearing at my shirt and dropping to my knees to bring it home. My big finish would invariably be a Jerry Vale or Perry Como number, usually in Italian, while my grandmother clapped along, laughing, her big gold teeth flashing in the soft basement lights.

There was always music in our apartment. My parents loved to dance the jitterbug and Lindy Hop to the big band music of their teenage days, and that became the soundtrack of my first couple of years. I loved it then, and I love it now. After every song my father would tell me who was playing, "That's Tommy Dorsey . . . that's Lionel Hampton . . . that's Benny Goodman . . . that's Glenn Miller . . ." The sophisticated, complex arrangements, the beautiful, memorable melodies oozed from the thick, warm pads of saxophones and clarinets were punctuated and slammed home by the bright blasts of energy from the brass sections. I still listen to the big bands today and to me, they sound like childhood.

·   ·   ·

When I was four years old my sister, Diane, was born. With my dad gone all day at work and my mom tending to the new baby, I would spend long afternoons and evenings at my grandma's nearby apartment.

Her name was Clementina DePalma and she was the mother of seven children: four daughters and three sons. Her husband, my grandfather, died the year I was born, so I never really knew him. The only thing I have to remember him by is a tiny $2.50 gold piece that he bequeathed to me for my first birthday. It was a magnanimous gift and I'm sure

No doubt from one of the countless talent shows I performed in throughout the 1950s. *(Courtesy John Oates)*

a huge sacrifice. My grandmother lived alone in a tenement in an Italian neighborhood, just around the corner from us, on Twenty-sixth Street between First and Second Avenues. She was a character. She didn't really speak to me in English, except when I would ask her where my mom was. That's when she'd chuckle and say, in her thick Italian accent, "She went-a to Cali-forn-ia." She thought that was just the funniest thing. It was her favorite broken-English punch line.

"Grandma, where's my mommy?"

"She went-a to Cali-forn-ia."

While Grandma cooked in the kitchen (and she was always cooking in the kitchen), I'd spend hours kneeling on a hassock, leaning on my elbows and staring out the third-floor window, gazing through the iron grate at life below, on the Lower East Side street. The neighborhood for a few square blocks was populated entirely by Italian immigrants and the air in the streets smelled like warm bread and pastries wafting from the local bakery. Down below, the occasional fruit vendor would make his way slowly down the block on a squeaky cart pulled by an old, worn-out horse. It was always cool, quiet, and sanctuary-like in that apartment. Grandma's dark wooden bureau displayed a carefully placed collection of religious icons: silver crosses and hand-carved wooden rosary beads along with small, framed pictures of Jesus and Mary, as well as other assorted, mysterious saintly figures. In the kitchen, Grandma would knead and roll pasta dough into flat, thin noodles that she then spread out on a white linen sheet on her bed. Later that day she would layer them with fresh mozzarella, ricotta, ground beef, and savory sausage, and cover it all in a fragrant red sauce that had been simmering for hours on the stove top.

The warm apartment would fill with tantalizing aromas from the fresh ingredients until finally, from the oven, the mouthwatering masterpiece would appear, hot and bubbling in the pan. It tasted like a religious experience. When she made spaghetti and meatballs, Grandma would always pick one or two meatballs out of the pot and present them to me on a plate. No one else was allowed in the kitchen. I was the first male grandchild, and in an Italian family, that made me the boy king. Nobody was ever spoiled more than I was by my grandma.

When Grandma was finished cooking, we celebrated with spumoni or cherry-vanilla ice cream, which she liked to eat straight out of the cardboard carton. A few years later, after she moved in with my Uncle Joe and Aunt Lou in Jersey, she added watching professional wrestling on a

Modeling my new Lone Ranger outfit at Christmas, early 1950s. (*Courtesy John Oates*)

small black-and-white TV to her list of life's simple indulgences. Anyone who really knows me will recognize that my tastes run along exactly the same lines!

After the war my dad had bounced around doing odd jobs, but in 1947 he was hired by the Transicoil Corporation. During this postwar period, Manhattan actually had an industrial base, and this upstart company produced electric motors used in the navigation systems of the burgeoning new guided-missile programs that were expanding as the Cold War era loomed. But by the 1950s, Manhattan real estate values were forcing the city's industries to relocate. Transicoil Corporation was moving its operation to a freshly built facility in rural Pennsylvania, located in a big field adjacent to a new Nike guided-missile base. Any employees willing to move with the company from New York City would be promoted, so my dad made a bold decision . . . one that would forever change my life.

IT WAS JUNE of 1952, just another ordinary hot summer afternoon in the city. In the middle of the block, some older kids had wrenched open a fire hydrant and were playing in the gush of water. A few doors down I was bouncing on an old discarded mattress on the sidewalk with another little boy who lived nearby, on Twenty-fourth Street. Suddenly I heard my mom calling, and I ran toward her. There, idling by the curb in front of our apartment, was a dull-green 1947 Chrysler sedan. It was my father's first car. I hopped into the back seat and moments later, with his young family settled inside, my dad pulled the car away from the curb and we drove west toward Pennsylvania. We were moving . . . just like that.

Our destination was the small country town of North Wales, about twenty-five miles north of Philadelphia. Going from an ethnic, urban, melting pot like New York City to this little village settled by Welsh immigrants back in the 1700s, where the community was made up primarily of folks with German-sounding names along with a scattering of Amish and Mennonites, was a true culture shock. We moved into a small upstairs apartment in a clapboard house adjacent to the Reading railroad tracks. The house was on a quiet tree-lined street in the old part of town. Not too far away was a huge pig iron foundry that belched black smoke and employed many of the local residents. Coming from New York City, my family and I were outsiders in a strange, small-town world.

I don't recall seeing much of my father after we moved because he worked two jobs. He seemed to be gone all the time. I'm sure my mother had her hands full dealing with a rambunctious four-year-old boy and an infant baby girl all by herself. She was only twenty-four years old, had no friends, and no family. . . . I'm sure it was very hard on her.

Eventually my father received the promised promotion and became a supervisor in the company. Shortly afterwards, courtesy of the GI Bill, we moved into a newly built house on Tenth Street, at the outskirts of town. Our yard backed up to a sheep farm with an old red barn decorated with huge hex signs. I wasted no time exploring this strange new world of woods and fields, learning how to trap muskrats in the creeks, making friends, playing war with the local kids, and just living the life of a transplanted country boy in this innocent and beautiful 1950s setting.

New York had yellow taxicabs. North Wales had black Amish buggies. You could walk the length of the entire town in about twenty minutes. And good luck trying to find sausage and peppers, linguini, and cannoli. This place was more about Pennsylvania Dutch food like Lebanon baloney, scrapple, pickled beet eggs, and the local regional delicacy, the famous submarine sandwich known as the "hoagie."

But thankfully, I had the best of both worlds, because we drove back and forth to New York City pretty much every weekend. My folks were homesick and missed their friends and family. The long drive was boring, but there was one saving grace: the radio.

My baby sister, Diane, and I would lounge on the sofalike backseat of the lumbering Chrysler. The musty, soft, fuzzy upholstery made the car feel like a rolling living room as I watched the Pennsylvania countryside pass until it gradually dissolved into the suburban sprawl of New Jersey. I would press my face up against the window when the majestic New York City skyline appeared, as we crossed the final bridge on the Pulaski Skyway before rolling underground into the Holland Tunnel.

There were dull metal slats on the bridge that, as I gazed through them from the backseat window, created a flickering illusion, much like an old-time black-and-white movie. As we approached the city, the static on the AM radio began clearing and big band music filled the car, making the perfect soundtrack to accompany the strobelike, hand-cranked, cinematic effect.

My dad would always tune the dial to a show called *Make Believe Ballroom* on WNEW radio. It was hosted by Martin Block, who was different from other announcers on the radio. He wasn't corny and didn't speak in a big radio voice. He was low-key and spoke just like a regular guy, which for some reason made me pay attention. Block's *Ballroom* also had a "Saturday Night in Harlem" segment, where Cab Calloway, Louis Armstrong, Duke Ellington, and other jazz musicians' music were featured.

When the big, roomy Chrysler would emerge from the darkness of the Holland Tunnel into the light of Canal Street and glide through Greenwich Village, my mother would invariably turn from the front seat and say, "Johnny, this is the Village. This is where the kooks live." We were driving through the heart of the Beat Generation's neighborhood and to my mom, that's what the Beatniks were: "kooks." Little did I know then, that years later that's exactly where I would end up living . . . a rock-and-roll kook! Perfect!

Around this time I attended my very first concert. My folks took my sister and me to the nearby Willow Grove Amusement Park, a circa-1890s park midway between North Wales and Philadelphia. One magical summer evening my life changed as I stood near the edge of the stage, under the arch of the bandshell where years before John Philip Sousa had regularly performed for more than twenty years. That night the headliner was Bill Haley & His Comets. The moon-faced Haley, with that famous spit curl, in his black pants and ivory-colored dinner jacket, backed by five guys all dressed exactly like him, kicked it off with his now-famous opening: "One, two, three o'clock, four o'clock *rock*!" With the distant roar and screams coming from the Thunderbolt roller coaster in the background, that was all it took. My clock was rocked.

Even at that young age, I was deeply affected by the performance. I pushed my way up to the lip of the low stage to get closer to the heat and the jacked-up rockabilly beat. Haley, with his honey-brown sunburst Gibson, cut a hypnotic and powerful image, filling the sultry moonlit night with punchy, early rock-and-roll classics like "Shake, Rattle and Roll," and "See You Later, Alligator." The upright bass player, Marshall Lytle, straddled his instrument and rode it like a wild bucking bronco. Wide-eyed, I took it all in. This was *not* big band music. It was something entirely new, young, and alive.

Bill Haley, whose show at a Philly amusement park made a deep impact on me. *(Courtesy John Oates)*

My next rock-and-roll epiphany came later that year, in November 1956, when my Aunt Mary took me to see Elvis Presley's screen debut, *Love Me Tender*, at the Paramount Theater at Forty-third and Broadway in New York City. As we approached the theater, weaving through the hundreds of teenage girls who were obviously infatuated with Elvis since his first appearance a month before on *The Ed Sullivan Show*, something amazing caught my eye. Gazing up through the throngs of bundled-up New Yorkers was a spectacular, two-story-high cardboard Elvis (with guitar) mounted on the building above the marquee. He looked Olympian and godlike to a kid like me.

The lights dimmed in the majestic theater and about twenty minutes into the Civil War–era western, many of the girls started screaming for apparently no reason, as three men rode up on horseback. Huh? None of these guys looked like Elvis, but then I figured it out. In the distant background, barely discernible, a young man and a mule were plowing a field—just a speck on the screen. Many of the girls had apparently spent the day watching the film over and over, and they knew. The plowboy was Elvis, and the mere hint of him on screen was enough to spark a primal kind of insanity. Later, when he performed the film's title song, many in the house wept.

Nobody cried at Bill Haley. This guy was different. This guy was reaching kids on an entirely different level.

Weeks later, I was back at the Voice-O-Graph machine at Coney Island, plunking down another couple of quarters to record my own aforementioned rendition of Presley's version of the Otis Blackwell-penned classic, "All Shook Up." I was all in.

BY THE LATE 1950s, my grandma had moved to New Jersey to live with my Uncle Joe and my godmother, Aunt Lou. Since that was where Grandma was, that's where our large family would gather, and we ended up spending many weekends in Bergenfield, New Jersey. Still the anointed one in my grandma's eyes, I was the only one allowed in the kitchen while she cooked, and she always made sure I got to taste the first meatball. She also spoke a bit more broken English by then, and would smile as she advised me, "Play-a violin, Johnny. Real musicians play-a violins, not-a guitars."

Besides my mother and grandma, my Aunt Mary, who had no children of her own, was probably my biggest fan. Family legend has it that when I was just old enough to talk, she would roll me in a baby carriage down the block, stopping in front of a bunch of mechanics who worked at the local garage on Twenty-fifth Street and making me sing for them. She also dropped me headfirst onto the concrete stoop in front of my grandma's apartment. The fall split my chin open, which didn't go over very well with my mom, who never really forgave her for it. Aunt Mary was pretty flamboyant. Her husband, Sammy, was a butcher. They drove a big two-toned Mercury convertible and were both incorrigible gamblers; she would babysit me by taking me to Belmont race-track to bet on the horses. I guess she was the black sheep of the family. Maybe that's why I loved her so much . . . she was fun.

But as I got a bit older, those family get-togethers became much less fun. I wanted to stay in Pennsylvania and practice my guitar and hang out with my friends.

The First Lessons

When I was about five years old my mom thought I might like to take accordion lessons. I'm not really sure why, other than because she recognized that I had some musical talent and the only music teacher in the small town of North Wales was a semifamous guy named Wayne Barrie. Mr. Barrie's claim to fame was that he had performed on the Lawrence Welk TV show, and rumor had it that he was one of the first people to build and play an electric version of the traditional bellows accordion. He was the only game in town, so I took my first lesson on one of his little student-model accordions. It was red, and I hated it. After my first lesson I put it in the front room closet and didn't take it out until the following week, when it came time for my next lesson. After about three weeks of no interest and no practice, Mr. Barrie kindly suggested to my parents that perhaps I wasn't very interested in the old squeezebox. Boy, was he right. I wanted to play the guitar, just like Elvis.

One of my best friends was a kid named Dick Reiner. He was a year older than me and lived down at the end of Tenth Street in North Wales. He had an older brother and the two fought like cats and dogs. While they ran around the house, beating each other with broom handles, I would sneak down into the basement and explore their father's wood shop. He made bass fiddles as a hobby, and over in the corner, tossed to the side, I found a crude guitar that he had made. The fingerboard was painted dull silver, and he had hand painted hearts, spades, clubs, and diamonds for fret markers. It called to me, and I asked him if I could borrow it. He told me I could have it! So with my first guitar under my arm, I walked home to ask my parents if I could take guitar lessons.

A few miles away, in the town of Lansdale, was a music store called the Betty Reichenbach School of Music. I remember my first lesson like it was yesterday, walking in with the handmade guitar and sitting in a small room and meeting a very large lady who would be my teacher. I remember that before we began, my mom mentioned to the teacher that I was left-handed. I'll never forget her saying, "Oh that doesn't matter he'll do just fine." She probably didn't want to deal with turning the guitar upside down and restringing it, and so to this day, I play in the conventional right-handed way. I often wondered what my playing would have been like if I had learned to play left-handed.

Upstairs in the same building a woman named Verna Kerr gave vocal lessons, so naturally my folks signed me up with her as well, and we would go to Lansdale twice a week, once for guitar and once for vocal lessons. Mrs. Kerr had a big, dramatic personality and presided over her little second-floor studio as if it was a portal to the Great White Way. She reeked of old-fashioned perfume, had a teased-up bubble hairdo, wore heavy makeup, and acted as though she was perpetually ready for her curtain call. A young, blond, high-school gal with a ponytail served as an accompanist and sat at an upright piano playing for all the students. I thought she was pretty and liked sitting alongside her on the piano bench while Verna pressed her hand into my stomach and forced me to breathe from my diaphragm. Hours were spent vocalizing assorted vowel sounds and performing the dreaded Broadway show tunes that she favored. Yes, I know them all . . . *Brigadoon, South Pacific, Oklahoma*, and of course the standards from the 1920s, '30s, and '40s.

My vocal teacher had a pipeline of sorts for her stronger students to audition on an amateur-hour-style live revue held at Atlantic City's famous Steel

Pier. It was called *Tony Grant's Stars of Tomorrow*. So when she deemed me ready we headed "down the shore." As we approached the boardwalk the first thing that hit me was the salty ocean breeze; from afar I could see the platform for the famous diving horse, the water circus, and other well-known attractions. But I was there to sing, not eat saltwater taffy, play skeeball, or gawk at the sideshow.

I'll never forget the audition. There was a hole on the stage, in front of the mark where I stood, and on cue, a microphone magically appeared from below; a prop elevator slowly lifted it up to the stage, stopping it at my lips. The bored-stiff pianist began reading my sheet music, and I dutifully did my version of the brand-new hit "Nel blu dipinto di blu," better know as "Volare," as recorded by the singer/songwriter Domenico Modugno. Just like him, I sang it in Italian.

I didn't make it past the audition, but the experience was a revelation, a childhood step up to a bigger stage, and a confrontation with the reality that I was not the only star in the show business universe. I was working through the process of honing my chops, paying some young dues, and learning what it takes to be a performer.

BEING A '50s kid, I wanted to sing the rock-and-roll songs that were just starting to be played on the radio at the time.

There was a teenage boy living in the house next door to us, and on Saturday afternoons he would wash his 1955 Ford convertible. He'd always have the radio tuned to WIBG, the first Philly radio station to program all rock and roll, which at the time was a big deal. I used to sit on the front lawn and listen while Fats Domino, the Everly Brothers, Buddy Holly, Elvis, Conway Twitty, Chuck Berry, and Little Richard screamed from the crackly little speaker. That was the stuff I wanted to sing, not those frumpy Broadway songs. But as long as Verna Kerr was choosing the repertoire and the chick with the ponytail was playing the piano, I was stuck. Unless I could learn enough chords on the guitar. . . . Fortunately, it only took three or four chords in those days, so it wasn't long before I was bringing my guitar to the vocal lessons and trying to accompany myself.

Once every summer, Verna Kerr would bring all her vocal students to perform at a small amusement park next to a river in Sellersville, Pennsylvania, about twelve miles from North Wales. My mom would dress me up in a red blazer. I can still hear her voice: "Johnny you look so good in red." The outfit also included white shirt, white pants, and dreaded white bucks that were impossible to keep clean. I'd catch hell for every smudge. Then I'd have to wait around all day to sing a song or two in the hot afternoon sun. All I wanted was an ice cream cone and to go on the rides but no . . . "Ice cream isn't good for your voice" said Mrs. Kerr, while Mom sagely nodded over her shoulder in agreement. Eventually they would trot me out on stage and I'd belt out the old Judy Garland tune, "For Me and My Gal," or "Five Foot Two Eyes of Blue" to the small audience of farmers and old ladies sitting on the grass in front of the band shell. That's when I really started practicing the guitar, so I could play and sing the kind of songs I wanted to.

My mom, being a bit of a stage mother, pushed me to perform at every opportunity in our area. Oddball shows like playing before the perversely entertaining Donkey Baseball game, the annual North Wales Lions Club Fun Fair, and an actual minstrel show with local parents and teachers in blackface. However nothing compared with the harrowing experience of doing a Christmas show deep in the bowels of the Norristown insane asylum (as it was called in those days). If I had a time machine I would love to travel back to 1956 for the chance to question the logic of the person who thought that it might be a good idea to bring a group of seven- and eight-year-old children to perform in such a place.

The Norristown State Hospital, built in 1880 and originally known as the State Lunatic Hospital at Norristown, was a massive stone building complex that resembled a haunted castle. It was dominated by an imposing red stone tower and populated with the mentally unstable patients marginalized by the medical profession or the legal system of Southeastern Pennsylvania. The idea was sold to little seven-year-old Johnny as just another Christmas show at a hospital, but after hopping out of our '55 Chevy Bel Air into the cold December air, I began to sense that this would be no ordinary holiday show. A burly uniformed guard was standing beside a heavy wooden door with a small, barred window in the center. Once inside, our little troupe was herded down a cold, dank, institutional, green-tile tunnel with an arched ceiling. At first the only thing I could hear was my footsteps tapping along the concrete floor, losing pace with the rapidly increasing beating of my heart. After what seemed an eternity, I began to notice strange sounds coming from somewhere up ahead. We emerged from the tunnel into a larger room and found ourselves facing a semicircle of inmate/patients dressed in what looked to be filthy pajamas or ill-fitting hospital gowns. Many were seated in wheelchairs and secured by thick brown leather straps. Behind them, along the back wall, were a group of green uniformed orderlies on guard, but they were of little consolation. My heart pounded and my mind reeled trying to process what my innocent eyes were seeing. All I could hear was moaning, unintelligible groans, and incoherent commentary coming from the twisted, tortured, and distorted faces. I was freaked out years before the phrase was invented: *Sing? Here? Now?*

I don't remember much more. I must have managed to make it through a Christmas song . . . but that's about it. An experience like this might well have wounded a kid for life, but when a wound heals, it leaves a welt of thicker, tougher skin behind. As time's gone by, when people ask me if I get nervous before going on stage, I always reply, "Not really."

The First Season

SERIOUS MUSIC
1960s

Racing

should have been studying . . . well, in a way, I was. Tucked away in the corner of the Pennbrook Junior High School library I had my geography book open, but was quietly concentrating on the tattered old *Road & Track* magazine hidden between the textbook pages, focused on absorbing all the minute details of the legendary Grand Prix racing season from that year. The issue was one of many that I found while walking along a tree-lined street in North Wales. The magazines, which dated to the early '50s, were tossed in a cardboard box destined for the dump, but became a source of inspiration and an education for me in 1962.

I lugged the box home and immersed myself in the legend and lore of the racing car. The exotic sounding names of the European Grand Prix circuits like Monaco, the Nürburgring, Spa, and Monza, as well as classic long-distance sports car events: Le Mans, the Mille Miglia and the Targa Florio were fascinating and intriguing to me. The drivers: Nuvolari, Fangio, Ascari, Moss, Clark, Stewart, and Hill seemed heroic. These were extraordinary figures whose triumph and tragedies I followed through the stories and photos on the pages. Oil-streaked machines—their drivers' faces covered with soot, white ovals where their goggles had been, surrounding clear, fearless eyes—alive in victory and defeat. It was a glimpse into an exotic world far from my little Pennsylvania town. It was as though I could smell the fumes and feel the ripping, crackling sound from the straight exhaust pipes as the daring *pilotes* manhandled their *bella machinas* to victory and, all too frequently, death.

From the quiet corner of the school library, I was transported. My youth and inexperience could not fully process the reality of this high-octane otherworldly place, but these larger-than-life figures and their exotic, deadly playgrounds gripped me with a passion I could not shake.

America's racing scene during that time seemed a bit more homespun. Yes, the Indianapolis 500 was and still is a legendary, world famous event, but at the core of the sport were the many local asphalt-and-dirt short tracks from coast to coast. These banked bullrings were the backbone of America's oval-track heritage. Just a few miles from the little town where I lived was such a track: Hatfield Speedway.

On most summer Saturday nights, the dusty haze kicked up by the race car tires filtered through the yellow lights suspended from the telephone poles lining the perimeter of the half-mile track, giving it a filmic quality. I had a friend whose father ran the hot-dog concession right behind turn four. We would sneak in by wriggling through a hole in the chain-link fence behind the concrete restrooms. The program would alternate between the tiny snarling midget race cars, clapped-together jalopies based on older model American coupes, and the always-entertaining Destruction Derby, where beat-up modified street cars would smash into each other until only one was left running. I loved it all. I watched future legend Mario Andretti and his brother Aldo from Nazareth, Pennsylvania, as well as other big names like A.J. Foyt, Len Duncan, and Parnelli Jones duke it out with the local hotshots.

I followed the sport as closely as I could and one day read about a world championship sports car race that was to be held at the Bridgehampton circuit out on Long Island New York. The year was 1964 and I was only fifteen years old, but I managed to talk an older friend of mine, who had a Triumph TR3, into driving there from Pennsylvania. I told my parents I was just going across the Delaware River to New Jersey to hang out for the day and promised to be back later that night. I knew that New York City was two hours away but didn't realize just how far the tip of Long Island stretched out into the Atlantic. We left early in the little roadster and by midday arrived at the track. Finding a good vantage point, we settled in among the fans on the sand dunes overlooking a fast downhill curve. At one point the Ferrari of Ludovico Scarfiotti sputtered to a stop directly below where we were sitting. There were no fences separating us from the track, and we ran down the sandy hill and helped push the stricken race car off the asphalt. The speed, the fragrant smell of Castrol, the exotic atmosphere . . . little did I realize that some twenty years later I would win my first national SCCA (Sports Car Club of America) race on that very same circuit. I was hooked for life.

Wrestling

My dad was a good baseball player. I played Little League with a right-handed glove by mistake (I'm a lefty) and got hit in the eye with a fastball. That ended that. Don't get me wrong: I appreciate the game and its tradition in America's history . . . I just sucked at it. I am also a fan of the synergy in great team play, but for me, there has always been more satisfaction in the self-reliant category of competition.

I tried to play football, but I was too small and really not into getting run over, mangled, and driven into the ground. Yet I still love to watch the game. I tried some track and field, managing to pull off the occasional slightly better-than-average broad jump.

Then there was wrestling.

Mano a mano, one plus one and done . . . wrestling is about as primal as it gets. And I loved it. I started in tenth grade and made the varsity squad for the next three years. In the 1960s, North Penn High School was just becoming a force to be reckoned with in the highly competitive Pennsylvania high school wrestling universe. Since then, the school has become a top program, having developed numerous sectional, regional, and state champions. That legacy can be traced back to one man: Ed Klavon. He was a biology teacher by day and a gifted wrestling coach by late-afternoon practice. He became a mentor to me, on and off the mat. Klavon had a tough-but-fair coaching style and pushed us hard. As a leader, he tempered his aggressive coaching with uncommon sensitivity. It was impressive and surprising for me to see an adult who was not afraid to wear his emotions on his sleeve. He was the first teacher I felt I could relate to on equal terms; he taught me how to turn suffering into success, and although I didn't realize it at the time, he was training me for grappling with life itself.

Through wrestling, I discovered that my diminutive height could have its advantages. This was a revelation, and I set about figuring out how I could play to my strengths. Working hard and training harder appealed to me. Throughout my life (if you don't count the past few years, when various important body parts have begun to outlast their useful lifespan) I've been unusually healthy, and I believe much of that is directly related to the strength base that I developed while wrestling. Wrestling will kick your ass but you *will* be in shape.

The Avalons

joined the band known as the Avalons near the end of ninth grade, about
1963. The guys, Jack Austerberry, Pat Collins, and Craig Minninger were all
a few years older than me and in high school. Jack played tenor sax, Pat played
guitar, and Craig was the drummer. A year or so later Alan Merico joined the
group. He played a Hammond B-3 organ and also owned a clapped-out Ford
van. When I joined the band as the lead singer and guitarist, Pat switched to
bass. Craig decided to leave, and we found a new drummer named Kent Longacre. We stayed together a little over five years, eventually changing our name
to the Soul Sound Continentals, and soon after that, the Masters. Eventually
we added a trombone player named Dave Rupp and enlisted my sister, Diane,
and my friend Nevin Harper to sing backgrounds. The Philadelphia radio
stations that I was listening to at that time were playing mostly rhythm and
blues, doo-wop, and gospel music. My two favorite stations were WDAS and
WHAT, AM stations with local DJs like Georgie Woods, "The Guy with the
Goods"; Joe Tamburro, aka Butterball; Jimmy Bishop; Hy Lit; Sonny Hop-
son, "The Mighty Burner"; and my favorite, Jerry Blavat, "The Geator with
the Heater." Blavat was the mother lode when it came to spinning doo-wop

My band the Masters circa 1967. Left to right, back: Jack Austerberry (sax), Nevin Harper (vocals), Pat Collins (bass); middle: Alan Merico (keyboards), Diane Oates (vocals and my sister), Kent Longacre (drums); front: David Rupp (trombone), John Oates (guitar/vocals). *(Courtesy John Oates)*

street-corner harmony groups, oldies, and obscure B-sides from 45-rpm singles. The songs that I heard on his show and danced to at his record hops at Chez Vous Ballroom and Wagner's have become part of my musical DNA, and to this day I often reference certain grooves and vocal styles when I'm writing and recording.

WHEN THE BRITISH Invasion, spearheaded by groups like the Beatles and the Rolling Stones, began to sweep the nation, Philly was not impressed. In fact, there was an unusual backlash to those groups and their sound, which was for the most part a rehash of American roots music, repackaged and resold to a new generation of American kids who thought it was actually something new. I had been listening to Muddy Waters, Chuck Berry, and Little Richard for years, and as far as I was concerned, most of the British bands sounded like

Strumming in sandals around the time I was also wrestling in high school. *(Courtesy John Oates)*

a ragged imitation of the real thing. In addition to that, the new Brit sound was not very danceable, and in Philly, if you couldn't dance to a song it pretty much wasn't worth shit. Years later I appreciated and became less small-minded about the value that these British bands brought to the world of popular music but as a teenager I wasn't into it.

Around this same time, I was playing solo acoustic shows at local coffeehouses, doing a mixed bag of Delta blues and primitive Appalachian folk songs. Meanwhile, my band's repertoire was based around 1950s and '60s R&B, leaning heavily on the Stax/Volt, Motown, Chicago, and Philly music that we all loved so much. This musical split personality has never really changed, and to this day the approach to my solo career and playing in a band is exactly the same.

In those days, band uniforms were important. Any group worth a rim shot had to have matching suits. So one day we took the Reading railroad down from Lansdale to Philadelphia in search of some cool threads. It was always an adventure just stepping out of the Reading Terminal onto Market Street and navigating the urban onslaught of drifters, bums, hustlers, and hookers. Our first stop was a shop called Slax and Jax, just off the square around city hall, on Somerset Street. From there we moved on down to South Street. Now, today, if you were to walk down South Street, you'd find trendy shops, cool hipster bars, restaurants, and of course the ubiquitous cheesesteak hoagie shops, but back in the mid-'60s it was a different world. The street was a shabby collection of dive bars, pawn shops, boarded-up storefronts, and a few clothing stores offering up the height of South Philly fashion: bold, striped, Italian knit shirts; jeff caps; fedoras with feathered hatbands; pointy-toed patent leather Italian shoes; and flashy sharkskin suits.

One of the hot spots was a well-known shop called Big Hearted Jim's. In those days, in that neighborhood, there was always a front-door hustler/salesman who would literally grab you by your arm if you tried to walk by and would physically drag you into the store, spewing a rapid-fire, big-city sales pitch—threateningly intimidating, yet friendly enough that you felt like you either had to buy something or there was a good chance that you might not make it back to the street in the same condition as you entered the store.

"Come on in fellas! You boys look like you got some taste and we got a taste for you . . . step right this way . . . make you look so fine that all the ladies will drop their drawers and fall in love, we got just the thing to make

My sister and me today. *(Courtesy Chris Epting)*

'em go *wooo* . . . you gonna walk out of here looking like a hundred million dollars."

On one trip to Philly, we took the bait and let the guy strong-arm us into seven, cheap black-and-white houndstooth suits. I'm sure the sales guys were laughing behind our backs as we walked out the door . . . "sold them hicks some shit" . . . but we thought we were styled. Hell, we had matching suits, that's all that mattered. We couldn't wait to hit the stage in those suits. My sister, Diane, bless her heart, had been recruited as our background singer. I kind of forced her into wearing her prom dress. She missed a lot of weekends with her friends while she was singing with the band in that prom dress. Sorry Diane. . . .

By the time I was in my senior year of high school we had been playing together pretty much every weekend and making some decent money, by 1960s-teenager standards. We'd make up to a hundred dollars a night playing high-school dances, a few local bars, frat parties at nearby colleges, and a regular gig at a place in Doylestown called the Hustle Inn. It was there that I first saw a guitar player, in a British-rock cover band, bending strings as he played. I thought it was cool, and it was something totally different from the R&B and Delta blues music that I was listening to. At the time I was using the standard jazz setup of medium gauge flatwound strings on my red 1964 Gibson SG Standard. I asked him how he was able to bend the strings so easily and he told me he had replaced his high E string with a banjo string, which was much thinner, so he could bend it. In those days you couldn't just go to a music store and buy different gauge sets of strings. It was a revelation of sorts, not only from a guitar player's point of view, but also as a subtle sign that there was a musical revolution on the horizon, beyond the stuff that my band was doing.

Summer of '66

After graduating from high school in 1966, I spent most of that summer growing a mustache, not cutting my hair, playing in the band, and looking forward to leaving the small town of North Wales. I was focused on making a record with the band, and we had been saving money from our shows. Since there were no recording studios anywhere near where we lived, I looked in the Philadelphia yellow pages and found the name and number of a place on North Broad Street called Virtue Studios. A phone call later, I was speaking with a guy named Frank Virtue. Frank had made a name for himself and his band the Virtues with an instrumental hit in 1958 called "Guitar Boogie Shuffle."

His recording studio was a cramped one-man operation on the second floor. It had a small live room for the band and a tiny control room with a quarter-inch two-track tape machine. In the summer of 1965 Barbara Mason recorded her big hit, "Yes, I'm Ready," and just a couple of years later, sweet-singing Eddie Holman would record the classic "Hey There Lonely Girl" in that same room, but for now, it was our moment. We struck a deal, forked over the dough, and booked a date in July to make our record. A few weeks before the session

Pat Collins and I had written two songs: "I Need Your Love" and "Not My Baby." I was influenced by the falsetto singing of Curtis Mayfield and Smokey Robinson, and the musical groove was a reflection of a current style that Philly R&B radio was playing at the time.

Making your first record is a big deal but we didn't have a clue and just walked into the studio and played the song the way we rehearsed it. Frank Virtue said, "Youse guys got talent but you need someone to arrange this for you" and handed me a simple business card with the name "Bobby Martin Musical Arranger" and a phone number. I called the number and Pat and I went down to center city Philadelphia to meet with him.

Of course, I had no clue at the time that I was reaching out to a man who would go on to be directly responsible for some of the greatest classic R&B arrangements that ever came out of the Philly soul-music scene. Martin became one of Gamble and Huff's go-to guys, and his arrangements propelled such classic songs—and some of my all-time favorites—as "For The Love of Money" by the O'Jays; "Bad Luck" by Harold Melvin and the Blue Notes; and "I'll Always Love My Mama" by the Intruders. Whether it was fate, luck, or destiny our lives intersected in that little office of his off of South Broad Street. Little did we know what life had in store for either of us later on. But it didn't matter. I just wanted to make a record.

It was a sweltering afternoon and I was more than a bit nervous as we climbed the creaky wooden staircase to meet with this unknown "professional" arranger.

Sweating, I cautiously tapped on the door and was greeted by a stylishly dressed man in his early thirties. He wore a striped Italian knit shirt, sharply creased dress slacks, and patent leather shoes. The room was stuffy and packed, with floor-to-ceiling bookshelves full of records, an old-fashion wooden desk cluttered with paper and, crammed next to that, a well-used upright piano. I introduced myself and explained that we had booked a session at Virtue Studios and were looking for someone to help us make the record. I recall that Martin came off as aloof but not unfriendly while exuding a big-city air of coolness and letting me know up front that he might be able to make some time to work with us. I'm sure he was waiting to see just what kind of kids and music he might be dealing with.

I had my acoustic guitar with me and he asked me to play him the songs. So I squeezed myself onto the edge of his swivel desk chair and he sat on the piano bench while I played both songs. He didn't say much, but he didn't kick me out either. He asked about the band instrumentation, and suggested that he could write a horn chart for us. We only had a trombone and sax, but he wanted to add a trumpet part as well. We went over the songs a few more times while he wrote up a basic chord chart, and he said he would bring a trumpet player and meet us at the studio for our session. All that was left was to negotiate his fee. He told me it would be $150, and even though the band could hardly afford it, I agreed . . . the recording session was on!

Finally, on a steamy day in mid-July, we drove the van into the city, lugged the big Hammond B-3, heavy Leslie speaker cabinet, and my Fender Twin Reverb amp up to the second floor. We set up in a semicircle in the recording studio while Frank placed sound baffles around the drum kit and amplifiers and pulled out music stands for the horn players. The plan was to play and record the songs live, all together, in one room. I was to sing on my own mike, and off to one side of the room Nevin, Pat, and Diane would sing around an overhead boom mike.

Frank Virtue sat behind the console looking through a small glass window separating the control room from the recording space. We played the song down a few times to rehearse the parts while Bobby Martin worked with the horn players, making small adjustments to the chart. It was really starting to come together. The arrangement felt tight, and after just a couple of takes, it was done.

This was cloud-nine time—we had finally, actually made a record. Little did I know at the time that the recording studio would become such an integral part of my life and, in a way, define who I would become as a musician. I was also just starting to learn how a song became a record, but the true depth of that education lay ahead.

Everyone always asks me, "When did you know you had finally made it?" Answer: The night I first heard my voice on the radio. It was one cool autumn evening in 1967, on a dark country road near Silverdale, Pennsylvania, parking with my girlfriend, Lynne. We were in a little green Renault Dauphine that I had talked my parents into buying because it was foreign and had two horns— a city horn and a country horn that you could switch with a little plastic toggle on the steering column, and, oh yeah, it had a radio.

At the time, there was a DJ from Norristown who called himself Super Lou on WNAP, 1110 on the AM (and only) radio dial. My band had played a few small shows for him at his record hops on the Jersey Shore, and he had promised to give our 45 a spin when we finished it, so we made sure he got the first copy.

There we were. The car was parked, the road was dark, we were kissing in the glow of the radio dial when I heard it, exploding from that little speaker in the dash: the slightly out-of-tune horn intro with the rushed drum fill from "I Need Your Love." It crackled and split the silence. Super Lou had honored his promise. I lost track of what we were doing during that fumbling, teenage make-out session on the side of the road, but I know whatever it was . . . I stopped doing it.

In that moment, one minute and fifty-one glorious seconds, my life truly changed. I could now legitimately call myself a recording artist, and somehow I sensed that something profoundly important had just happened. I had a record out. I was on the radio.

My life would never be the same again.

First Year in Philly

When September rolled around, while I was still playing in the Masters, I began my first semester at Temple University, commuting from my folks' house in North Wales. Each morning I would take the Reading railroad, get off at the North Broad Street station, and walk south down the left side of Broad toward the campus. It was, and still is, a predominately African-American neighborhood. Each morning I'd nod to the men and women as they opened their clothing stores, five-and-dimes, and barbershops.

I never felt any racial animosity or fear, the black-power movement had not become much of a factor and at least musically the city was for the most part integrated.

In the early '50s, the Uptown Theater had become a major venue on the "chitlin' circuit," a collective name given to theaters where R&B performers could appear during the age of racial segregation. And by the mid-'60s, the Uptown was the epicenter of soul music in Philly.

I'd always pause on the sidewalk to check out the upcoming shows advertised on the box office window. If there was a great lineup, and there always was, I'd take the train or drive down and catch every show. I wish I could bottle the thrill of walking down the dark, dirty Saturday-night sidewalk as the brightly lit Uptown Theater marquee beckoned me. The featured performers' names in thick block letters read like a pantheon of the gods in my musical heaven: The elegant sophistication of the Temptations with their precision dance steps and sharply cut suits; the liquid falsetto of Curtis Mayfield and the Impressions; "Mr. Dynamite," James Brown; the Four Tops; Sam and Dave; the suave and uber-professional Smokey Robinson and the Miracles; the Coasters, with their entertaining and comical pantomime routines; the jacked-up tempos of Otis Redding and "Mr. Excitement," Jackie Wilson; the wicked Wilson Pickett; and the Mad Lads, their white gloves glowing under the ultraviolet lights . . . the harmonies were transcendent, the energy was propulsive, this was my church and the religion that took hold of me, shook me, saturated my soul. There is no doubt that the shows I witnessed at the Uptown affected and informed my performance and musical sensibilities on every level.

The girls went wild when Tommy Hunt, formerly of the Flamingos, dropped to his knees at the edge of the stage and ripped open his shirt. There was pandemonium the night that Little Stevie Wonder played "Fingertips" when he was thirteen, laying down that classic harmonica solo then jumping behind the drum kit and doing a five-minute solo. Watching all the groups and solo artists bringing it at the Uptown was an education in Saturday-night stagecraft. I paid very close attention, not only to the singers and stars, but also to the dramatic use of dynamics within the musical arrangements of the backup bands—a powerful combination of technique and emotion that could make the girls cry one minute, then have them howling with orgiastic ecstasy the next.

The train ride back and forth from North Wales soon became a drag, as I was drawn more and more toward the city. I began to seek out places to stay, and spent a few weeks at the Newman House, at the edge of the campus. It was a sort of hostel run by the Catholic Church, but I didn't last long when I noticed one of the guys a bit too obsessed with a large poster of Julie Andrews hanging over his bed. Occasionally I'd meet a girl who had an apartment, and

I'd crash there on weekends or until she kicked me out. I just wanted to be in the city as much as possible.

I managed a low *B* average that first year of college. However, my grades deteriorated over the next three years mainly due to the fact that my academic choices were totally predicated on the principle of the path of least resistance. The formula was to avoid science and math, focus on English and history, stay in school long enough to be deferred from having to go to Vietnam, and keep playing music. I finally chose to major and get a degree in journalism, mostly because I was good at typing and there was very little homework.

The Record Deal

In those days, when a recording session was finished, the only way that you could hear what you had done was to request a copy of the song on a small plastic reel of quarter-inch tape, or cut an acetate—a soft black plastic disc that was good for a couple of spins on a turntable before it deteriorated.

Studios were equipped with a large machine to cut these acetates. The engineer would send the recorded music signal from the studio tape decks to the machine. The sound would vibrate a sharp, pointed stylus at the end of the tone arm, which would then physically etch and cut grooves into the blank acetate spinning on the turntable. Thus the term "cutting a record."

I believe we walked out of the recording studio with both a reel of tape and the double-sided black disc with the distinctive yellow label that said Virtue Studio. We couldn't wait to hear the results on our keyboard player's Zenith tape recorder, and to play the test pressing on our record player.

A few days later we took the train to Philly and headed straight to a store called the Record Museum on Chestnut Street. The entrance to the Record Museum was three steps down below street level. Inside were rows upon rows of 45-rpm singles, with their multicolored labels, arranged in alphabetical order by the artists' names. I loved flipping through the bins searching for the obscure doo-wop and R&B records that I heard on Jerry Blavat's radio show. I actually didn't know at the time that he was a part owner of the store, along with a guy named Jerry Greene. But this trip was different. I had my own record in my hand and was trying to figure out how to release it.

Trying to appear as professional as possible, I introduced myself to the man behind the cash register, told him about our group, and that we had just cut

That's me with the legendary Philly DJ, Jerry Blavat, aka "The Geator with the Heater." (*Courtesy John Oates*)

our own record at Virtue with Bobby Martin. I handed him the acetate and he placed it on the shop's turntable and dropped the needle. For an anxious few seconds that felt like an eternity I tried to gauge his reaction, then I noticed his head starting to bob, and then his body began to slowly sway to the groove of "I Need Your Love." When the song ended he turned and with a grin said, "Cool. . . . Who owns this?" I piped up, "We do," and he lifted the wooden hinged countertop and ushered us into the back room, which was cluttered with even more records and cardboard boxes. The Record Museum had its own label, Crimson Records, and had released its first single, "Expressway to Your Heart" by the Soul Survivors, which had been written and produced by Kenny Gamble and Leon Huff. After a little small talk, and after the guy figured out that we didn't have a clue about the record business, he handed me a wad of paperwork, told me to look it over and get back to him. In the meantime, he'd hang on to the disc and get some feedback from his partners and some radio folks. We walked out of the shop into the inner city sunshine with a record contract . . . but I'm not sure if I even knew what had just happened. Hell, I was ready to just sign the paperwork right there on the sidewalk, turn around and hand it back to him without reading it. This ignorant, impatient attitude was to be a portent of things to come in many more ways than I could have ever imagined at the time.

After finding some local yokel lawyer who didn't explain much but was eager to take our money, we all signed the paperwork and returned it to the guys at the Record Museum. Soon they began to press copies of our 45 single. They assigned a guy to take us around to the radio stations, where we were stared at by DJs who were more than a little surprised by this goofy group of white kids who obviously didn't know shit from Shinola. Part of the promotion campaign (if you could call it that) was to appear at the Adelphi Ballroom on a Sunday afternoon for a record hop that was hosted by the well-known DJ and program director of WDAS, Jimmy Bishop. Little did I realize that a seemingly insignificant Sunday afternoon would lead to a chance encounter of profound significance that would forever change my life.

Meeting Daryl

In the winter of that year, a group called the Temptones had performed for the Freedom Show at Convention Hall. The concert was hosted by popular WDAS DJ Georgie Woods ("The Guy With The Goods") and the acts included Arthur Conley, the Delfonics, Barbara Mason, and the new psychedelic soul group, Sly and the Family Stone.

The Temptones opened the show in their slick, blue suits, sang a few Temptations covers with choreographed dance steps, and ended with their single, "Girl I Love You." Their vocal harmonies were tight, but the tall, skinny, blond lead singer stood out immediately to me as having a particularly outstanding voice. His name was Daryl Hohl, and we would meet a few weeks later on a fateful Sunday afternoon at the Adelphi Ballroom in West Philadelphia, when both of our groups were booked to lip-synch our respective singles for a WDAS record hop.

For my group, the Masters, this was a big opportunity. We had been getting airplay on both WDAS and WHAT, the most important AM R&B stations in the city. One of the guys from our record label drove us to the venue, and we all piled into a rickety service elevator, emerging on the upstairs into a small, cramped, backstage room.

The artists who were to perform that afternoon were all there: The Five Stairsteps, ("World of Fantasy" and "You Waited Too Long"); Howard Tate ("Look at Granny Run Run"); and over in the corner, the five white dudes in their blue-silk suits that I had seen at the Freedom Show, the Temptones. I was a bit uncomfortable being thrown into that mix of what appeared to be seasoned professionals, and we all kind of kept to ourselves, waiting to be called up onto the stage to mime our single.

I remember hearing the funky hits of the day pounding out of the speakers in the packed hall beyond the backstage walls. Jimmy Bishop's smooth patter filled the gaps in the music but then . . . *POP! POP! POP!* The muffled sound of shots rang out, followed by screams and the unmistakable stamping of foot-steps as a gang fight broke out between rival West Philly gangs in the ball-room. I had never heard the sound of any gun other than a hunting rifle, so at first I had no idea what was happening. One look on the faces of everyone back-stage told me, though, and before I could process that, we were hustled into the service elevator along with Daryl's group, the Temptones. There wasn't a lot of small talk, just a quick acknowledgment that we were "gettin' out while the gettin' was good," and that since we were both going to the same school we just might see each other again . . . sometime.

A FEW WEEKS after that episode, two of the founding members of my band joined the air force as an alternative to being drafted into the army, and that was the end of the Masters. Shortly after that I ran into Daryl somewhere on the Temple University campus, and after a quick recollection of the trouble we had dodged at the Adelphi, I told him that my group was finished.

By some seemingly predestined twist of fate, he told me that he had lost the Temptones' backup rhythm section and asked me if I could play guitar behind them. I knew all the songs that they were doing, so I replied with a quick "yes" and presto . . . I had a new gig. I honestly can't even remember if we rehearsed. I'm sure Daryl just told me what songs they wanted to do, and since their repertoire was based on the Temptations' records, I already knew the tunes. A short time later Daryl told me that we had a New York showcase booked at the Village Gate, on the corner of Bleeker and Thompson Streets in Greenwich Village.

The Village Gate was a landmark venue that over the years played host to everyone from John Coltrane and Billie Holiday to Miles Davis and Aretha Franklin. Bob Dylan wrote "A Hard Rain's A-Gonna Fall" in September 1962 while living in the club's basement apartment. It was hallowed ground.

Having spent so much time in New York City growing up, I was very excited to be playing with a new group in what seemed to me like a big-time, big-city gig. My first thought was that I had to upgrade my guitar. In those days, R&B guitarists in backup bands usually played a semihollow, jazz-style electric guitar; it was the sound, it was a "thing." I convinced Daryl that we had to make a stop before going to the gig in the Village. So around midday we drove into Manhattan through the Lincoln Tunnel, headed uptown, and parked in front of Manny's Music on West Forty-eighth Street. That one city block between Sixth Avenue and Broadway was musical-instrument central. Manny's was the largest and most well-known store, with an enticing front window chock-full of amps, guitars, brass instruments, and drums. Inside, the walls were lined with eight-by-ten glossy publicity photos of famous musicians. There seemed to be salesmen everywhere, behind the counters and scurrying between aisles full of equipment. This wasn't my first time at Manny's. A few years earlier, my folks took me there to buy my first electric guitar. As we walked along, we passed a pawn shop on that same block, and a golden-brown sunburst Fender Stratocaster displayed in the window caught my eye. I dragged my parents inside and told them I wanted to see that guitar. I could feel that my mom was reluctant to go inside the cluttered, dimly lit pawn shop, and wasn't happy about me being attracted to that particular guitar. I loved it and asked the guy behind the counter if he would take it out of the window and let me play it. The neck of that guitar just felt so natural in my hands, and I wanted it badly. However, to my parents it just looked like an old, beat-up piece of junk.

"Don't you want a new guitar Johnny?" my mom kept insisting, while pointing out the big cigarette burn on the headstock, where some dude must have wedged his Lucky Strike during many a late nightclub set. Being a little kid without his own money, there wasn't much I could say, and I dejectedly handed the Strat back and followed my parents outside and up the street toward Manny's. I remember meeting the owner, Henry, and we settled on a new guitar called an Alamo Titan that came with its own matching amp. Imagine what that early '60s Strat would be worth now!

But now I was back again, with cash in hand that I had scrounged together from teaching guitar lessons and selling my red Gibson SG Standard. There were a lot of choices, but my eyes locked onto a big, flashy Gretsch Viking with a brown sunburst and a gold Bigsby vibrato . . . *sold!* I didn't even change the strings; we jumped back in the car and headed downtown to do the show. On the drive over from Philly, Daryl had casually mentioned that after our showcase he had been invited to take us all up to Harlem, to the Apollo Theater, where the Temptations were playing. Okay . . . that was all I needed to hear! A gig in the big city, a new guitar, and going to the Apollo to hear the Temps. I was alive and in heaven—so much so that I hardly remember much about the Temptones showcase, other than that I didn't fuck up. Oh, and anticlimactic as it seems now, that was the very first time Daryl and I ever performed on a stage together. After playing our little showcase, we rushed out of the venue and headed up toward 125th Street in Harlem.

What Daryl didn't mention was that not only were we going to catch the Temptations show at the Apollo, but also we were going in through the backstage entrance, straight into their dressing room. Yes, Daryl was cool, and I was impressed. We milled around in the dark alley in front of the stage door, and when it opened, we stepped inside.

The first person I saw was the man himself, David Ruffin, wearing his trademark thick-framed glasses, leaning casually on the banister in the stairwell smoking a cigarette, his custom-tailored classic black tux perfectly fitted to his rail-thin frame. He didn't speak and just gave us a slight nod as we passed and entered the dressing room. When we walked in, the group's famed baritone,

Paul Williams, who had "discovered" the Temptones and actually bought them the iridescent blue silk suits that they performed in, greeted Daryl and the guys warmly, and I was introduced to my idols. Eddie Kendricks, Melvin Franklin, and Otis Williams were all friendly and exuded an air of successful profession-alism. At that moment in time they were at the top of their game and their songs were at the top of the charts. That year alone they'd release three smash albums: *Temptations Live! The Temptations in a Mellow Mood,* and *The Tempta-tions With a Lot O' Soul.* In my book they were *it*!

After a little small talk, we were guided out of the side stage door into the front row of the theater and we watched the show from there. I had seen the Temptations perform many times before but this was different—this was being on the inside . . . a musical rite of passage . . . the real deal. This Daryl Hall guy, he seemed like he had it going on.

Drive-In

Around late 1968, a few years before our official musical partnership began, Daryl and I began to hang out, got to know each other, and did a lot of the dumb shit twenty-year-olds tend to do. Today it might be called "chemistry building." We were both still going to Temple University and traveling back and forth between the city and the countryside where we grew up. There were some times when we casually fooled around with some music in my parents' basement, and we got hung up on playing some Vanilla Fudge songs, like "Season of the Witch," in a lame attempt to sound like a white rock band and experiment beyond the comfort zone of the R&B we were both so familiar with. But mostly we just got wasted and laughed a lot.

One summer night we decided to go to the drive-in movie and we brought along Daryl's sister, Kathy, to see the controversial George Romero film, *Night of the Living Dead*. Horror movies in the 1950s and '60s were for the most part silly B-movie fare like *The Blob* and *Attack of the 50 Foot Woman* and other kitschy flicks that stoked midcentury repression and Cold War paranoia. But Romero's shocking black-and-white classic was filmed in a quasidocumentary style, and the setting—Western Pennsylvania near Evans City, just outside of

Pittsburgh, where Romero had attended Carnegie Mellon University—looked identical to the area where we were sitting in the drive-in. That alone would have made the experience something to remember. But we thought it might be fun to take it to another level and Daryl and I dropped some acid as we drove to the movie.

Oh boy . . . bloody, slack-jawed, bone-crunching zombies staggering and lurching around a grim Pennsylvania town in a movie shot in grainy 16-millimeter, and the three of us sitting in the old sedan, eyes big as saucers and brains pulsing on what the fuck is happening. The fact that the movie was narrated by a well-known local newscaster named John Facenda (who many football fans will recognize as the longtime NFL films' "Voice of God") made the jacked-up realism even more intense. In fact, we were more than a little freaked out, alternating our attention between the undulating outdoor screen and the car's side windows . . . paranoia washing over us with a growing, genuine terror that the zombies might actually be right outside the car. . . . *"Wait . . . what was that?!"*

The only way the night could have been weirder would have been for us to be wearing our kaleidoscopic pink-prism eyeglasses that fractured the world into hundreds of identical images all with a soft, rosy hue . . . but it was nighttime so we didn't need much more in the way of sensory enhancement. It was one of many memories that comprised much of the late '60s haze for both me and Daryl. But for some reason, to this day we both remember this night well. And we still look at each other and laugh about it.

Rocky Mountain. High.

One day in the winter of 1968, while I was a junior at Temple University, I saw a three-by-five card tacked to a bulletin board in the student union. It read: "Ski Trip to Aspen, Colorado! Airfare, lodging, lift tickets included: $125.00."

This caught my eye. I had been skiing since I was a kid and could handle the low East Coast hills with confidence. But "blue ice" skiing in Pennsylvania and upstate New York is a far cry from tackling the legendary majestic slopes of the Colorado Rockies, and so my interest was more than a little piqued. I had always dreamed of skiing out West and here was my chance . . . and for a hundred and twenty-five bucks . . . are you kidding?

I couldn't get that little three-by-five card off of my mind, so when I filed into my journalism class a few minutes later, I casually mentioned it to a guy sitting next to me. "Hey man, I just saw an ad on the student-union bulletin board about this crazy skiing deal? A hundred and twenty-five bucks to Aspen, and everything's included." He didn't hesitate, replying, "Well what the hell . . . I can ski, let's go!" We hardly knew each other but that's what you did in college, right? You didn't overthink things. If it felt good, you just did it. So over the next few weeks, I scrounged up what little money I had from guitar lessons, sold a few things, and packed my gear. This would be my first time leaving the confines of the East Coast, and my first time on an airplane. Little did I realize that although the destination was the Rocky Mountains, Colorado would be my destiny and would have a much more profound impact on my life than I could have ever imagined.

Upon arriving at the old Stapleton International Airport in Denver, we quickly learned that this too-good-to-be-true ski package didn't include any way to get to Aspen, which was a good four or five hours away by car. While waiting for our bags and skis at the luggage carousel, not knowing what to do, we struck up a conversation with a couple of guys who were a little older, probably in their thirties, who were renting a car to drive to Aspen. Hearing our predicament, one of them said, "Hey if you can throw a few bucks in for gas, we'll take you with us." We were on our way.

But getting there would be an adventure in itself. We left Denver in the late afternoon. Light snow began to fall as we climbed higher into the hills to the west of the city. In 1968, neither the Eisenhower Tunnel nor Interstate 70 had been completed. We cruised on Highway 6 through the old mining towns of Idaho Springs, Georgetown, and Silver Plume, and gradually gained altitude as the treacherous, serpentine, two-lane road led us toward Loveland Pass. The route to the top of the twelve-thousand-foot pass was a series of seemingly endless white-knuckle drop-offs and dizzying hairpin switchback turns. We moved cautiously along as the snow continued to increase in intensity. We were in a 1960s sedan, just a run-of-the-mill rent-a-car with no snow tires. I was on the edge of the backseat, holding my breath most of the way. Snowflakes swirled and danced hypnotically in the headlights until finally tapering off as we descended into the small cluster of buildings that made up the newly built resort of Vail. We stopped for some coffee and then continued, following the Colorado River into the mouth of Glenwood Canyon. The darkness obscured the dramatic, towering, red-stone walls of the canyon as we forged on at a crawl through the blizzard that came and went in fits of intensity, one moment clear and the next blinding and nearly impenetrable.

We arrived in Aspen around midnight, and our heroic driver dropped us off in front of a lodge that looked like it had been airlifted from Austria and plunked down in the center of Aspen. It was classic. Stepping in through the heavy oak door was like walking in to another world. Sprawled next to a sunken, open-hearth fire pit was a giant Saint Bernard, straight out of central casting, small barrel around his neck and all. The sleepy proprietor with the German accent checked us in and directed us toward our room, which had four bunks. Inside we found one longhaired hippie dude from Los Angeles who would be sharing our space. He graciously took out some hashish and we all spent the night warm, high, and safe from the storm outside.

The next morning, I opened the door to look around and couldn't believe what I saw. Like some fairy tale, overnight everything had been quietly blanketed with more than a foot of fresh, fluffy, powder snow. (I would later come to understand that Aspen has these magical days on a regular basis, and over thirty years later, I'm still blown away by it.) The sun was shining brightly, suspended in a deep-blue sky unlike anything I had ever seen . . . this was too much, but exactly like I hoped it would be. Skiing fresh powder is every skier's Holy Grail, and here it was served up on a platter. I was stoked to get up on the hill but at the same time more than a little bit intimidated. "Where is the easiest place to ski around here?" I asked the guy behind the front desk. He sent us down the road to Buttermilk, the smallest of the local mountains, where I spent the first day struggling to adapt my East Coast hardpack technique to the dry, soft, powder snow.

I was on a pair of stiff, yellow Blizzard skis, wore leather lace-up boots, wool pants, and a nylon jacket . . . all I can say now is God bless the breathable fabric known as Gore-Tex. We dragged ourselves back to the lodge at the end of the day, exhausted from the high altitude and soaked from falling our way down the mountain in the unfamiliar, challenging conditions.

Then we skied Ajax, now called Aspen Mountain, which back in 1968 still featured just a single chairlift, the historic Lift 1-A, built back in the 1940s, in part by the army's Tenth Mountain Division. When you hopped aboard the creaking wood seat, the attendant threw a heavy blanket over you for the forty-five-minute ride to the top. Again I spent the day alternating falling down, snowplowing, and basically trying just to survive the steep slopes and thickly wooded glades on this challenging mountain.

Once back at our lodge, our roommate from California clued us in to where we could buy some pot. He directed us to a rundown place downtown on East Main Street called the Hotel Jerome. Today it has been renovated and is now a first-class, five-star hotel, but back then, the circa 1880s building had become much like a rundown youth hostel. Gone were the days when vacationing celebrities like Gary Cooper and John Wayne would drink, dine, and hang out at the famous J-Bar. I must say, I thought I was hallucinating when I saw actual horses tied to the rail by the front door and actual cowboys with revolvers slung from holsters sitting at the bar. My friend and I walked through the shabby Victorian lobby, climbed the creaky staircase, and wandered along the empty hallways of peeling wallpaper, following the dim yellow glow from hand-blown glass wall sconces until we found the room we were looking for. We got our Rocky Mountain high on before John Denver got around to writing about it.

When we finally floated out of the Jerome onto the snow-covered street, I looked back over my shoulder and felt the hotel watching over us with a majestic air, its facade a faded reminder of Aspen's glory days during the silver boom of the late 1800s.

The year before we got there, the Snowmass Village resort had opened a few miles down the road from Aspen. There wasn't much there except a few bars and a couple of ski lifts. I had overheard someone in town raving about a local singer/songwriter who was playing out there, so one night I hitched a ride to Snowmass, wandered into a cozy saloon, and grabbed a seat along the bar. A blond-haired singer with wire-rimmed glasses sat casually in the corner and, in an engaging folksy style, began playing and singing some beautiful original songs. One in particular stood out. He said he had written it a couple of years before but that he was all excited because the well-known trio Peter, Paul and Mary would soon be recording it. Then he played it, a yearning and plaintive ode to the pain of leaving someone you love and hitting the road. He had originally titled it, "Babe, I Hate to Go," but the song I heard that night became much better known as "Leaving On a Jet Plane." Now I understood why there was such local buzz about this guy. He was just genuine, warm, and talented, although I did think it was odd that here was a guy named John Denver actually performing in Colorado. I didn't know then that his real name was Henry John Deutschendorf, Jr., and that only a few years later we would both be signed to the same record label, RCA, and a few years after that, living in the same town.

The entire week for me was powerful and indelible. Every moment seemed expansive and ripe with unlimited possibilities. The deep blue sky from eight thousand feet felt closer to heaven. The crisp, clear, thin air was euphoric, sweet, and transformative. This high-altitude world was unspoiled and awe inspiring. I returned to Philadelphia a different person.

Moon Walk

We all have those "do you remember where you were when?" moments by which we chart our lives. For instance, I remember being in seventh grade when astronaut John Glenn first orbited Earth. They marched us into the auditorium and we watched the famed CBS newsman Walter Cronkite narrate the story on a small black-and-white television they had propped up on the stage. That really fascinated me; the thought of a man being strapped into a tiny capsule atop a cylinder of explosive fuel, blasting into orbit, and hurtling around Earth through space blew my mind. A few years later, in 1963, I was sitting in Spanish class when the principal popped his head in to announce the tragic news of John F. Kennedy's assassination in Dallas. While I hate to admit it, and I certainly felt terrible, my first thought was, "Wow, I guess this means we get to ditch JV football practice?" Which I guess is a commentary on my callow teenage mentality, and perhaps just how tough those Pennsylvania high school football practices really were.

As I got a little bit older, another defining moment was the first time man walked on the moon: July 20, 1969. Do you remember where you were? Well, unlike many people who huddled transfixed in their living rooms around their television sets, riveted by the shaky, unearthly, black-and-white images being transmitted from about 240,000 miles away, I recall that monumental event in a somewhat different manner: tripping on mushrooms.

Hey, it was 1969 and Woodstock was less than a month away. This was the Age of Aquarius, and in the hippie subculture of downtown Philly, marijuana, hashish, psilocybin, and LSD were just part of everyday life. I was struggling through my junior year in college, and even though they had been declared illegal three years earlier in the United States, psychedelics, as well as other mind-altering substances, were everywhere and easily procured.

Hanging out with my then girlfriend while neighborhood freaks blasted a good stereo, listening to the latest album by Dylan or Hendrix, the Beatles or the Stones, was a sonic experience to be celebrated. Gathering around a little TV to witness the moon landing was another "high" social event. At the time, I was living in this little hovel in Philly, on Arch Street, between the Franklin Institute and the art museum. I thought I knew what was happening on TV that historic night, but after gulping down some magic mushrooms, all I could do was bounce off the walls, deliriously repeating over and over, "He's walking on the fucking moon! That guy is walking on the fucking moon!" Over and over and over. . . .

Eventually, I wandered out on the street, still babbling about what Neil Armstrong and Buzz Aldrin were doing up way, way, way up there, and mindlessly began heading down toward Center City. Off to my left, something unusual attracted my befuddled attention. I stopped and stared at the famous and ornate Swann Memorial Fountain. Also known as the "Fountain of the Three Rivers" (in honor of the Delaware, the Schuylkill, and the Wissahickon), it's one of the most famous sculptures in the city and features many quirky pieces of art, including a series of sculpted frogs and turtles which spout water toward a fifty-foot geyser in the center.

During the hot summer months, splashing around in the Swann Memorial Fountain was a long-standing Philly tradition for neighborhood kids. But on this sultry July night, there was something different going on, and it stopped me in my tracks. The normally clear water in the fountain was seething and overflowing with iridescent bubbles, popping and bursting in the breeze as they floated into the nighttime air. Giddy with euphoria ignited by both the acid and the incredible news of the moon walk, I jumped in alongside the screaming, laughing children and assorted seminaked hippie freaks frolicking among the bubbles. As I lay on my back, staring up at the stars, immersed in the soapy water, I began alternating between hysterical laughter and terrifying panic as the bubbles began to swallow and overwhelm me in layers of froth. Who knows who dumped the bubble bath into the fountain—in fact, maybe it was just me lying on my back in the clear water, cackling like a lunatic . . . but I swear to this day it was real . . . or maybe not.

After a few minutes the cops arrived to chase everyone out of the fountain. I ran down the street, dripping in suds, cleansed, and still tripping. They had walked on the fucking moon; I swam in a liquid space of bubbles.

Valentine

In the last few years of the 1960s, a colorful and eclectic community of artists, freaks, drug dealers, and musicians inhabited Center City, Philadelphia, mostly concentrated within a few square blocks from west to east between Eighth and Twenty-third Streets and north to south between Walnut and Bainbridge Streets. I must have trod a million footsteps in funky wooden-soled clogs or filthy leather sandals on the cobblestone streets and tree-shaded old sidewalks. I loved walking through the city—along the way strange faces became familiar, girls became lovers, hustlers worked in the shadows, and dealers dealt in euphoria and finality. There were more than a few months when I actually didn't have an address and would often wake up on some hardwood floor covered in a tattered blanket in a room draped in diaphanous Tibetan prayer scarfs, with American flags and Day-Glo posters serving as wallpaper. If I stayed anywhere for more than three days in a row . . . well I guess that would be considered a long-term living arrangement.

. . .

ONE OF THOSE familiar faces
was a guy with long, thin,
blond hair, who walked with an
odd bouncing gate and always
seemed to be lugging a battered
tweed Fender bass case. He was
known around town as John the
Baptist. We got to talking and
he told me about his band Valentine. They were a country-
rock band in the style of Moby
Grape or Poco. Noticing the guitar case perpetually dangling
from my hand, he asked me if I
wanted to jam with them. They
had a rehearsal space set up in
the basement of an old church on
the other side of the Schuylkill
River, near the University of
Pennsylvania. I was teaching guitar and playing the odd solo show

As a member of the band Valentine, late 1960s.
(Photograph by Barbara Wilson D'Andrea)

and thought it might be fun to sit in with a band for a change. I grabbed the
'59 Les Paul Special I had bought from my buddy's older brother for a hundred bucks and went over one day to check them out. The band had a charismatic and quirky lead singer named Frank Stallone (Sylvester Stallone's
younger brother), Gary Goff on piano, Jack Daley on drums, and John "the
Baptist" McGettigan on bass. They had a few original songs, and I just slotted in as lead guitarist and added some vocal harmonies. It clicked immediately, and I joined the band. It was the first time I had played in a band that
wasn't an R&B-oriented unit, and it was an interesting challenge for me to
use my folky repertoire and guitar style and basically just play the same

The folky days. *(Photograph by Barbara Wilson D'Andrea)*

licks a bit louder on electric guitar through one of their spare Fender Twin Reverb amps.

Valentine had some gigs lined up and had been building a reputation around town. After a time, I began to share lead vocals with Frank, although he always made it clear that he was the lead singer—and he did have a really distinctive, powerful voice. I started bringing song ideas to the group, and I came up with an electric band arrangement to an old traditional southern field holler called "Another Man Done Gone." It turned out to be a kick-ass song in the set, as I worked on pushing the guys toward a harder-edged, bluesy style. We played a few small clubs around Philly, many of which I would return to a few years later with Daryl. The band's big break came when we were booked for two nights, February twenty-eighth and March first, at the city's premier rock venue, the Electric Factory, opening for the group Rhinoceros. We had a loyal local turnout and the band played really well; somewhere there is a recording of that show; I have no idea what became of the tape, but I wish I had it. For Valentine, that was about as big as it was going to get. Eventually

I could tell Frank was not happy with the direction of the band, and I knew my days were numbered.

This was only a few months before I would graduate from college, and my mind was focused on something way beyond Philly and local gigs. I was dreaming about the Old World to the east, over the Atlantic.

Jerry Ricks

In September of 1969 I was trying to figure out a way to earn a little money while still struggling to get through Temple University. I had heard about a woman named Esther Halpern who ran a folk-music school on Walnut Street, near Twenty-third. I thought perhaps I could get a job teaching guitar, so I walked over to see her.

Esther had long dark hair with streaks of gray that she wore in elaborate twists held together with inlaid mother-of-pearl Spanish combs and what looked like long black chopsticks. She favored long dresses of indeterminate ethnic origin with multiple jangly bracelets and necklaces. Her studio was in the bottom floor of a brownstone on the north side of Walnut Street. She and her husband Ed ran the Gilded Cage, which was Philly's first coffeehouse, and they had been founding members of the Philadelphia Folk Song Society, that was the seed for the Philadelphia Folk Festival, still going strong today after more than fifty years.

I introduced myself and asked if she needed a guitar teacher. We sat and talked for a bit, and I played her a few fingerpicking numbers from my folky repertoire—some Carter Family, Dave Van Ronk, and Joan Baez songs that I thought she might like—and lo and behold, I had a part-time job. Most of the students she sent me were beginners, and although it was boring, it was better than working in a restaurant or a factory.

As we got to know each other better, Esther turned me on to the folk scene in the city. She introduced me to the guy who ran the door at the Second Fret on Sansom Street, the premier folk venue in the city, and turned me on to the person who ran the door at the Main Point in Bryn Mawr as well.

As much as working at the guitar studio was an entree into the local folk scene, more importantly, Esther introduced me to another one of her part-time guitar teachers. His name was Jerry Ricks. He was a soft-spoken man with a ragged afro who played a vintage Martin D-18, and meeting him would change my life.

Jerry had worked as a short-order cook and eventually became the booking agent at the Second Fret in the early '60s. There he got to meet and hang out with all the legendary artists who were booked at the club. Most of the traditional musicians, especially the ones from the South, were not familiar with the culture of northern cities, and the meager appearance money they made was seldom enough for them to afford a hotel room. Many of them would come and perform for a week or more, and Jerry offered to let them stay at his place on Bainbridge Street and sleep on his sofa. Seminal artists such as Skip James, Doc Watson, Mississippi John Hurt, Robert Pete Williams, and others would stay with him while they gigged around the area. Jerry had been playing the guitar since the late 1950s and had learned a lot from listening to records, but hosting these authentic traditional musicians gave him the key to the musical kingdom. They got a free place to sleep, and Jerry picked their brains and watched their hands.

Jerry and I bonded over our mutual love of this roots music, and I quickly realized that I could learn a lot from him. Jerry was a direct link to the creators of this uniquely original American musical and cultural treasure chest, and I wanted to get to the source. I asked him if he would show me a few things, and without much formality, he invited me to come by his place and we could "pick a bit." Thus began the next critical phase of my musical apprenticeship and mentorship.

In those days I walked everywhere, carrying my guitar down the narrow colonial alleys in the footsteps of the ghosts of the founding fathers. In the shadows of Independence Hall, where the radical concept of democracy was molded and realized, my personal journey of musical enlightenment was about to blossom, and with it, an experience that would link me in the most direct way to another part of American history.

Ricks lived in a small brick townhouse with his wife and two children, across the street from another luminary in the roots music world: Dick Waterman. Dick was a traditional music enthusiast, archivist, and photographer in the mold of Ralph Rinzler and Alan Lomax. He acted as a de facto manager for many of the aforementioned artists, helping them by booking shows and facilitating their introduction to a new generation of folk-music fans, and all the while documenting the era with his wonderful images. Often, Dick would ask Jerry to travel with and look after these artists, many of whom were not familiar with living and surviving in the big city.

In between, Jerry took on several students, and I became one of the lucky few. I'll never forget my first lesson: pressing the doorbell and walking up the stairs into his eclectic, nicely decorated living room, adorned with folk art and African wood carvings. In an adjacent alcove, he sat on a small sofa, dressed in soft, loose pants; a tan, well-worn corduroy sport coat with leather patches on the sleeve; and a wool pinstripe vest. Before him was a dark wooden coffee table scattered with scrap paper, pencils, and a Native American bowl filled with metal and plastic fingerpicks as well as a collection of flat picks. Off to the side, within an arm's length of the sofa, was a low cabinet filled with vinyl albums, and an open-top turntable. But what really attracted my attention was the rich, golden wood on Jerry's well-worn Martin D-18, casually propped up against the front of the sofa.

He motioned for me to sit down across from him and we made some small talk until he finally suggested I open my guitar case and play a little bit. I can't remember what I was playing in those days, it might have been a Guild F-40, but it wasn't a D-18! There was no formal lesson plan and there never would be . . . he just asked me to play a few things for him and so I began. The next thing I remember, the rich, deep thump of his Martin filled the room. Suddenly my guitar parts just began to sound better. Jerry tastefully plugged the sonic gaps of my playing style. I was being transported to another musical plane; his deft and subtle accompaniment elevated what I was doing in a way that I had never experienced. I was so blown away, I believe I stopped to watch him, and he just laughed and we smiled at each other. His effortless playing had a rhythmic fluidity and groove that made everything I was doing sound so much better. This is a quality that in later years I would come to appreciate and experience with many of the great instrumentalists that I've had the privilege to work with.

Jerry had a quiet presence and he let his playing do the talking. From the sound hole of that vintage Martin the echoes of the Delta dirt, the Smoky Mountains air, and the big-city blues reverberated and enveloped me.

Jerry had mentioned to me during one of our lessons that Doc and Merle would be performing at the Main Point, a popular folk venue in Bryn Mawr just outside of Philadelphia, and even though he couldn't go, he suggested that I go by myself and he would let them know I was coming to see the show and hang out in the tiny downstairs dressing room with them. Hell yeah, I was going! That evening I hauled my guitar to the station and hopped aboard the train to the Mainline.

Arriving at the Bryn Mawr station it was just a short walk to the Main Point, a venue that I had been to many times to see such legendary performers like Sonny Terry and Brownie McGee, Jim Kweskin Jug Band with the sexy Maria Muldaur, Reverend Gary Davis, Dave Van Ronk, Buffy St. Marie, Phil Ochs and so many more, but this time I was entering the inner sanctum of my hero. The gal working the door gave me the high sign and pointed me toward the low staircase that led to the small basement dressing room.

There, on a sofa, sat the man himself, holding his acoustic guitar in his lap almost exactly like the photo on his album cover, while his son Merle was talking to another fellow over on the other side of the room near a small table with fruit, muffins, and a tea kettle. Merle interrupted his conversation for a moment when he saw me and I introduced myself as a "friend of Jerry Ricks." Doc spoke up almost immediately saying, "You must be John, come set a spell, thank you for coming by." His deep soft voice was warm and his distinctive North Carolina accent instantly put me at ease. He asked me how Jerry was doing as his milky blue eyes stared straight ahead, gazing over my shoulder at something unseen beyond me.

Somehow Doc knew that I had my guitar with me and asked me if I wanted to "pick a bit." In the corner of the room I noticed Merle reaching for his guitar, and he came over and sat next to me with his father facing us across the small coffee table. Doc began to strum the opening melody of "Little Sadie" and I joined in tentatively. All those hours dropping the needle and learning every song all came together in that magical moment as the three of us traded rounds in between the verses of that classic mountain murder ballad. I guess I did OK because everyone was smiling. If I could have pinched myself and not dropped a beat I would have. Then I asked if he'd pick me "Bye Bye Blues" and he did, in two different keys, as well.

A diary entry of mine from this magical night adds even more long-ago color and detail: *We were all sitting and drinking and Doc slapped his knee and spoke about intolerance and humans and their inhumanity. The things that even the blind can see. Stories from Deep Gap and how his brother David left the oxen in the field, one day bound for the big city. Doc's daddy knew he'd be back and home he came with his "tail between his legs." Doc also said that Dan Crary was the best flat picker he'd ever heard . . . "Nobody should pick that good," were his words.*

I was very conscious of not wearing out my welcome, and I recall making some small talk about what a big fan I was and how I had seen him perform at the Second Fret and Philadelphia Folk Festival. Then all too soon, it was show time and, wanting to give them some space, I headed back upstairs. Their show was flawless as usual, with Merle featured on a classic Mississippi John Hurt song called "Spike Driver Blues," still one of my favorites to this day. I stayed for both sets and caught the last train back to the city. It must have been close to midnight by the time I began walking with my guitar toward Daryl's little Father, Son, and Holy Ghost house on Quince Street, where I was staying.

There I was, clip clopping down the empty Spruce Street sidewalk in my dirty, worn out clogs nearing the corner of Twelfth Street when I noticed three dark shapes heading in my direction. The natural high of the amazing evening was suddenly snuffed as I realized that these approaching shapes had materialized as three young boys, menacingly moving shoulder-to-shoulder straight for me. I heard one of them say, "Hey you got a light?" My street sense kicked in and I mumbled "No" and quickly stepped off the sidewalk between two parked cars into the street. . . . Right move but wrong answer . . . they were on me like a pack of coyotes and before I could run, one of them had latched onto my long hair and began pulling me down to the asphalt. I immediately began to yell as I was whirled around in a desperate attempt to keep from having the hair yanked out of my head. As I swung around the other two began punching and kicking at me. My only weapon was my heavy guitar case, which I had clenched in my hand . . . and I wasn't about to let that go. Around and around we tussled while they pummeled me until suddenly I heard another voice from the darkness down the block . . . then as quickly as the attack had come, the three boys were gone and I collapsed in a heap still clutching my guitar case. I looked up toward the sound of the voice and to my amazement there, under the dim yellow street lamp, I saw a man standing with a framing hammer held high above his head, and then without a word I watched as he turned and slowly disappeared back into the darkness.

When I got back to the house, Daryl's reaction was, "what the hell happened to you?" and I told him about the attack in the street but I think I was in such a state of shock that the amazing experience with Doc Watson became almost insignificant. The next day, Daryl sat down at his little Wurlitzer electric piano and wrote a great song called "Fall in Philadelphia." A week before, his bicycle had been stolen; the little hippie neighborhood that we lived in was crawling with drug dealers and ne'er-do-wells, and he cleverly crafted the real little world that was all around us into a very cool song . . . artfully capturing a slice of life and immortalizing a moment that might have gone unnoticed by the average person but not to a great songwriter. The truth is where the best stuff comes from. After all these years, I always find it so amusing when the Philly fans request that song as though it's a celebration of the city; I guess they really don't listen too closely to the lyrics. But it really does capture a moment in time in a city that I would only call home for less than a year.

The Second Season

MELODY FOR A MEMORY
1970s

The Draft

graduated from Temple University in June of 1970; the Vietnam War was
still under way, but the loss of so many young men was wearing on the psyche
of the American public and public opinion was turning. The antiwar sentiment
was expanding beyond the hippies and college campuses to the general popu-
lation. I have always thought of myself as a patriotic American with the con-
stitutional right to dissent, and this was a dark, critical time and pivotal moment
for my generation. It was my opinion that the Vietnamese conflict was really a
civil war, and as such the United States had no strategic basis for becoming
involved. Attempts to craft the legitimacy of our involvement by invoking the
Cold War-era fear of ideologies between communism and democracy sounded
like bullshit to me. This was my mindset at the age of twenty-two. Statements
from then-Secretary of Defense Robert McNamara, stating that our involvement in Vietnam would be "a laboratory for the development of organizations
and procedures for the conduct of sub-limited war" only reinforced my beliefs.
The get-out-of-Vietnam movement was strong and in full swing around the
country, including on the Temple University campus. Casualty rates were high
among the boys my age. The fact that many of my closest friends from high

school were either wounded or killed only served to heighten my feelings of the urgency and seriousness of the situation. This was not a war to defend our country from a clearly defined threat to the United States; it was a senseless, deadly chess game endorsed and encouraged by the military-industrial complex, played and promoted by arrogant former World War II generals with the lives of young American servicemen and women as pawns on their board.

One of those boys was my best friend and fellow co-captain of the North Penn High School wrestling team, Ron Murphy. Ronnie was a quiet, strong, but gentle kid who after high school graduation enrolled at East Stroudsburg State College. After his freshman year he dropped out and joined the Marine Corps. I never heard from him again. Then, a few months later, word spread around my hometown that he had been killed by a Claymore mine. What was left of his remains were flown back to the States, and shortly thereafter his flagged-draped closed coffin was displayed front and center at the foot of the Lansdale Catholic Church altar.

We had been really close during high school, and for a time I even dated his sister Sharon. His parents asked me if I would sing at the service. I really didn't know if I could hold it together but couldn't say no. It was difficult to choose an appropriate song, and I thought long and hard about the selection, finally settling on "The Battle Hymn of the Republic." That song had historic military gravitas, and I wanted to honor him and make a statement at the same time.

I stood alone, upstairs in the vacant choir loft of the church, next to the pipe organ, peering down at the families and friends gathered below in the pews. Up to this point in my young life, it was without a doubt the toughest thing I had ever had to deal with. I was nervous and very emotional. On a cue from the priest I began to sing, but my throat closed almost immediately as tears welled up in my eyes and I stared at Ronnie's coffin lying in state before the tabernacle. The blood-red stripes on the flag that cloaked his coffin were but a blurry vision. All I could see was the face of my childhood friend, who had lost his future in a senseless war in an unforgiving foreign jungle. It was my first taste of mortality.

In those days, the government draft had a provision that would defer college students as long as they remained in school, but as my graduation approached, I duly received my draft notice in the mail. I couldn't eat, sleep, or even bathe for weeks prior to the day of the required physical. When that day finally came, I reluctantly dragged my emaciated, reeking body to the address on the draft notice. I slowly climbed the steps of a foreboding, brownstone building in Center City. My thick, dark mane of hair hung well below my shoulders, I was unshaven, and my ragged clothes reeked of body odor. I silently took my place in line with a bunch of boys straight out of high school. To my twenty-two-year-old eyes they appeared so young and innocent and, like me, scared shitless. I spoke to no one.

I filled out the required medical form, careful to check the boxes that applied: allergies; asthma; insomnia—anything truthful enough to look bad. For hours we stood in line to be herded through various physical and mental tests by burly army MPs with crisp, brown uniforms. Finally, we were all instructed to line up, drop our trousers, turn around, and bend at the waist while a doctor in a white lab coat approached from the rear and, with rubber gloves, spread our butt cheeks to inspect our anuses. Was he checking for possible contraband or did the army have a preferred anal profile for soldiering? Who knows . . . but he didn't spend a lot of time in front of my ass.

After pulling up our pants, we were individually directed to enter a series of green-curtained cubicles. Inside was another white coat, sitting behind a small desk covered in official-looking documents. I handed over the sheaf of papers clutched in my hand and sat on the edge of the chair in front of him. As he silently began to peruse my paperwork, I noticed a look of consternation on his face.

My fate was well and truly in his hands. After a long moment he looked up at me and said, "Son, you seem to have a lot of problems. Will you be willing to sign this document and confirm that everything you listed on this form is true?" I nodded in the affirmative, and as he pushed the forms across the desk toward me, he continued. "The army is no place for someone like you. I suggest you pull yourself together and get some help." I signed my name and he dismissed me. I emerged from the booth and approached a long desk with three or four sergeants wielding large rubber stamps. As each of the boys filed by, they pounded a big red 1-A on their forms while shouting out loudly, "Accepted! Report for duty!" When it was my turn, I placed the paperwork on the table in front of the soldier. He paused then looked up at me with an odd expression. Then he slowly reached for another stamp, and as he mashed it onto the page he made a point of bellowing, "UNACCEPTABLE!" I walked out of the building and went back to my apartment.

Europe

wanted to travel after I graduated from Temple University. Other than the brief ski trip to Colorado during college, I had never really ventured beyond the northeastern United States. My dream, like so many young Americans before me, was to fulfill a time-honored postcollege tradition: Make the passage and journey through Europe. Free from the regimen of four years' university study and with no job and no timetable, I decided to embark on a loosely conceived plan to spend the summer traipsing and tramping around as many countries as I could. I'd travel light, with only a backpack, my guitar, and a couple of blank journals to help document the journey and satisfy my new passion for writing.

As the last few months of my senior year in college began counting down, the itch to put Philadelphia in my rearview mirror grew stronger. I yearned to breathe the air, touch, and feel what life was like in the Old World, the one my family came from. Encouragement to make the trip blossomed through conversations with a girl named Barbara Wilson, a very creative photographer and equestrian who was graduating from Moore College of Art and Design at the same time as I would graduate from Temple. Her plan was to spend the summer in England, working with racehorses, and we agreed to meet there before I continued on my own to the Continent.

Earlier that spring, I had what could have been a very serious motorcycle accident. One late spring afternoon, I hopped on my bike en route to a guitar-teaching job in Glenside, just outside of the city. As I accelerated from a stoplight near the entrance to Fairmount Park, my peripheral vision was suddenly filled with a flash of shiny metal and glass as a large sedan appeared out of nowhere. To this day I can still see the shock and surprise on the driver's face, frozen in my vision for a split second through the car's passenger window. My bike and time did not slow down when I hit the brakes. The motorcycle plowed straight into the back door of the car at a ninety-degree angle. Upon impact I must have reflexively stood up on the pegs, and I was catapulted over the roof of the car, finally coming to a bloody and battered stop after somersaulting down the road. The skin had been ripped from my arms and back, my T-shirt was torn to shreds, but luckily the helmet I wore prevented a more serious injury. Sprawled in the street, I dimly recall a voice asking, "Are you all right? Don't move." Standing above me was a Philadelphia policeman. He said, "I saw the whole thing, he came out of a one-way street the wrong way, it wasn't your fault." He then carefully helped me to my feet, but I couldn't stand up, my legs were shaking, and I collapsed back onto the curb. Twenty yards away my bike was a twisted, mangled, smoking mess wedged beneath the car. Even in my shocked state I realized that it could have been me under there. By some miracle I had been spared. As the years went on I would have more close encounters with the grim reaper . . . but for that moment I was battered and shaken but still alive on the streets of Philadelphia. A small legal settlement awarded me five hundred dollars; now I could now make my trip to Europe a reality.

Never having had that much money, one of the first things I did was buy some real food; in those days my diet consisted mostly of classic Philly staples: soft pretzels, hoagies, and Tastykakes. After a few good meals, I folded the remaining money into a Fodor's map of Europe, packed a little blue leather-bound Berlitz phrase book with a change of clothes into a backpack, and, guitar in hand, took the train from the Thirtieth Street Station to New York City, where I boarded a flight for London.

Before leaving, I made an arrangement to sublet the apartment I had been sharing with my ex-girlfriend, Mimi, to Daryl's sister, Kathy, and her boyfriend. I knew them well, I trusted them, and I figured my place would be in good hands.

And then I was off.

After arriving in London I made my way to the American Express office near Piccadilly Circus to try to connect with Barbara Wilson, who had traveled on her own to England. In those days before cell phones, the only way to leave a message for someone was to tack a note on the bulletin board at the local American Express office and hope they might see it. I hung around for a few days but we never connected, and I was anxious to explore and get moving. I would be returning there to spend more time later in the trip.

First stop: France. I took a wild, stomach-churning ride on a huge hovercraft across the channel to Calais and from there hopped a train to Paris. Written on the inside cover of my little blue Berlitz phrase book was an address given to me by an acquaintance in Philly. He advised me to go to that address and said the people who lived there would welcome me and let me crash there.

From the moment I arrived in Paris it was apparent that the language barrier was going to be a problem. To say the Parisians were unsympathetic to my inability to speak the language would be an understatement. I was greeted with disdain and for the most part ignored as I did my best pantomime and phonetic linguistic butchering in an attempt to get directions or something to eat. My little Berlitz phrasebook didn't do me much good, but somehow I managed to find my way to 129 Rue du Maine. I approached a heavy wooden door and rang the bell with trepidation. Finally, a rugged-looking thirtysomething man answered the door, eyeing me with an uncomfortable and confused look. There I stood, this frumpy, freaky friend-of-a-friend from Philadelphia with nowhere else to go. That he even invited me into his home still astounds me to this day, but times were different then . . . the peace and love ethos still existed. He reluctantly led me inside his quaint, bohemian-styled apartment. I set my guitar down in the entryway, when suddenly from another room his gorgeous girlfriend appeared. They began a tense exchange, and although I couldn't understand a thing, I sensed that he was doing his best to explain why this weird-looking little foreigner was standing in their living room for no apparent reason. Language barrier notwithstanding, it was obvious that she was not thrilled with the prospect of hosting this longhaired vagabond in their home. There was a long, awkward moment while I considered tossing off some Benjamin Franklin and Lafayette references to break the ice, but I wisely held my tongue while their conversation played out.

Incredibly, they agreed to let me stay and showed me to a tiny room. I'm sure they had their regrets right from the start, after I asked to use the toilet and would make the first what would become many ignorant American missteps: I entered what I thought was the bathroom and proceeded to take a piss in what I thought was an exotic-looking urinal. I had never seen a bidet before, and when I emerged into the hallway, my host, realizing what I had done, just stood there shaking his head. Welcome to Europe!

Despite that faux pas, for several days my hosts were nothing but gracious and generous with their time and energy in helping me find my way around. I tried my best to reciprocate by playing and singing for them, and learned that the gal was a well-known actress and her husband loved American folk music. Things were looking up in the City of Light. I set about speed sightseeing, squeezing in the Louvre, Notre Dame, the Champs Elysees, and the Left Bank in two days. All the while I had my ears tuned to the music in the air.

In my journal I wrote:

Music in Europe is a strange combination of old American music, both good and bad, and their own—but not much. Dylan even more than the Beatles is the most popular artist—his words—or just what is it? Everyone sings his songs—with his or her peculiar accent etc. It's very beautiful.

One specific event I did not want to miss was the French Grand Prix, which was taking place at the Circuit de Charade near the town of Clermont-Ferrand,

a classic race track in the Auvergne Mountains, about four hours by train from Paris. Witnessing a European Formula One Grand Prix had been extremely high on my to-do list ever since I first fell in love with racing back in the early 60's, inspired by those old magazine articles.

My Parisian hosts directed me to the proper train, and after several hours and a lot of hiking, I finally arrived at the track. The racing circuit, built in 1958 using public roads surrounding the sides of an extinct volcano, was littered with loose rock, which caused all sorts of problems, from punctured tires to drivers being hit in the face with pieces of basalt shot like bullets from under the rear wheels of the cars ahead.

I bought my ticket and couldn't wait to experience my first European Grand Prix. However, after the initial excitement wore off, I found myself lugging my backpack and guitar through the crowd while my freaky appearance elicited more than a few odd looks from the thousands of race fans scattered about the hillside overlooking the track. I struggled without success to string together enough French words to order food, so with hunger as a powerful motivator, I formulated a plan: Standing patiently near the concession stand, my stomach growling, I listened carefully to how people ordered and figured when it was my turn I would simply mimic them and see what happened. The best I could manage came out sounding like: "Un coca, Un burga si vous pleas." Close enough . . . I got a burger and a Coke and sat on the hillside to watch the race.

I had been following the Grand Prix circuit for many years and knew the teams, the cars, and the drivers by heart. As a Yankee, I guess I was pulling for Dan Gurney, the California driver who ultimately came in sixth that day. The race was chock full of guys who would become future racing legends. Among them was eventual three-time world champion Jackie Stewart. That day he struggled with an ill-handling March Ford. Sitting on that hillside in 1970, I never could have imagined that one day I'd meet him and become friends with his family . . . but more on that later.

Journal entry: There is nothing like a European world championship. . . .
Rindt in his Lotus won the race. And now it's 8:30 P.M. I'm sitting on a

stone bridge about 5 miles west of Clermont in the middle of these beauti-
ful mountains. Evergreen but also hordes of skeeters that are driving
me nuts.

The next day I tried hitchhiking and didn't have much luck. People must have thought I looked like Jesus, with my long hair and mustache, because as they sped past, they would honk their horns, laugh and point while making the sign of the cross. I walked for miles until I finally came upon a little farm-house. I cautiously walked down the lane, and when I knocked on the door, a kindly old woman patiently waited while I mumbled and mimed that I was desperate for a drink of water. She filled a glass, handed me some bread, and I kept on walking.

My fortunes changed later that day and I was finally able to string together a couple of rides into the town of Toulouse. There I got a quick bite to eat and boarded a rickety old train bound for Spain. I wedged my way into the packed, dirty, and smelly second-class car. It was an extremely humid summer day, the heat was oppressive, the car was packed—not an empty seat to be found. I tried wandering from car to car, but the smell of body odor and rotting food drove me to finally find an equally odorous spot next to the toilet in the clattering metal space between the two rail cars, where I ended up sitting on my guitar case for most of the twelve-hour journey.

When I arrived in Barcelona, I immediately fell in love with the city. It was Old World and mysterious, with structures from the Romanesque, Gothic, and Renaissance periods. It was late in the afternoon when I arrived, and the first thing I did was take a dip in the warm blue Mediterranean. Since I had nowhere to stay I decided to sleep that night in a park near the city center. The following morning, after rolling up my sleeping bag, I used the facilities at the park information center, and on my way out stopped to look at their collection of huge black scorpions—all of which were found in that same park where I had just spent the night.

I would need other accommodations quickly.

Hanging out on Las Ramblas, Barcelona's famed tree-lined pedestrian

mall, I began to meet lots of
other young people who, like
me, had decided to play the
part of summer nomads. We
were like leaves, scattered
and random, all being blown
throughout these beauti-
ful countries. There was an
unspoken trust among us;
strangers shared food, wine,
sex, dope, water—the essen-
tials of life, as the wayfarer
spirit was alive and well that
summer of 1970. Many of us
also exchanged travel plans
so that we could reconnect

at some point down the line. I met many fantastic people. A guy named Jim,
from Winnipeg, even sketched me one night, and his portrait remains in an
old diary of mine.

Being in Spain, it seemed sensible to attend a bullfight. I really didn't know
what to expect. Of course I bought the cheapest ticket available, which put me
in the direct sunlight on a very hot summer afternoon. It was broiling, but I
was curious and soon very unsettled by the spectacle about to unfold below
me in the bullring.

Journal entry:
I went to the bullfights.
Three men killing six animals

*For sport? For money? For the crowd? For their heads? It goes on, and
has for many years. There is an appeal, the romance with a challenge of man
against the great, thundering beasts. But the contest is decided long before the
two foes meet. There is danger for the man but there is only death for the bull.*

After that bloody, unsettling experience I needed to mellow out and treated myself to a sit-down meal at a harborside restaurant. I decided to try the classic seafood-and-rice dish called paella and wash it down with some cool sweet sangria, an intoxicating concoction made of wine, chopped fruit, a little bit of brandy, and a lot of sugar. I had never had anything that tasted so refreshing and I guzzled it like water . . . bad mistake. As I stumbled my way back toward the pension where I was staying, I stopped every few feet to puke my guts out in the street. Somehow I made it back to the pension. When I finally laid my head back on the creaky cot, the abstract design of peeling paint on the ceiling spun around and around all night. It was awful.

After a few days in Barcelona I hitchhiked south, down the coast to the picturesque town of Sitges, which had gained a reputation as an artistic community back in the late nineteenth century, when Catalan painter Santiago Rusiñol took up residence there. Actually a lot of hippies and backpackers had the same idea, and shortly after I arrived I met an English couple named Jules and Gabby who were camping in a tent on the beach just outside of town. They invited me to crash with them for a few days, and I took them up on their offer. After the first night we noticed machine-gun-toting military patrols harassing the hippies and herding them off the beach. Near our campsite, I had discovered what looked to be a broken-down, ancient stone jail cell with rusting iron bars. For the next few days this became my "beach house," where I hid out from the intimidating patrols.

One day word spread throughout the drifter community that a bunch of freaks and squatters were having what could be loosely described as a barbecue up in the hills above the town. In a dusty, dry arroyo, a ragtag group of kids were grilling slabs of lamb (at least they said the wild-tasting, strangely shaped meat was lamb) on filthy iron grates over makeshift fire pits. Free food was always welcome and it seemed really appetizing at first, but a few hours later, after scarfing down what was either a piece of uncooked or simply rancid meat, I became violently ill. Sangria sick is one thing, but this was dysentery, and it was a whole other level of ugly.

I managed to make it back to my jail cell on the beach where I lay for the better part of three days. I was so sick I actually thought I might die. Retching and shitting uncontrollably, doubled up on the dirt floor until there was nothing left to purge. When I could finally summon the energy, I stumbled down to the ocean to rinse off, only to return to the jail cell with my hair a tangled, matted mess and my deeply tanned skin crusted white from the salt water.

After a few days I made my way back into Sitges and found a restaurant that would pay me with a meal if I played guitar on the patio. I was starving and needed some decent food. I did that for two nights, and after my strength returned I was ready to move on. Next stop: Rome.

Throughout my life I have always been interested in the history of ancient Rome. As a young kid I would cover my school notebooks with doodles of Roman Centurion helmets, SPQR regimental banners, and the Romans' iconic architecture. I read everything I could about the epic one-thousand-year span of the Republic and Empire. Now finally I had arrived on hallowed ground amidst the sunken ruins of the Forum. Running my fingers across the finely carved marble columns, I strolled the ancient cobbles, passing the crumbled remains of buildings where commerce and law, life and death, myth and everyday life intersected eons ago. Now that they were no longer one-dimensional images from the pages of history books, I felt my surroundings come to life. Closing my eyes, I was transported in my mind back in time to 47 BC, during the reign of the Caesars, feeling the heat on my skin from that same sun that beat down on the citizens and slaves of what once was the center of Western civilization. The elaborate fountains, piazzas, and basilicas were no longer merely a historic backdrop. A thousand years of technical innovation, world military domination, architectural genius, and the polytheism that yielded to Christianity, enveloped me in that moment. The sensation was more visceral than mere imagination could conjure.

Everywhere I went felt eerily familiar. Running my hands over the exquisitely carved statues of Gods and demigods and descending into the bowels of the Coliseum and the Catacomb crypts gripped me in a profound way. This was no longer a tourist experience. I was overwhelmed with a sense of returning home.

Snapping out of the reverie of the past one afternoon I made the requisite pilgrimage to Vatican City. I was curious, as a lapsed Catholic, to find out whether my former faith might be rekindled or reconfirmed. First impression: overwhelming awe at the opulence and ostentation that surrounded me everywhere I turned. Saint Peter's Basilica appeared to me not as a shrine to holiness, but rather more like an anti-monument to the essence of spirituality. At the entrance to the Sistine Chapel priests with coin belts were collecting fees as they herded and hustled the long lines of tourists into the rotunda, to crane their necks upward toward the ceiling while trying to view and appreciate Michelangelo's masterpiece before being hurriedly shooed back out into the hot Italian sun. Be in awe, pay up, bow down, believe, and keep moving . . . two thousand years of contradiction and implausible myth, an empire of power in the guise of imperious faith left me wondering if the dogma and doctrine of man can ever be truly divine.

Faith not renewed, I found myself back on the street, still a wanderer, still in Rome, but still with the urge to keep moving. After all, didn't the Romans build their elegantly designed roads with the express purpose of moving their armies north to conquer the land of the Goths? I too was feeling the urge to hit the road and head north as well.

IN THAT SUMMER of 1970, in every city throughout Europe, the American Express office was the place to connect, mail and receive letters, catch up on the latest news from back home, and make friends. The group of guys and gals from the Detroit area that I had met earlier that week invited me to join them in their Volkswagen van heading to Florence. They dropped me off on the outskirts of the city at dawn and I made a quick visit to see the famous statue of David. There I reunited with my Dutch friends, hopping a ride in their van up toward the Italian Alps. After many kilometers of being lulled to sleep by the sound of tires droning over the road, I was awakened by cathedral bells tolling dream tones across the water of exquisite Lake Como. Scattered about the hillsides, palatial villas shimmered and glowed through the van's dust-covered windows, unapproachable in the distance. This was a world separate both physically and culturally from my vagabond existence, but the villas, too, segued into the past as the little Volkswagen's anemic engine wheezed and struggled its way up the Italian foothills and on into the mountains of Switzerland. We chugged our way up and down the dizzying alpine switchbacks, passing picturesque chalets with stones on their roofs, and cows with bells around their necks. A cliché of sensory scenic overload but beautiful beyond description all the same. My companions were bound for Holland, and after exchanging addresses with them, I hopped out and was on my own in Switzerland.

After a few days of exploring around St. Moritz I took the lift up to the Corvatsch glacier above Lake Silvaplana. After skiing on the meager strip of midsummer snow and fortified by the requisite local chocolate and cheese, I stuck out my thumb once again, bound for Germany.

During my brief stay in Hamburg I heard rumors about a hippie commune in Copenhagen called Christiania where everyone was welcome, and so I booked myself passage on a ferry to Denmark. Arriving in Copenhagen I wasted no time finding this supposedly utopian paradise of free love, music, and hashish. Instead, I discovered a bleak, end-of-the-world dystopia—a blown-out, apocalyptic set of rundown buildings on the edge of town, commandeered by junkies, dealers, hustlers, and other desperate layers of a heavily drugged-out fringe society. I wandered around and ended up settling into a dirt-floor basement inhabited by a kaftan-wearing Turk and his mute girlfriend, who huddled in a shadowed corner and never seemed to move. They spent all day and night puffing on a clay chillum packed with Moroccan kief. For several days I shared that depressing, dank hovel, always on guard, for in Christiania, thievery was rampant. If there was ever an antidote for the illusion of a hippie society of peace and love, this was it.

During the day I emerged from the darkness of Christiania and wandered around the quaint streets of Copenhagen. Passing by the historic Tivoli Gardens amusement park (which dated back to 1843 and was the place said to have inspired Walt Disney to build a theme park of his own), I saw a poster advertising a Joan Baez concert that evening. I bought a ticket to the park and strolled its pathways, hoping to catch the eye of any one of the many gorgeous young blond girls hanging out that summer evening. No such luck . . . considering I hadn't had a shower in weeks and looked like a wild man from planet Weirdo, I never got a second look. But soon dusk fell, and thousands of tiny lights began to twinkle and glow in the trees, giving the park a fairytale milieu. I made my way toward the front of the small stage just as the concert began. I had been a Joan Baez fan from the first time I heard her back in 1960. I spent hours learning every song on her first Vanguard album by heart, and even more time mastering the unique, bushy, index-finger strum that she used on "Silver Dagger," "The Lily Of the West," and the classic Carter Family standard, "Wildwood Flower." Through her, I discovered the Child Ballads and became aware of the Scotch-Irish link to the music of Appalachia. Baez was the quintessential queen of folk music, and her ethereal voice was in full command that night, floating through the summer air, singing all of her best-known anthems, including "Joe Hill," "Oh, Happy Day" and "Swing Low, Sweet Chariot." It took me back to those days, a few years earlier, of sitting on the grass of the Old Poole Farm at the Philadelphia Folk Festival in the hills near Schwenksville.

I escaped Christiania and Copenhagen frail, weary, and disillusioned. The naive dream of finding a hippie paradise now felt like nothing more than a mass hallucination, something that only existed inside my generation's collective imagination. But there was one more mind-altering mecca yet to be experienced, and so I made my way to Amsterdam.

By now I could feel the energy of my journey running out. I hung out on the Leidseplein Square with kids from all over the world; hit the two infamous nightclubs Melkweg (Milkyway) and Paradiso, where I watched the debut of the Beatles' movie *Yellow Submarine,* smoked some Nepalese black hash, and gorged myself on sweet apple pancakes covered with powdered white sugar. Then one day, and don't ask me how, Barbara Wilson seemed to magically materialize. She had traveled over from England. Remember there were no cell phones and no way to keep in touch and she had no idea that I would be in Amsterdam on that exact date . . . but there we were, coincidentally reunited. We spent a few days swapping tales of our solo adventures.

On the streets of Amsterdam, 1970. *(Photograph by Barbara Wilson D'Andrea)*

ONE AFTERNOON I visited a record store in Amsterdam that featured private listening booths where you could give albums a spin before buying them. I grabbed a few records by Doc Watson, the Delmore Brothers, and Bill Monroe. Donning a pair of headphones, I closed my eyes and let the raw beauty of the bluegrass music fill my mind and swirl through my soul. A flood of emotions hit me and to describe it as merely feeling homesick would be to diminish its impact. For months I had been running so hard, trying to absorb everything the Old World had to offer, but now, alone in the record store's phonograph booth, an overwhelmingly thick and textural longing for something familiar welled up from deep inside. It washed over me, and like a siren call from the hills so uniquely and undeniably American, it beckoned. At that moment, low on cash and even lower on energy, I knew it was time to go home.

I figured it would be easier to get a flight to the states from London, so after a few more days in Amsterdam, I jumped on the ferry and crossed the channel.

The day after I arrived, I awoke to the news that Jimi Hendrix had died from a drug overdose only a few blocks away from where I was crashing.

I wandered down King's Road and strolled toward World's End, observing the parade of rock-star wannabes teetering along in their platform shoes and flashy flamboyant fashions. Stopping to have a coffee, I searched the classified section of a local paper and found an ad that read, "Flights to New York just one hundred pounds." I headed straight to the address in the ad and arrived at a little brownstone apartment in a down-on-its-heels residential area. There, in a sparsely furnished makeshift office with a simple desk, were two sketchy-looking Indian guys just hanging out. "Oh yeah man, we got jet flights to New York, best deal in town." Damn! I scored. . . . Jet flight to New York for a hundred pounds. . . . I'm as good as home.

I handed over the last of my cash, and while they were processing my ticket, I couldn't help but notice the music that was playing on the turntable in the background. The melodies were infectious, with clever, thoughtful lyrics brought home by a very musical production focused simply on a piano and vocal. "Who is that?" I asked. "Brand new album by a piano player named Elton John."

"Take Me to the Pilot," "Sixty Years On," and especially "Your Song" were instantly stuck in my head. I was completely entranced and impressed by the music I heard that day in that grim little office. Soon I would be seeing him in a small club in Philadelphia during his first tour of America. Years later I would sit with him recounting these stories, musician to musician. But those things were down the road. Right now I had to get home.

A COUPLE OF days later I arrived at Gatwick Airport and was sitting anxiously in the waiting area, preparing to board the plane. Suddenly, out of nowhere, four uniformed police officers appeared and ordered us to separate and form two lines, men on one side of the hallway and women on the other. I shuffled to the back of the line and began to panic when I realized that they were starting to pat down and body search the passengers. I had a big chunk of hash stuck in my sock. These guys were already looking at me funny, so I knew they were going to give me a pretty good going over. I had one way out. Reaching down and pretending to tie my shoe, with my hands hidden by my guitar case, I pulled the hash out of my sock, put it in my mouth, and swallowed the entire thing. They frisked me and checked my passport, and with my heart pounding I walked out of the terminal and across the tarmac. As I approached the airplane through the early evening mist, the advertised "jet flight" to New York turned out to be an old, worn-out-looking Lockheed Electra turboprop. These planes were probably great when they were built back in 1957, but as I climbed up the stairs that September evening in 1970, I began to sweat. By now it was way too late . . . the hash began to kick in, and a creeping paranoia concerning the prospect of a long flight high above the North Atlantic swept over me.

After squeezing myself into a cramped middle seat, sandwiched tightly by passengers on either side, we took off, and so did I. Between the bone-rattling turbulence, the undulating drone of the prop engines, and my now near-hallucinogenic state of mind, I was doing my best to not freak out and to hold it together. Whatever happened out there at thirty thousand feet over the gray and bitter-cold ocean, I was along for the ride.

Miserable, claustrophobic, and nearly suffocating in the stale cabin air, I managed to survive the eight-hour ordeal, and we finally landed at Gander, Newfoundland to refuel. But hey, we would soon be in New York, right? Well, sort of. . . .

See, my budget ticket wasn't exactly getting me to New York City. I had taken that for granted. The ad read: NEW YORK. The truth was that we would soon be landing in Buffalo, New York—about an eight-hour drive from Manhattan. This trip could not end fast enough.

Finally on terra firma, stranded in the Buffalo airport terminal, I meekly called my folks collect, and through Western Union they sent me enough money to hop a flight to Philadelphia.

Home at last.

Again . . . sort of.

The apartment on Quince Street. *(Courtesy Chris Epting)*

WHEN I ARRIVED back at my old apartment at Twentieth and Spruce Street, I didn't find Daryl's sister or her boyfriend but I did find a padlock on the door and an eviction notice. During my absence they hadn't paid the rent, so now I was locked out and homeless. Utterly exhausted and out of options, still lugging my guitar and backpack, I walked over to Daryl's house at 406 South Quince Street and knocked on the door. When he answered I said, "Hey, your sister and her boyfriend kind of didn't pay the rent. I've got nowhere to go." He laughed and said, "Come on in, man. You can live here."

So I moved into his place, where he lived with Bryna, whom he had recently married. It was an eighteenth-century Father, Son, and Holy Ghost house, as I wrote earlier—called that because it had three floors and three rooms, one on top of another. I would be staying up on the third floor, where Daryl kept his electric piano. And my roommate would be their dog, Jo.

Safe, snug, and happy to be back, I recovered from the trip, and for Daryl and me as musical partners, this is where it all really starts. This is the moment when our lives truly changed.

After my summer-long sojourn, I was ready to buckle down and get more serious about my life and my music. But that trek will always stand out in my mind. It taught me how to travel, how to truly explore, and how to survive. It was my first real look at the world. And it was the last time in my life when I would be so untethered that I could wander for months without a care in the world.

The end of that trip was the beginning of a much more interesting and rewarding one.

Back in Philly

Back in Philly, after almost four months in Europe, my life was settling in.

During the time I was living upstairs at Daryl's place, both he and I were frustrated. He was unhappy with the new band he was in, and I was fed up with having nothing to do. So he quit the band. Then we sat up on the third floor and started kicking some music around, Daryl on his piano and me on my guitar.

Many afternoons and evenings I would take up residence with my guitar on the stoop outside the front door and play traditional blues and bluegrass. Not wanting to be left out, and since he couldn't carry his piano out there, Daryl picked up a mandolin. He was so naturally gifted musically that he figured the instrument out in no time and began to learn a bunch of the folky stuff I was into. Meanwhile, upstairs by the piano, I began to adapt my guitar playing to accompany his unique piano style and chord progressions. It was a mutual sharing and learning experience.

Then we started writing songs together, which we played out in front of the house, for all the hippies and bums in the neighborhood. We wanted to get back to basics and thought it would easier if we just played together, two singer/songwriters with their instruments. It was a simple solution born from frustration, and it seemed like an easy and natural way to test the creative waters.

One autumn day I noticed some posters around town announcing the debut performance of Elton John at the famed Philly concert venue, the Electric Factory. Remembering that I had heard his record just before leaving England, I decided to go and check him out. Just a few weeks earlier, he'd made his U.S. debut at the Troubadour in Los Angeles. His weeklong run there had blown away both fans and the critics, who heralded his stand as an instant classic. He did one other show in San Francisco, and then he arrived in Philly. Elton, performing as a trio with drummer Nigel Olsson and bassist Dee Murray, was actually *opening* for Tracy Nelson and Mother Earth. I came to hear the music, but what I witnessed was triumph and disaster on stage.

I didn't know what to expect from the show, but from the downbeat, like a sonic smack in the face, I knew Elton was out to make a statement. He ran out to the long, black, grand piano at center stage wearing his soon-to-be-trademark exotic eyewear and a bright-yellow jumpsuit. Oh, and he also had a toy monkey on a string dangling from his crotch. The band was on fire, and the crowd in the Electric Factory went bonkers. Hendrix, Zappa, and many others had graced this stage before, and Elton and company were now there to stake their claim. They were loud, musical, and exciting. Near the end of his set he put one leg up on the top of the piano, and when he reached down and pulled the string on his crotch monkey, the arms waved up and down and its eyes lit up . . . it was insane! The applause was deafening and he came back for multiple encores—the audience would not let him off the stage . . . that was the triumph part.

When he finally finished, and after what seemed like an eternity, the evening's headliners, Tracey Nelson and Mother Earth appeared. She walked slowly out to the center of the stage, dressed in her floor-length flower-power dress and stood, visibly upset, almost apologetic in a way, as a front-row fan handed her a bouquet of flowers. Before the music began, the first thing she did was softly mumble a cryptic apology to the audience in a sweet, quiet way for taking so long to come onstage. But I knew what was going on in her head and the reality of what had just gone down . . . there was no way the laid-back country-folk rock that they were about to play could ever match the intensity and energy that Elton had just unleashed on the crowd. While she was singing their first song, a large majority of the crowd began to walk out. That was the disaster part. I learned a big lesson that night, and I never forgot it.

My journal entry on November 4 includes a prophetic sentence:

> *Daryl and I have begun to get our songs together in a more serious way with performing in mind.*

But first we needed a name. The label on the mailbox of the apartment we first shared back in 1968 had both of our names listed on it: "Hohl—Oates." So we simply gave ourselves the name "Whole Oats." (He'd soon change his name to Hall.)

The next couple of months were a busy, creative, productive blur. Daryl and I were writing, doing some session work, and whatever we could to shape our careers as musicians. Of course once we both committed to working together seriously, the next logical thing was to try and play some shows.

Another diary entry from that month:

> *I hope that Daryl and I get it together soon . . . we've got to get out and play for people just to see what happens—the reaction is what is important at this point.*

Saturday December 5, 1970, as Whole Oats, Daryl and I performed our first official show together at a little club in Germantown (northern Philly) called Hecate's Circle. The club was a remnant of the old folky days, run by a bear of guy named Danny Starobin. He was well known in the inner circle of Philly rock musicians as the lead guitar player of a blues band called Sweet Stavin' Chain. When we booked the show, little did we realize that our audience would be pretty much the same kids that roamed the Center City neighborhoods where we lived. It was strange to play our songs with all our friends sitting in front of us. But it was a start.

WE BOOKED A few more shows at Hecate's in January, as well as a handful of shows at the Main Point. Our reputation was grow-ing amid the small Center City hippie crowd, and out of nowhere, we were asked if we'd like to be part of a telethon to be broadcast on KYW-TV. We showed up at the TV studio among all the tap dancers, comedians, and local per-sonalities. We set up and did three or four songs before a small studio audience.

Whole Oats era, 1971. *(Courtesy John Oates)*

I didn't understand the power behind the unblinking eye of the TV camera. When the show was finished, we became minor celebrities overnight . . . people stopped us on the street and effused about how good our songs were. The TV show was a major step in our quest for the "invisible carrot"—the phrase we adopted to describe the unknown goal that we were hard at work to reach, like the donkey that trudges forever onward, pursuing a carrot on a stick.

We booked some time at World Control Studios in Philly to record some tracks, as well as cutting some demos up at Regent Sound Studios in New York. I had a working list of songs then that included "I'll Be Bye," "Past Times Behind," "Run Rabbit Run," "Lady Rain," "If That's What Makes You Happy," and a few others. Daryl had his own list of songs as well, and we just traded off singing and playing.

We were entering a strange phase as the bitter Philly winter settled in around us, enveloping us like a cold, wet, gray blanket. Daryl and I were working hard, writing, starting to perform and find our way.

Making a Move

In the early 1960s Philadelphia pop music dominated the AM airwaves, and a lot it came from the Cameo-Parkway label. It was a pre Gamble and Huff Philadelphia hit-making factory with artists like Bobby Rydell, Dee Dee Sharp, the Orlons, the Dovells, and the biggest star in their constellation, "Mr. Twist" himself—Chubby Checker. As the decade began to wane a few of the honchos from that organization branched off and created their own mini production and writing companies.

One of them was a guy named John Madara, and his right-hand man was Harry Chipetz, who formerly served at Cameo-Parkway as general manager and who enjoyed telling stories about how he bought Pat Boone his first pair of white bucks, and passed on signing the Beatles because of something to the effect of, "kids can't dance to that crap." His hits and misses were based on the correct, yet provincial, concept that Philly was the epicenter of teenage culture in America. Every afternoon after school, kids all over the country flicked on the nationally syndicated TV show Dick Clark's *American Bandstand*. It was a teen dance-craze phenomenon in glorious, blurry, black-and-white. The show truly was a phenomenon, starting as a local Philadelphia show hosted by a guy named Bob Horn. Mr. Horn was fired in 1955 after being charged with drunk driving. But when television-friendly and business-savvy Dick Clark became the host in 1956, *American Bandstand* exploded in popularity. Every week, the same dancing kids would appear on the show. That was because each after-noon, at a certain time, the TV studio would open its doors for the teenage audience, and of course the kids from the closest school had an advantage. School bell rings and whoever lines up first on the sidewalk alongside the studio . . . well you know the rest.

In a way, these kids were the first teenage reality-TV stars. The way they dressed and danced to the latest hits influenced teenagers all over the country. Now, for the first time, teen culture had a unifying focal point. So as myopic as it first might seem, there's real meat on the bones of the idea that mid-'50s teenage zeitgeist did, in fact, emanate and originate from the City of Brotherly Love.

I could never figure out exactly what Harry Chipetz actually did, but he was always around, acting like the friendly front man. He had huge mutton-chop sideburns and favored shimmering sharkskin suits, shirts with high col-lars, loud ties, and white patent-leather shoes. He presided over a small desk in an alcove near the door that led from the fourth floor elevator of the Shubert Theater building on South Broad Street into the warren of small cubicles that made up John Madara Productions. Along the narrow corridor that led from Harry's desk to Madara's office was a small writers' room with a worn-out up-right piano, a tacky floor lamp, and a wooden chair. It was in that room that the small stable of Madara's songwriters would meet and bang out new songs, or rework current hits to sound like something original.

Daryl and I spent quite a few hours in that room, writing songs even though he was on salary and I wasn't.

Every once in a while the boss would pass by on his way in or out of his office and poke his clean-shaven, perpetually tanned face into the room and listen for a moment, usually making some sagely simplistic "I speak from experience"-type comment like, "Sounds great guys, could be a smash," before quickly slipping out, leaving a whiff of some expensive cologne in his wake, along with the muted tinkle of the crucifix and Italian cornicello he wore on gold chains that hung low in the deep open neck of his pastel shirt. Then he was gone, down the elevator and into his waiting cooler-than-everyone-else's car parked on the street below. Of course I didn't realize at the time that his brief stop in the doorway during a writing session automatically made him a co-owner of any song that was being written at that moment. I wasn't getting paid by the week and didn't have a contract with him. . . . Old-School Music Business Education 101 had begun.

Madara had written and produced a number of big hits back in the early '60s with his partner Dave White, including "At the Hop" by Danny and the Juniors, "You Don't Own Me" by Lesley Gore, and Chubby Checker's "The Fly," the record on which Madara proudly recounted his quasi musical contribution of swirling an electric razor around the microphone to create the buzzing effect. Dig up that old 45 and take a listen . . . you wouldn't want to miss one of the great moments in recording history.

Day after day he could be counted on to impart his wisdom on the secrets of making hit records to us struggling writers, spouting off such invaluable gems like, "If you want to write a hit, just make sure you have the word 'magic' in the title . . . works every time." He was also a big fan of tropical fish and was always bragging about his latest exotic aquatic acquisition, which seemed like a frivolous and extravagant hobby to me, especially when my idea of a worthwhile pastime was finding something decent to eat.

For the first few months I wrote for free with the promise of a salary, until I finally badgered him into paying me twenty-five dollars a week—but only after enduring yet another tale about his latest two-hundred-dollar pet fish.

Then one day Madara made a big announcement: He was bringing in a partner by the name of Allan Sussel, who had co-founded the successful labels Jamie Records and Laurie Records, named after his daughters. He had some huge hits with Dion and the Belmonts and the Chiffons. Although I didn't realize it at the time, I guess John Madara needed an influx of cash. I started to figure it out after a week or so because the walls were thin and I couldn't help overhearing heated discussions coming from behind the closed doors of Madara's office. Seems the new partner figured that if he was ponying up the cash, he should be entitled to the big office.

You can imagine how well that went down, and after a few tense weeks, Sussel was seen no more on the fourth floor. A short time afterwards John Madara announced that he had made a deal with the well-known music publishers in New York City: Chappell & Company. He indicated that this could be a big break and a chance to play our original material for his potential new partners.

When the day came for the meeting with Chappell, Daryl and I met Madara at his office and hopped into his station wagon for the two-hour drive up the New Jersey Turnpike. Madara was a master at parlaying his copyright and publishing royalties from his early hits to keep his cash flow alive. The two long-haired songwriters in the backseat were his way of sweetening the deal, to show the folks at Chappell that there would be more hits coming from the John Madara organization in the future.

Chappell was founded in England in the early 1800s and had offices in midtown Manhattan. The company had the entire floor of an older office building, and we found ourselves in an understated but nicely appointed waiting area. We were ushered into the offices with much handshaking and introductions. After some small talk, we adjourned to a conference room that had an upright piano and a large oval table and chairs. There were about four or five guys in suits who all appeared to me to be around middle age, except for one short Italian-looking kid with slicked-back hair and an aquiline nose.

After a brief introduction we were given the cue to start playing. Daryl and I went through our limited selection of new songs, alternating lead and harmony vocals. We didn't treat it as a big deal and pretty much just did what we did in the house on Quince Street. After we were finished, the suits applauded and seemed pleased but not overly excited . . . after all, they had on their roster songwriters like Cole Porter, George and Ira Gershwin, Hoagy Carmichael, and Irving Berlin. These were the legends and lions of American songwriting history. While I was packing my guitar and Daryl was sitting on the piano bench, Madara and the older executives walked out of the room in deep discussion.

When I looked up, the slick little Italian dude was standing there and, with a hint of a smile on his face, he introduced himself. "Hey you guys, I'm Tommy Mottola, you sounded great." We had heard that before but he seemed genuinely excited. "So you're from Philly . . . cool tunes, you got more?" All this was delivered in a very engaging, rapid-fire patter that was appealing enough to make us continue the conversation. Daryl and I spun the *Reader's Digest* version of our career, and as we were getting ready to leave Mottola asked, "Who's your manager?" "No one" we answered. No sooner did the words leave our lips than Tommy winked and said, "Not anymore . . . I'm your manager." He quickly wrote his phone number on a slip of paper that I tucked into my overalls. A few moments later we were on the busy city street and hopping back into the car for the ride back to Philly.

We didn't say a word but were a bit stunned by what had just happened and sat silently as John Madara drove and chatted about the great new deal that was going to happen with Chappell. When we got back home Daryl and I were both a bit confused as to what our next step would be, and whether Tommy Mottola was for real or just giving us the big-city schmooze.

Over the weeks that followed we were informed that there would be more trips to New York and chances to perform at various showcases around the city. Madara told us that he could get us a record contract with Chappell's help. He acted very positive, and that enthusiasm rubbed off on Daryl and me. We hadn't really considered that there was any chance of a career outside of Philly unless we stayed with Madara or went up to the sixth floor to work with Kenny Gamble, Leon Huff, and Thom Bell. We had a bird's-eye view of Ben Franklin on top of city hall, but if I squinted my eyes real tight, I thought I could imagine the skyline of New York City in the future.

We began taking the train to New York, sometimes alone and sometimes riding with guys like Thom Bell or Leon Huff, whom Madara had also signed to a publishing contract that attached him to Huff for years afterwards, even though Leon had partnered up with Kenny Gamble. John Madara had a knack for locking in talent and publishing rights. The train rides were fun, and it was cool to listen to all the tall tales from the recording studio and the street, laughing while Thom Bell pontificated on his personal dietary regime that included never eating shellfish. "The roach of the sea, the roach of the sea" he'd shout in a high-pitched voice, over the rumble of the Amtrak train.

On some of those trips to the city we played on a few recording sessions and squeezed in a lot of small cabaret-style venue showcases, where we'd set up with piano and guitar and perform our songs.

Tommy Mottola was at every show, standing in the back but making his presence felt, introducing and promoting us to everyone there after the performance. I started to get the feeling that every showcase was a winner . . . there was never a negative vibe or even a noncommittal response. It always felt like a musical lovefest.

Taking the train back to Philly, both Daryl and I began to actually believe that we could be on our way and that the phone would ring and some big-time record exec would be offering us a deal.

But time dragged on. We kept pressing John Madara for a response and would be crestfallen to hear, "They passed." I'd respond, "What do you mean they passed?" Was I operating in a separate reality? I know we played well . . . the showcases went great, everyone told us how much they liked our songs. "Don't worry about it," he would say. "You just gotta keep trying harder."

Little did we realize that there was genuine interest in us and that legitimate offers were coming from the New York record labels. We had signed an exclusive with Madara's production company. It was his view that he had the authority to sign a recording contract on our behalf, and he was negotiating every aspect of the deals that were being proposed, while we remained mostly in the dark. We would later be told that he was driving such a hard bargain for upfront money that even the hardcore New York guys got scared off. This went on for quite some time and even in my hippie-hazed brain I knew that we weren't getting anywhere.

Desperation Leads
to Action in LA

By mid-November, exasperated by the lack of response from the New York record folks, we began to reach out to Chappell music directly through Tommy Mottola. We wanted a record contract and wanted to sign directly to a label as artists. I don't recall who came up with the idea of going to Los Angeles initially, but we had tapped New York and Philadelphia dry. Frustration leads to desperation. Perhaps it was because we had nowhere else to turn, and because the musical world had shifted its focus to the cult of the singer/songwriter that had been bred and was flowering on the West Coast. Or maybe it was as simple as the vague hope that a change of scenery might just feel good.

In the fall of 1971 the airlines had initiated a student fare that was basically a half-price ticket. Neither Daryl nor I were technically students, but rules were easy to bend in those pre-computer days. So around the second week of November we just showed up at the ticket agency with some diversionary patter, and with a sleight-of-hand-style flash of our expired Temple University student IDs, we soon were winging our way to the West Coast.

Los Angeles California . . . another first. Everybody in the airport looked

One of our first promo shots. *(Courtesy John Oates)*

famous, the cops looked like characters from a TV series, everyone was tan and wore sunglasses and the girls looked healthy and beautiful. As I approached the luggage carousel, on cue, a tan guy with mirrored shades wearing a Technicolor Hawaiian shirt stuck out his hand. "Hey, I'm Jon Devirion from Chappell." Perfect. Gathering our bags, we jumped into his convertible and cruised out into the bright midday sunshine of LA.

Weaving out of the airport, past sandy hills dotted with oil rigs shaped like grasshoppers, the car nosed its way toward West Hollywood. Wide, bumper-to-bumper boulevards with twenty-foot semi-naked chicks calling down from garish billboards loomed overhead, tattoo parlors, clog shops, Fatburger, trashy lingerie, Porsches flirting with Rolls Royces . . . heaven and hell battling for my attention all in one big, fabulous traffic jam.

Here again, why our destination was the Tropicana Motel on Santa Monica Boulevard I couldn't tell you, but that's where we ended up, in two small adjacent single rooms overlooking the pool—and it was the exact right place to be. In the '50s it had been a hotbed for character actors, but after Los Angeles Dodger southpaw legend Sandy Koufax bought it in 1963, somehow or another it became the ultimate rock-and-roll crash pad. Jim Morrison and Andy Warhol—both made this their glittery basecamp over the years. The hotel was funky and so was the vibe; everyone was a character straight out of central casting. Cowboys, hookers, junkies, prom queens—Hollywood, hell yeah!

Adjacent to the lobby on the street level was a greasy-spoon eatery called Duke's Coffee Shop. Even the short-order cook looked like a star. A cramped room filled with a continuously rotating cast of wannabe actors, musicians, and other assorted starving artistes passing scripts and cassette tapes across the Formica countertops into the hands of would-be kingmakers.

Can't say I wasn't blown away by the fabulosity of it all because I was. I felt a bit like an East Coast cockroach that scuttled out from a hole in the wall and was teleported in a blinding solar flash into another, way more good-looking universe. Those first few days in LA we saw Cher, Milton Berle, Andy Williams, and even drove by Elvis's house. The star chamber was real. But it was hard to believe that anything good would come out of the trip.

Our new friend from Chappell told us he'd come by in a few days and show us around but in the meantime, "Relax . . . it's Southern California."

OK let's hit the street and check out this boulevard of dreams.

Rule Number. 1: you need a car. Mistake Number. 1: I didn't know that. In Philly I walked everywhere; I could make it across the entire breadth of Center City in twenty minutes. In LA, *nobody* walks. Figured that out the first day, when I noticed that the sidewalks were totally empty. The guy at the hotel mentioned that there was a cool bar not far down the street to the left. I guess he assumed I had a car. After hoofing it for what felt like a mile on an uninhabited planet, and barely surviving crossing La Cienega Boulevard, I spied a big square yellow-and-orange sign that read BARNEY'S BEANERY AND ducked into the low white building with the green awning.

A cold blast of air-conditioning and the smell of stale beer hit me as I entered. The interior was dominated by a long, dark, wooden bar choked with more memorabilia and random ephemera than I could absorb; multicolored plastic-covered booths; and the feel of an ersatz movie set doing business as a real establishment. Built in the 1920s right off Santa Monica Boulevard (the old Route 66), Barney's Beanery was a favorite haunt of many silver-screen legends, from Clark Gable to Errol Flynn. Seedy, well-oiled, and tailor-made for long nights of heavy imbibing and equally heavy debauchery, Barney's to this day is haunted and hemmed in by myths, riddles, and lore. The year before we walked in there, Janis Joplin carved her name into a wooden table, knocked back a vodka, and then headed back to room 105 at the nearby Landmark Hotel, where she shot one last dose of heroin and left the stage for good. Morrison, "The Lizard King" himself, was tossed out for pissing on the bar. Years later Quentin Tarantino supposedly scratched out the screenplay for *Pulp Fiction* while sitting in his regular booth. The joint just bleeds its own history.

I tried to blend in, but I was sure my East Coast roots were showing, and I didn't really hang too long . . . the place had a local's vibe and I had the street sense to know when and where I don't belong. A half a block away was the International House of Pancakes and I popped in for a cheap and filling meal before the long walk back to the Tropicana.

True to his word, Devirion came to collect us the following day and we did a nonstop marathon of lunches that I quickly learned was a thinly disguised method of doing business, Left Coast style.

ABC Dunhill, A&M, Warner, Epic—it was a mind-bending whirlwind of handshakes and how-do-you-dos. There was some interest here and there but nothing firm. We ended up at a rustic-style club called the Troubadour just down the street from our hotel and hung out at the bar with Jackson Browne, Linda Ronstadt, J.D. Souther, and a slew of '70s starlet/waitresses . . . oh yes, Hollywood can suck you in. And who knew we had stepped smack into ground zero of the Southern California sound that would soon be dominating the air-waves on the wings of the Eagles and all the other great songwriters hanging out at the Troubadour bar?

Our West Coast handler told us that he found a gig for us up north. Why not? Driving for hours up the scenic Pacific Coast highway, taking in the incredible vistas over the ocean, and soaking up the California experience. We ended up in San Francisco but that was a blur, and a little further south, outside of San Jose, we pulled up to a place called the Bodega. We had no clue, but it was a relatively famous music club in the area; Joe Cocker, Elvin Bishop, Iron Butterfly, Jesse Colin Young, and Bo Diddley were among the acts who had played there at one time or another.

There was a bit of a red flag when we pulled up behind a long row of gleaming Harley-Davidson motorcycles lined up across the parking lot. Inside, the bar was packed with Hells Angels and their girls. All Daryl and I had was an acoustic guitar and an electric piano. Oh boy . . . this was going to be very weird. We set up on the small stage with a big pole in between us and started playing our folky singer/songwriter set, all the while expecting to be heckled and hit on the head with a beer bottle or worse by the gnarly crowd of bearded, leather-clad bikers. But it was like a really good acid trip . . . they loved us! It was crazy—they started clapping and howling and sending the waitress up to the stage to hand us drinks. . . . I was so drunk by the end of the set I could hardly walk, and after the show we hung out with the Hells Angels for the rest of the night, drinking and smoking reefer in the parking lot.

We headed back down to Los Angeles the next day, where we had one more audition set up, with a guy named Earl McGrath. He had a small custom record label called Clean Records, distributed by Atlantic Records, and was a personal friend of the president of the company, music-business legend Ahmet Ertegun.

Earl's day job could be best described as art gallery owner, raconteur and connoisseur. He had a vine-covered, ultracool, classic old-Hollywood bungalow very close to our hotel, and we went to meet him for lunch and to play some songs. Sophisticated, laid back, and worldly, he welcomed us into a lush garden surrounded by flowering plants and large colorful paintings. A very relaxed conversation eventually led us to getting down to the music.

I remember seeing a sparkle in his eyes and a semi-amused look on his face as we performed. He twirled his bushy mustache and made unusually insightful comments in between the songs. I recall him saying things like, "Are you guys serious . . . are you for real?" in a puzzled but very friendly way. Almost as if he thought we might have been putting him on. I found his response odd but not rude in the least; he was acting as though we might be testing him by doing a wickedly clever performance that could have been a parody of the sensitive singer/songwriter genre. He said we reminded him of a musical Andy Warhol. I took that as a compliment, but the bottom line was that he loved what we were doing.

After we finished, he became noticeably animated and excitedly told us that he would call his friend Ahmet Ertegun back in New York, and that he wanted to sign us to Clean Records. Holy shit, did that really just happen? Yes! A few days later it was back to the East Coast and straight up to New York.

The Audition—11/22/71

Soon after we played for him, Earl McGrath got in touch with Mottola, and within just a few weeks, there Daryl and I were, on a cold, monochromatic day in Manhattan, huddled in the backseat of a cab heading uptown from Penn Station. We hopped out of the cab on the corner of Broadway and Sixtieth Street. I doubt any of the bundled-up bodies filling the sidewalks noticed the two longhaired singer/songwriters entering the building at 1841 Broadway, near Columbus Circle.

We'd now been friends about four years and were confident in the chemistry between us. We'd been learning from each other and filtering our experiences through our songwriting but the time for dreaming was growing short.

Stepping into the narrow vestibule and reaching for the elevator button, we felt a thick sense of gravity and pressure. If this meeting didn't go well, I'm not sure we would have had many more roads ahead together as performers. We'd just been through too many of these auditions. It felt like the end of the line. The steel elevator door slid closed, and a moment later there was a lurch as we arrived at the second floor. Atlantic Records.

Both Daryl and I had been deeply affected by the recordings stamped with that iconic red-and-black Atlantic label. Ray Charles, Aretha Franklin, Otis Redding—now we were being invited into the home of some of the best rhythm and blues on the planet. Being a guest at the door is one thing . . . being part of the family is something entirely different.

The company goes back to the mid-1940s, when two Turkish brothers, Ahmet and Nesuhi Ertegun, decided to stay in the United States after their father, the Turkish ambassador to the United States, passed away. The brothers adored American music, collecting literally thousands of jazz and early R&B records. Ahmet studied music in college, and in the late 1940s he convinced his family dentist to invest in his dream. That dream became Atlantic Records.

In the early 1960s another American-music-loving Turk named Arif Mardin joined the staff at Atlantic. A graduate of Berklee College of Music in Boston, he had an encyclopedic knowledge of classical music and an even deeper respect and love for the giants of American roots music, jazz, R&B, folk . . . to him it was an aural mirror of this country, his new home. He looked at music from a completely pure point of view, without prejudice concerning style, fad, or trend . . . his was a sensibility based on the true meaning of soul. He began working at Atlantic Records in 1963 and quickly worked his way up the rungs to become one of the most influential producers at the label.

Mardin, along with Jerry Wexler and Tom Dowd, basically established the Atlantic sound during the 1960s and onward. And what a sound it was. The day we walked in the building, one of the top-ten songs in the country was Aretha Franklin's "Rock Steady," produced by Arif Mardin.

We didn't know what kind of situation we were walking into. The room was rather small, cramped, and dimly lit; there was grand piano and a few folding chairs. Tommy Mottola made some introductions as the principles—Jerry Greenberg, Mark Meyerson, and Arif Mardin—began to file in. I'm sure there was some small talk as we got ready to play but it's all a blur. There was too much at stake to remember unimportant details.

As auditions go, this one could not have started off much worse. Daryl was sick as a dog with some kind of cold or flu, and I'd just gotten over one. The piano had a few keys sticking and was out of tune. Things did not look too promising. I recall Arif making a quiet and comforting apology about the piano before we began.

All of those days and nights Daryl and I had spent working out songs in a tiny third-floor room, playing music on stoops and in small clubs night after night after . . . it all came down to this.

Daryl sat down at the piano, coughed and cleared his throat. I pulled out my acoustic guitar, and we start playing our handful of songs, just like we did for Earl McGrath a few weeks earlier in Los Angeles. But this felt different, this felt like a sing-to-survive kind of moment.

After a couple of songs, I started getting a faint sense that Mardin actually liked us, although the suits sat silently. I know now that they were deferring to Arif. In between songs he spoke up, making brief comments that seemed to indicate that he understood what we were about, that he got where we were coming from. His references were musical, with no consideration for commerciality or business. He was studying us. Measuring us. Processing our potential. The suits sat there stone-faced, typically not wanting to commit one way or the other. But Mardin had a light in his eyes, and he was not shy about expressing his feelings. After we finished playing a song called "Laughing Boy," which was one of Daryl's most elegant numbers, he exclaimed, "This is like Delius!" He was referring to the English classical composer who was influenced by African-American music he heard in the late 1800s. A good sign.

Still, we didn't feel very well and this affected our performance. We actually apologized at the end of the audition. We thought we'd blown it. Bombed. It just wasn't our day, but if it was any consolation, at least this time, for once, we would get to hear a rejection firsthand before heading back out into the bleak, bitter chill for the long train ride back to Philly.

AND THEN ARIF Mardin stood up. He paused. He said slowly, carefully, in deliberate syllables, with his thick and exotic Turkish accent, "I want to produce you."

Here we are signing our Atlantic Contract in 1972. Left to right: Mark Meyerson, Earl McGrath, Ahmet, Tommy Mottola. I bought that gag pencil on the way to the office from a gift shop on Broadway. *(Courtesy John Oates)*

It was November 22, 1971. Thanksgiving was just three days away, but all of a sudden, we were ready to celebrate a little early. What easily could have been another end of the line for us instantly became a step into a future of un- limited possibilities.

Philly Mean Streets

So now we had a record deal, but we still had to deal with John Madara. The street where Daryl and I lived was like a miniature family compound with everything you could possibly need to sustain life: a hoagie shop, a head shop, and Granny Takes a Trip, a hip English clothing store on the corner of Twelfth and Pine Streets. On one corner, in a neat, newer brick townhouse lived a married couple that actually had real nine-to-five jobs. A few doors down lived an insane speed freak named Steven who barricaded his door one day, screaming that he could talk to the cockroaches and that they were controlling him. The cops finally came, broke down the door, and hauled him away. On the other side of the street was a rundown apartment house where lived one crazy-hot girl who always seemed to have someplace to go, and a rotating group of South Philly street kids who used the pad for drug deals and free-love sex parties. It was a fun neighborhood.

I spent many a warm night sitting on the stoop in front of the Quince Street house talking with Daryl and trying to figure out what we could do to extricate ourselves from our now toxic connection with John Madara Enterprises.

One afternoon, a few days later, when we were back in the old Shubert building writing room another one of Madara's other songwriter/artists dropped in. We knew him casually, and on this day he was livid, menacing, and muttering out loud to no one in particular, but it was quickly obvious at whom his wrath was directed. "I found my record in with the panty hose . . . in with the fuckin' panty hose!" he kept repeating. He was pacing back and forth outside the doorway in a very threatening manner, and in between his rant about how he had found his new 45-rpm single tucked in with the ladies' hose at his neighborhood convenience store, I noticed a black pistol tucked into the waistband of his continental-style suit pants. At that moment I realized that he might have a philosophical problem with the method that John Madara was using to promote his record, and he was incensed enough to take it from the theoretical to a very real and personal place. He abruptly whirled around and without warning threw open the door to Madara's office. All I remember was hearing him shout, "My record's in with the fuckin' panty hose!" and John Madara pleading for him to calm down. "We can work this out man . . . cool it . . . whatever you want. . . ." A string of desperate words, the babble of survival sounds that spew from the lips of someone who has a gun pointed at his chest.

After a few suspenseful seconds, I fully expected to hear the crack of a shot that would end the conversation for good. But Madara finally said the words the angry artist wanted to hear, "I'll tear up your contract . . . whatever you want," and with that, I watched in amazement as the singer appeared, walking backwards past the doorway of our room, the pistol cocked, held steadily at his waist, still pointed into the office. "Tear the motherfucker *up* or I'll tear your ass up, motherfucker!" As soon as he was gone Daryl and I packed up and quickly split from the building. That experience left me shivering with the cold chill of shock, but coated with a warm thick layer of awe and respect. He actually pulled it off, holy shit! That's how you conduct business, Philly style.

THE WORD ASSASSIN is said to be a derivative of the word hashish. Stories of bloody Bedouin and Moorish tribal warfare bolstered by the compressed, highly potent marijuana product are legendary. There was a lot of it in our neighborhood.

That night on the front steps, Daryl and I retold the story of the pistol-packing singer while a rapt gaggle of neighbors listened intently; they were our friends and our first fans. Finally, everyone started talking at once. "Fuck him . . . you should dump him, too." The mob mentality quickly morphed into a plan for Daryl and me to get out of our contracts as well.

Well, we didn't have a gun, but we did have a tough, hulking South Philly hitter dude as a next-door neighbor, and he offered to come to the office and help us convince John Madara that we wanted to part ways. His name was Tom and I described him back then as an "inner-city angel of sweet, merciful justice."

Wow, what where we thinking? Raw emotion, desperation, and ambition blended with a healthy dose of youthful bravado were a full, rich fuel mixture. All we needed was a spark. In my diary, the words were naked and sharp:

> *We're making our last stand against him . . . win or lose. While he's buying $100 parts for his sports car, I walk with the snow in my face . . . had just enough change for a candy bar. Tomorrow—get it done first thing. . . . Face the man, stand eye to eye, show the hard lines on your face. Demand with mind, heart, and hand. Cause him to understand. . . . The bloodsuckers can't go on forever . . . you can shit on someone once, but you can't rub it in.*

The very next day Daryl and I went to the offices in the Shubert building a little later than normal, just to make sure Madara would be there. Trailing along behind us was our thickset one-man goon squad dressed appropriately for the occasion in a heavy gray trench coat, dark glasses, and black-leather fingerless gloves. We were going to spring an unannounced meeting with John Madara and fully expected to walk out with our contracts in hand, free and clear, just like Mr. Badass Panty Hose had the week before.

Screwing up courage and ignoring any semblance of common sense, we opened the office door and walked in. John Madara sat behind his wide wooden desk, phone cradled in his neck, shuffling paperwork. He was in the midst of a conversation so he didn't pay much attention when we entered and sat down in front of his desk. The South Philly muscle followed silently behind us and stood with his arms folded, leaning against the back wall. After a long moment Madara glanced up from what he was doing, placed the phone on the receiver cradle, and with a puzzled look asked, "What's going on here?"

I can't remember who spoke first because it was at that exact moment that time began to accelerate and slow down simultaneously. If it was my voice speaking, it felt as though I had become a marionette, wooden mouth moving, fervent emotions flowing, reason unchecked. I have no precise recollection of the words but meaning was conveyed: It's over . . . we've had enough . . . we want out. One thing I do remember very clearly is Madara saying, "What the fuck are you talking about and who the hell is this guy?" as he began to slowly rise from his chair.

His movement cranked the electrified machismo in the room to critical mass and the space-time continuum fractured. "I'm the motherfucker who is going to tell you how this thing is going down," came a growl from behind us, and like a jump cut in a horror film, the trench coat that was once leaning against the back wall was instantaneously transported across the room and flying over the desk. Madara was a fairly big guy, but he was like a skinny wide receiver being hit by a 230-pound linebacker with bad intentions.

Papers flying, cursing and flailing, the trench coat clinched the silk shirt, delivering thudding black-gloved body punches. I stood up and watched in shock as Madara was driven back into his leather office chair and as our guy's gloved hand began frantically groping around the desk, finally latching on to a long, gold, stiletto-shaped letter opener. It felt like watching a family movie in a cozy darkened room and then being suddenly blinded by a flash of white light when the old 8-millimeter movie-projector bulb melts the film. Adrenaline jolted me back to the reality of the moment . . . this was no movie, this was happening, and in a split second, my mind grasped the fact that there would be no rolling of the credits and no leaving this theater. I threw myself across the desk and with both hands grabbed on to the trench-coated forearm as the flashing letter opener plunged toward John Madara's exposed rib cage. I yelled, "Come on! Go! Go! *Now*!" We scattered out of the office. I could hear Madara screaming, "He broke my fuckin' glasses," and then nothing more except the hollow clattering of our footsteps as we beat it down the emergency stairwell before bursting out of the building into the sunlight of Broad Street.

There was no talking, just running, breathing, and heart beating as we bolted across traffic to the other side of the street and hustled underground, into the nearest subway station. Could we go back to the house, could we surface and survive? Scrounging around in our pockets for some coins, we found a pay phone, and I pulled a piece of crumpled-up paper out of my pocket and began to dial the number that Tommy Mottola had written down in the Chappell office. He said, "Get your asses on the train . . . I've got a lawyer." An hour later we were hunkered down on the Amtrak to New York. . . . There was no going back to Philadelphia.

THE TRANSITION TOOK a while, and during that time Daryl and I made a bunch of trips to New York, always showing up near the end of the work day at the Chappell Music building. After the employees had all gone home and the offices were empty, Mottola would work the phones and work on becoming our manager from his publishing office. I would walk into an adjoining office and use the telephone to call friends, family, basically taking advantage of the free long distance calls. One day, between calls, while I was leaning back in someone else's office chair with my feet up on the desk . . . *ring! ring!* I impulsively snatched up the receiver and put it to my ear. The voice on the other end of the line had a thick, gruff, old-time New York accent. He said, *"Who's this . . . who's this?"* I didn't know what to say, but before I could answer, with an exasperated tone he went on, *"This is Irving . . . Irving Berlin*! I think I mumbled something inane about just passing by the office or some such drivel, then just slammed down the reciever, with the dubious distinction of having hung up on Irving Berlin!

The First Album.
The First Real Tour.

Debut LPs which indicate "promise" are one thing, but those who actually start making good on their word from the start are another. This
Philadelphia area duo could well become a reference point for future
comparisons, as have Joni Mitchell and Cat Stevens in recent years.
Their music is broad in scope but always subtly stunning and bittersweet.

That was from one review of our debut album on Atlantic, *Whole Oats*,
which came out in the fall of 1972. Oh, that the sales had matched some
of the gushing. But it was cool to be on a major label, and Atlantic hadn't signed
two hit makers. Rather, they signed a pair of artsy hippie songwriters with a
casual, half-assed concept called "Whole Oats." In a way, it epitomized getting
back to the essential organics of music. . . . It was a '60s thing.

Atlantic, like us, viewed the album as a stepping-stone to the next record.
They had a great philosophy about all of their artists being part of a musical
family. The idea was to nurture acts and make them better and more interesting

with each album. *Whole Oats* simply comprised what we were playing in coffeehouses and art galleries at the time. It was a hodgepodge of songs, including some I wrote, some Daryl wrote, and a couple of collaborations. Getting signed and going into the studio all happened so fast that we didn't even have time to come up with much else. We just thought: This is where we are right now, so let's capture it. After all, that's what Atlantic had signed. We had played all of the songs for them and they had liked them. For the moment, we were in the raw and essential singer/songwriter mode of trying to invent ourselves.

Arif knew what he was getting into with us and so his production approach was sensitively subtle, adding only delicate and carefully chosen elements that would enhance and not distract from the purity of the songs. The potential energy of our collaboration would be tapped in the near future. But for now, with Daryl on keyboards and mandolin, we had ourselves a basic rhythm section from Philadelphia: Mike McCarthy on bass and Jim Helmer on drums. We added a couple of other players, including Bill Keith (one of Bill Monroe's Bluegrass Boys) on the pedal steel, and my old friend and mentor Jerry Ricks, who came in from Philly and brought with him a very special instrument . . . Mississippi John Hurt's actual Guild F-40 guitar (that the Guild Company had given to Mississippi John before he died) . . . then it was passed on to Jerry. I played that guitar on the entire album.

Releasing your first record is a big deal, but the real accomplishment was getting on the road and learning how to tour. Every band that truly wants to make it has to go through this rite of passage without knowing if it will ever lead to anything bigger. But before we hit the road, we made the move to New York City full time. We have always been tagged as a Philadelphia band, and we are. A musician's skin is hung on the bones of the music of their youth. There's a unique soulfulness in Philly that is the very marrow of those bones, but while that's where it started, it was in New York where we truly began our professional recording careers. In late 1972, Daryl, his new girlfriend, Sara Allen (although most folks called her Sandy), and I moved into a dreary, windowless first-floor apartment on East Eighty-second Street, between First

This was the Whole Oats Band opening at the Bijou Theater in Philly on a bill that night with Dan Hicks and His Hot Licks. Daryl is at far left and I'm at far right (note early Mellotron behind me). Then we have Jim Helmer (drums), Mike McCarthy (bass), and Neil Rosengarden (keyboards). *(Courtesy John Oates)*

and York Avenues, on the Upper East Side. (Interestingly, this was the same building where the great novelist Harper Lee kept a secret apartment through much of her adult life. Had we only known then!)

We never really settled into the apartment on Eighty-second Street, just threw in some old, thrift-store furniture and hit the road for our first tour as album artists. As soon as all the recording and mixing was done, and months before the album came out, we set off to play our music live—and forty-five years later, we're still doing it! These early days are still some of my fondest memories as a musician. The first few road trips with the band, when each new experience was a story in the making, bonding through the good and the bad, exploring, paying dues, and working like dogs . . . that's when you learn to survive, pedal to the metal all night, in search of dreams just beyond the headlight beams.

When we first hit the road with the band I talked my parents into selling us their 1968 Pontiac GTO; it was yellow with a black vinyl top. Then we rented a small panel van for the gear, and all five of us—Daryl, me, and three other musicians—started driving up and down the East Coast. I was behind the wheel pretty much all the time; one, because I love driving, and two, because there was no way I was going to sit on the hump in the backseat of that GTO.

Bringing up the rear of our ragtag convoy was a clapped-out, early '60s, blue Ford van driven by our two roadies and packed with gear. One of the guys was an Italian from Long Island named Joey "Boopa" Verga. He was a big kid with an easy laugh and a real New York attitude. In those days Daryl used to sit near the front lip of the stage, behind his black Wurlitzer electric piano. One night some joker in the front row kept reaching out and messing with Daryl's foot pedal, and then actually tried untying his shoes while he was singing . . . it was a really uncomfortable situation. I could see Boopa watching all this from the wings. Daryl was really getting pissed off, when suddenly, out of the darkness, from the back of the audience, Boopa comes running down the aisle, headed right for the guy in the front row! He grabbed the asshole by the neck and the back of his pants, spun him around, and manhandled him back up the aisle, throwing him straight into the snack bar at the back of the room. I could hear the body slam from the stage! We could barely keep playing we were laughing so hard. Backstage after the show, we all got together to congratulate our quick-thinking roadie. Boopa stood there with a shit-eating grin, waved a beat up billfold in his hand, and said, "Yeah, do you believe this shit . . . his wallet must have fallen out of his pants and ended up in my pocket!" That's what the early days were all about.

Long nights bled into even longer days, piling up the miles driving the interstates and back roads from north to south, playing every joint from seedy clubs to college cafeterias—anyplace that would book us. We were everywhere and we were nowhere, chasing shadows and hopes all over the Eastern Seaboard.

For all the forgotten hit-and-run one-nighters we racked up, there were also the bigger opportunities. In August '72 we were booked for a run of gigs in Florida, opening for Dan Hicks and His Hot Licks and headliners Cheech and

Chong. So we loaded up the vehicles and trucked down from New York. The first show with them was in the old Miami Convention Hall. Backstage, the Hot Licks played strip poker in the dressing room, but the smoke was so thick you couldn't see any skin. There were Coconut Grove dealers with giant iguanas sitting on their shoulders and barely dressed hippie chicks everywhere . . . oh, and Cheech and Chong were freakin' hysterical. Man, if this is touring, give me more! (Two months later we were on the bill with Hicks again, this time on the very first night the Bijou Café opened in Philly. Everyone from Marley to Muddy would appear there over the years, but we were the first band to ever play in what became a legendary Philly venue).

I THINK THE most influential show we opened for that year was on September 24 in Memphis. David Bowie had just arrived in America for his first tour,

Backstage at the Bijou in Philly with members of Dan Hicks and His Hot Licks. Tommy Mottola and Larry Magid standing on right. *(Photograph by Jamie Eric Eisman)*

and we were booked to open for him on his second show of the tour. After our opening set, I went out into the crowd to watch and see what all the Ziggy Stardust buzz was about. The house went dark, then blood-red spotlights started crisscrossing over the jam-packed Ellis Auditorium crowd. The strains of the theme song from *2001: A Space Odyssey* came wafting through the PA— majestic, heralding, yet ominous. Once Bowie and the Spiders from Mars hit the stage, I knew something extraordinary was about to happen. Bowie, with his shock of red-orange hair, glittery makeup, and skintight, spangled costumes, was electrifying and otherworldly. But it was the power of the band coupled with the dynamic stage theatrics that captured my attention. I had one eye on the stage show and one eye on the crowd absorbing the energy of the moment. The connection was visceral and intense. This was the writing on the wall. I knew from that night that our days as a laid-back acoustic act were numbered. Soon we would be revamping both our sound and performance style into something more aggressive and imaginative.

But in the meantime, we rocked and rolled our way across the countryside, I watched midnights melt into dawn from behind the wheel of that GTO.

In November of '72 we went to LA and played a week's worth of shows opening for Harry Chapin at the Troubadour. We even talked Harry into joining us on stage to perform a weird, ironic, comedy song that we had come up with, called "Whistling Dave." Our reviews were strong:

> Whole Oats has a vitality not found in too many new groups and appear to like what they're doing and are not just going through the motions onstage. Oates' *(good chance the writer didn't know Daryl from John!)* high tenor voice really stands out in the group's harmonizing. The fact that they received an encore from a group which for the most part had never heard of them before is a tribute to their zest and talent and not the work of a publicity department or a hit recording.

Daryl at the wheel of our GTO, the car I bought from my folks for the early tours. I'm in the backseat. *(Photograph by Barbara Wilson D'Andrea)*

After the New Year we were still hitting forgotten clubs and obscure colleges, zigzagging the map and playing for whoever wanted us. Appalachian State University, Pfeiffer College, Clarion University—we played and played, in between hitting more truck stops and BBQ joints than I can recount. The colleges were especially fun to play. After the shows we'd party with the crowd, crash on some girl's floor, bum meals, and collect phone numbers for the next time we'd roll through town. One week, back in New York City, we shared the bill at Max's Kansas City with another newcomer named Bruce Springsteen. He was just like us, trying to grab that next rung up the ladder. We were dues-paying, gig-hungry road warriors, notching thousands of miles on our belts each month. And I loved every minute of it.

But in the midst of the fun and madness there was a sudden and unprecedented issue to deal with on a daily basis: the oil crisis of 1973. The Organization of Arab Petroleum Exporting Countries began cutting shipments to the United States so that gas priced at thirty cents or so a gallon prior to the embargo quickly doubled in price. In many instances, there was no gas available, regardless of the price. The gas shortage strained the US economy and had a hellish effect on everyone, especially road warriors like us. Draconian restrictions were imposed. For instance, on certain hours of the day only commercial vehicles could get filled up. But most problematic for us was the decree that gas would be sold on alternating days based on the last odd-or-even number of your license plate! So every other night, while we were in the middle of playing our set, our road manager Randy Hoffman would jump into the Pontiac and make sure he got to a gas station to fill up before the clock struck midnight and we lost our high-octane glass slipper. Somehow we kept the tank filled, and the shows did go on.

Parkas

The *Whole Oats* tour wrapped up in late 1972 with a southern swing, starting down in Florida and working up through Georgia, the Carolinas, and into Virginia. Those last fifteen shows (which included easily as many pecan pies) represented a solid finish to a memorable year in which we really got our feet wet when it came to touring. The band, which I referred to in my journal as the "Whole Oats Chickenhouse Conservatory Orchestra," had come together nicely after guitarist Chris Bond joined us in October. Things were really looking up as 1973 approached.

Soon after I got home and unpacked at the apartment on Eighty-second Street, Tommy Mottola and his wife, Lisa, invited us to his place up in Scarsdale for a little preholiday cheer. Daryl, Sandy, and I drove up to Westchester County. An Italian feast with expensive wine was served and enjoyed by all around a very festive and beautifully decorated table. The food was rich and sumptuous but the dessert was even richer. Immediately after dinner Mottola left the table and quickly reappeared, beaming with a million-dollar smile and holding huge gift-wrapped boxes.

It was the dead of a frigid East Coast winter, and the way both Daryl and

I dressed was much more oriented toward looking cool than staying warm. Tommy liked to hunt and was very much into the high-end outdoorsy style. We ripped opened the huge boxes and inside were brand-new Eddie Bauer subzero Arctic parkas. Wow, wasn't expecting that! "You fucking guys need some warm coats," he laughed. "Try them on." The parkas were puffy and down filled, rated to thirty degrees below zero. Mine was big enough to use as a sleeping bag. I recall flipping up the fur-trimmed hood and basically disappearing inside the huge coat. It was quite comical, but I stopped chuckling when I reached my hands into the pockets and felt something thick wrapped in a rubber band. I pulled it out and I'm sure my eyes couldn't contain my surprise . . . there in my hand was a big, tightly rolled wad of hundred dollar bills. I'd never seen that much cash. I looked at Daryl, then over to Tommy . . . I was dumbstruck. What a way to end the year: a record contract; a first national tour; and now, warm new jackets, cold hard cash, and someone looking out for us. What a feeling, to have someone taking care of you like that.

She's Gone

The Upper East Side in 1973 was then as it is even more so now: a high-rise neighborhood of the buttoned-down descendants of author John Cheever's Manhattan. I knew I didn't belong from the moment I moved in. Every chance I got, I would take the subway or a cab downtown and wander among the "kooks" prowling the streets of the East and West Village.

The early '70s were a pretty extreme time for rock-and-roll fashion; if you don't believe me, just look at the album covers! Boys dressed like girls and girls looked like hookers. My personal version of fashion forward at that time could now, in retrospect, perhaps be best described as, "Oh, what the fuck was I thinking?" It consisted of a few key go-to pieces, one of which was an outlandish, oversized fluffy, white Afghan shearling coat. When wet, it smelled like an old stray dog abandoned on a riverbank. I wore it everywhere that winter, and took perverse satisfaction in the stares that it drew from the more conventionally business-attired east siders. Looks that were, at their worst, glares of hostile disgust and, at best, wary, bemused curiosity, similar to how a visitor to a zoo might view an exotic South American capybara. Strolling along the uptown sidewalks with my shoulder-length mop of dark curls on top, red-white-and-blue five-inch-platform clogs on the bottom, and that outrageous coat in between, you could say I didn't exactly blend in.

As the violet-gray shafts of early evening light oozed between the buildings, I could be found threading my way downtown, slipping through the rush-hour throngs of bridge-and-tunnel people disappearing into Grand Central station and descending into howling subway entrances.

Where I was headed was not unlike a medieval village within a walled city. Ramparts imagined and not clearly defined on a city map are its northernmost border somewhere below Twenty-third Street; its eastern border at Alphabet City; the Hudson River to the west; and Canal Street to the south. This was the historically recognized art-freak-zone neighborhood of Greenwich Village, and I felt right at home there. In a way I felt born to be there. A native. In this world, no one blinked an eye at my appearance as I made the intoxicating rounds of Max's Kansas City and the Mercer Arts Center in perfect stylish sync with the late-night crowd, prowling around downtown, absorbing the street life and listening to music that was everywhere but on the radio. It pulsated downtown, buzzing and humming with an almost electromagnetic power, tugging you in all directions.

One frigid December late night morning about 3 A.M., as 1972 was drawing to an end, I was rambling around in need of a bite to eat. It may seem strange today, when one thinks about the city that never sleeps, but back then, despite the evolving art scene, there were hardly any eateries in downtown New York that stayed open that late, much less all night. However on Bleeker Street between Grove and Bedford there was this great little all-night soul-food restaurant called the Pink Tea Cup, a cozy joint that had been there since the early 1950s. And at that hour of the morning it was the only place on that darkened block where a light glowed. Ham hocks, chicken-fried steak, biscuits and gravy with '60s soul on the juke box. Perfect.

No sooner had I settled into a back booth facing the street when the door flew open and in from the cold wafted this willowy, beguiling girl, incongruously wearing a pink tutu, cowboy boots, and no coat. In the middle of winter! My first thought was, "She looks like fun." She glanced my way, seemed to make a snap analysis of my getup and figured that she had found a kindred spirit. With nothing more formal than a big smile and a story to tell, she glided smoothly into my booth.

Originally from North Carolina, she claimed to have lived with the British folk star Donovan in his castle in England when she was fifteen, and said she had been flitting about the rock-and-roll universe until downtown gravity put our planets on a collision course in the sparkly vinyl booth of the Pink Tea Cup.

We started dating that night—hey it was the '70s and things happened fast—so with New Year's Eve approaching we made a plan to hang out. Daryl and Sandy were out of town so I had the apartment all to myself. She said she would come over, so I settled in on the sofa and began strumming my acoustic guitar to pass the time. Nine o'clock became ten o'clock became eleven o'clock. No girl. I had been stood up. When I finally realized that she was going to be a no-show on that night of nights, I thought to myself, "If she's not coming tonight . . . then she's gone."

Simple as that, I started singing this folky little refrain: "She's gone . . . oh, I better learn how to face it . . . She's gone, oh I . . ." The disappointment of getting stood up didn't last long, but that simple melody and chord progression was about to go on forever.

The very next day Daryl came back and there I was, still sitting on that sofa, still plunking away at that little chorus idea. He said, "What's that?" So I gave him the Cliff's Notes version of my no-show date, and he sat down at his black Wurlitzer electric piano and spontaneously began playing the classic alternating chord riff with the pedaled bass note that is now so well known as the intro and verse to the song. We started tossing around ideas about love and loss and how to personalize a well-worn universal subject. Propelled by an odd but provocative opening line, "Everybody's high on consolation," we were off and running. Like manna from heaven, the lyrics manifested themselves as we pooled our collective emotions, focusing on relatable, everyday imagery. "I'm worn as a toothbrush hanging in the stand"—a line both evocative and so real that anyone could picture it. Building on that theme, the song almost wrote itself through our hands. In less than an hour, "She's Gone" was born, and, in a way, so were we.

The song would take a circuitous route to popularity via radio; a couple of years passed before it finally became a hit. But however long it took, once it struck, things changed. I just don't think our lives would have been the same without that song. It still feels so timeless, a most incandescent moment. And in a way, it defines Daryl's and my musical partnership.

Abandoned Luncheonette

I n April of 1973 we gathered song ideas in preparation for recording our second album with Arif Mardin at Atlantic Records. While the *Whole Oats* album was a cobbled-together collection of assorted folky singer/songwriter-style tunes with no coherent theme or direction, this new album would be more focused, since the material was written entirely during the previous ten months.

Looking back now, I'm astounded by how little preproduction there was with Arif or anyone from the record company prior to walking into the studio. I believe we did spend one afternoon with Arif in the empty studio—just me and my acoustic guitar and Daryl at the grand piano. We played him our new songs and, for the most part, he responded very positively. I do recall one idea I had been working on that Arif rejected and dismissed, saying, "It sounds like (the novelty song) 'Three Little Fishes,'" because of the ascending bass line. We dropped that song without question; I'm sure he was right.

That fact that there was so little preparation is even more amazing when you consider how most records are made today. It's a classic case of the tail wagging the dog that has turned the current creative environment upside down. For most contemporary artists, regardless of the genre, the fate of their careers

In the studio with famed Atlantic producer Arif Mardin during the *Abandoned Luncheonette* sessions. *(Photograph by Barbara Wilson D'Andrea)*

is in the hands and at the mercy of corporate marketing teams, layered with
opinions by A&R staffers who consult with virtual tastemakers and radio focus groups. These days, it's all about the bottom line, and of course it always
was, but at least back when we started, most record companies approached
the decision to sign artists predicated on the belief that they fit the mold and
style of the company, and that they had the potential to have a long and lucrative career. It was a business model that would be mutually beneficial for both
parties. But over the last twenty years a new business model has emerged with
no artistic center and no real commitment to career building, even though it is
commonly understood that creative personalities need freedom take the occasional experimental side trip and the support to make mistakes in order to
evolve and blossom. I am so thankful to have had the good fortune to have
started a career during a time when musicians made the music and the record
company's job was to figure out how to sell it, staying out of the way of the
creative process.

Even though the passing of years and countless turntable spins have confirmed that *Abandoned Luncheonette* is a classic in our catalog, the sessions began in a most inauspicious way. For everyone involved, it was business as usual at the famed Atlantic studio.

Our producer, Arif Mardin, was the go-to guy, and he always had multiple productions happening simultaneously. Our sessions usually began around noon, and we'd work until the early evening, sometimes going later into the night if Bette Midler, Bob Dylan, John Prine, Donny Hathaway, Roberta Flack, Willie Nelson, Dr. John, Yusef Lateef, or Danny O'Keefe weren't booked as well. Robert Plant and the Stones would also pop in when they were in the city, to visit with Ahmet Ertegun. We'd just casually pass in the elevator or hallway with the Atlantic recording studio seemingly open 24/7.

The people who worked at the Atlantic studios were a heady collection of great musicians, and not just the recording artists, but also the cream of New York's session players. All of them cycling in and out of that one studio—it was like a star-studded musical circus all presided by ringmaster Maestro Mardin.

He was a true gentleman's gentleman, the son of a cultured Turkish family, Berklee-educated, urbane, polite, and totally in control. He presided over the sessions with an unchallenged, effortless grace that was never domineering yet never questioned. He orchestrated the recording sessions and the musicians with the same deft and skillful touch that he brought to his brilliant arrangements. Blending a comprehensive classical and fundamental musical knowledge with humor and deep respect for American roots music, he was able to bring out the best in everyone around him. Could you ask for a better mentor and partner to help you start a career? I think not.

The Atlantic studio in New York was the first in America to feature multitrack tape-recording machines. The room itself, designed by the engineering genius Tom Dowd, was a simple rectangle. The basic rhythm section instruments were set in a loose semicircle: Drums on the left, backed up to the west wall with low baffles to prevent sound leakage; bass, plugged into an Ampeg B18 amplifier, sat to the left of the drum kit against the north wall; in the center was a full-size black Steinway grand piano with an electric Wurlitzer and Fender Rhodes adjacent to it; guitar stations with various Fender amps were

Me, during the recording of *Abandoned Luncheonette*. *(Photograph by Barbara Wilson D'Andrea)*

slotted in between the bass and the pianos; percussion and any additional players found space on the floor on the right, near the south wall. Inside the control room we had our Mellotron and Arp 2600 synthesizers.

For this album Arif had booked a few top-notch session players who would
form the backbone of the rhythm section. First and foremost was the great Bernard "Pretty" Purdie on drums. He was at the height of his career as a session
drummer and took command of the grooves from the count off. His tempos
were exactly right . . . always. Wherever he counted it, that's where it was going
to be. He owned that indefinable sweet spot on the backside of the beat that
musicians crave and understand. Although casual listeners might not realize
what's going on, it's that subtle, infinitesimal shift in time that makes all the
difference, the space where the groove and the funk lives. He'd done it for James
Brown and Aretha Franklin and so many others, and now he was doing it for
us. Steve "Fontz" Gelfand from Philadelphia and Gordon Edwards shared the
bass chair. This bass-and-drum team was locked up and tight. With the ex-
ception of one song, they were the foundation. Ralph MacDonald, another

New York session legend, held down the percussion for the majority of the tracks. Chris Bond, who was touring with us at the time, played electric guitar and synths, while Daryl played piano and mandolin, and I played guitar. There were other very important players on assorted instruments who made appearances throughout the sessions, including drummer Rick Marotta, Pat Rebillot on organ, and Richard Tee on piano.

IT IS VERY difficult to remember the exact order in which we recorded the songs, so I won't even try, but a typical session went something like this: The musicians would arrive around 10:30 or 11:00 A.M. and the light banter and familiar small talk would set the mood. It was like a family gathering, with plenty of good-natured ribbing, the joke of the day, and tall tales shared before getting down to work. Since the engineers were so dialed into that studio, it didn't take long to get the basic sounds up, and, as usual when dealing with seasoned professionals, their instruments always sounded good. A treasure trove of high-

Goofing in the studio during the *Abandoned Luncheonette* sessions. *(Photograph by Barbara Wilson D'Andrea)*

quality microphones was wired through a well-worn MCI analog mixing console and then finally routed into a sixteen-track Ampex two-inch tape machine.

Chalk it up to the energy and fearlessness of youth combined with the professionalism of the surrounding cast, but there was magic in the air. The sessions were effortless, and we usually cut at least one and sometimes two songs per day. The songs were worked out by the basic rhythm section in a style known as head arrangements. By that I mean Arif would stand in the middle of the room while we would talk through the various sections of the songs. Some of the sections were dictated by the composition itself, and some elements were created on the spot with input coming from all the musicians. Of course Arif, Daryl, and I had the final say.

Arif would return to the control room with our engineer, Gene Paul (the son of the legendary Les Paul who invented multitrack recording), while we focused on cutting the basic tracks. The band would break the song down section by section: introduction; verse; chorus; bridge; discuss if there was to be a solo, etc. From behind the glass divider Arif would occasionally hit the talk-back button and add his suggestions. We would eventually get around to the ritual of deciding which deli to order lunch from.

Recording sessions can be very long and drawn-out affairs, and Arif had a quirky habit of making paper airplanes to pass the time. He derived a childlike kick out of sailing them around the control room. For his birthday I went to a bookstore and found a paper-airplane construction book, and from that his wispy aircraft took on a whole new level of sophistication.

When we'd finally nail down a great take, we'd all go into the control room and gather around the console to listen and eat our deli food.

And so it would go, day after day, until we finally had enough tracks to set aside and move into the overdub phase of the recording process, adding things like extra guitar parts, background vocals, and sweetening, which was Arif's specialty . . . his brilliant string and horn arrangements. There were lots of other unique overdubs added along the way, like the harp on the title track; the flugelhorn on "Laughing Boy"; the eccentric Vitar (five-string solid-body electric violin) on "Lady Rain." The instrument was invented and played by a bald wizard named John Blair, who arrived in the studio wearing a cape. It was during these overdub sessions that our collective creativity could soar. Arif seemed to have a little black book of the greatest, most diverse musicians in the city, and he was like a great film director, casting the musical characters for our album.

Our touring guitarist Chris Bond's real ambition was to become a record producer, so his time with us and Arif Mardin in the studio was his master apprenticeship. A few years later he would bring this experience to bear on the albums that we would record together in Los Angeles.

Chris was a very early advocate of electronic instruments, and we owned the first portable Mellotron imported into the United States from England. The best way to describe the Mellotron would be as a series of tape strips attached to spring-activated roller mechanisms. The tape mechanically passed over individual magnetic tape heads. Each of the strips of tape was connected to a piano-style keyboard. You could record anything you wanted and assign that sound to a strip of tape, and then play it with the keyboard. Each tape loop only lasted for a few seconds; it was a primitive yet exciting polyphonic instrument. It was also complex, finicky, and it broke down constantly.

Another very important piece of gear was our ARP 2600 monophonic synthesizer. This was Chris's baby, and we experimented with sending signals from various conventional instruments through it. Chris would modulate the sound manually by rotating knobs that activated harmonic filters that would modify the original sound. It can be heard to great effect during Joe Farrell's emotive oboe solo on "When the Morning Comes" as well as his tenor sax solo on "She's Gone." This was groundbreaking stuff in 1973, and early on we were very involved with the blending of traditional and electronic instruments. To Arif Mardin's credit, he was enthusiastic and excited for us to experiment with this new technology; as long as the results were musical and served the song, that's all that mattered.

He would often comment that he felt that songs and styles that Daryl and I brought together had a unique musical point of view, with a wide range of influences, from old-world classical to traditional Americana to urban R&B. The blending struck him as quintessentially American.

Pensive pose in the studio during the *Abandoned Luncheonette* sessions. *(Photograph by Barbara Wilson D'Andrea)*

The leadoff song on the album is "When the Morning Comes," a catchy acoustic groove driven by Daryl's mandolin rhythm figure and hooky background vocals. It would go on to be recorded by a number of other artists and became a classic in the Hawaiian Islands when it was covered by the band Kalapana in 1975.

ONE OF THE last songs that I wrote in Philadelphia before moving to New York was, "Had I Known You Better." I was standing on the corner of Broad and Spruce Streets in Philly when a city bus pulled up in front of me and through the dirty window a girl's face caught my eye. She looked at me through the gray glass veil—enigmatic, hauntingly beautiful. For a moment, time stopped. Seconds later, the bus pulled away from the curb, leaving me choking in blue-black exhaust. As I crossed the street, something about her face sparked my imagination. What if we had met, what if we had fallen in love, what if I hadn't arrived on that street corner at that exact moment, what if I didn't have the chance to say "those three old words." In reality, the experience was pure fantasy, but my songwriter mind spun a scenario that I'm sure was deeply influenced by the anxiety of leaving Philadelphia and the daunting move to New York. That song will always take me back to that street corner and remains for me a personal metaphor about moving on.

Another inspiration: One early evening, while still living in Philly, I was sitting on the steps in front of the house on Quince Street playing my guitar when two lovely young ladies strolled by. They stopped to talk for a while and told me they were airline stewardesses. This was before the politically correct era, when the term became flight attendants. They mentioned that they were about to fly a planeload of gamblers on a Las Vegas turnaround. I had never heard that phrase, and it immediately lodged in my head. After I jotted down their names and learned that they lived just a few blocks away, they were off . . . and so was I, with a great idea for a new song. Turns out one of the gals was named Sara, and as fate would have it, she would become very much a part of the Hall and Oates story in so many ways. Before the night was over I had written "Las Vegas Turnaround (The Stewardess Song)." It's based on a Philly-style chord progression performed on acoustic guitar, which gives it a little twist.

When the recording of the *Abandoned Luncheonette* album was completed, it was obvious to everyone that the standout track was "She's Gone." Every facet of the song refracted a perfection that was unselfconsciously inspired and professionally performed. Yes, Daryl and I were responsible for the composition, but the music that resulted was the collaboration of the masterful rhythm section: Daryl on Wurlitzer piano, me on wah-wah guitar, Bernard Purdie on drums, Steven "Fontz" Gelfand on bass, Chris Bond on guitar, Ralph MacDonald on percussion, Joe Farrell on tenor sax, a classic string arrangement by Arif Mardin, enhanced by the indefinable magic of the legendary Atlantic recording studio environment, captured sonically with old-school analog quality engineering by Gene Paul, and mixed by Jimmy Douglass and Chris Bond.

From the downbeat, Ralph MacDonald's eighth-note claves entrance opens the door for Daryl's signature Wurlitzer riff, my wah-wah guitar part plays off him, and Chris Bond's mournful guitar lead completes the introduction. Singing the lead vocals in octaves was something that we had never done before or since. The background vocal arrangement was not pre-planned, and we sang it spontaneously in the studio around one microphone. There are many unique things about this song, which has been so important to me over the years. First, the lyrics walk a fine line between being cryptic and very ordinary, in a poetic way. The opening line for instance, "Everybody's high on consolation," sets the bar—somewhat unusual yet a very clear statement of where the song is going. Lines like, "Worn as a toothbrush hanging in the stand," an everyday image that anyone can relate to, further reinforce the theme. And then the chorus . . . two simple words—"she's gone"—embellished by the background vocal answers that slot in like big-band horn stabs—"oh I, oh I"—and tied together with, "I'd pay the devil to replace her." For me, it is love lost personified. The arrangement builds to a surprising three-step modulation from the key of E to the key of G for the final dramatic fade out. Even more unusual is the fact that the tonic chord of the song is never heard. Mardin's classic string arrangement provides the finishing touch, and I recall him spending a lot of time on the chart. Somehow he knew that this would be a very special moment for all of us. Now, after forty-plus years, this is the song that defined both Daryl and I, and introduced us to the world. It sounds as good today as it did the day it was recorded. My journal on 3/2/73 says it all:

Session #4—She's Gone—I'm putting it down. In writing. This is the one. I believe in this one.

Yes, "I believe in this one." I did. I do. And I always will.

I GOT THE idea for "I'm Just a Kid" one night, standing in the back of the Capitol Theater in Passaic, New Jersey. I can't recall who was performing that night but as the crowd was filing out after the show, I had the strangest sensation that everyone seemed much younger than me. I was only twenty-three years old, so there was no logical reason for the feeling or why it stuck with me all the way back to Manhattan that night. It was as if the passing crowd was youth

In the studio during the *Abandoned Luncheonette* sessions. *(Photograph by Barbara Wilson D'Andrea)*

personified, and rather than standing among them I felt as if I was an old man removed and watching from above. The words came to me as I emerged from the Lincoln Tunnel: "Will you survive, learn to drive, I know you can't describe the dreams you want to be." The song wrote itself, an acoustic R&B feel under a blend of lyrics both sung and spoken, with an angst-ridden, eerie, confessional tone and a kickass Bernard Purdie drum groove.

STARTING OFF THE *B* side of the vinyl album is the title track "Abandoned Luncheonette." This is a wonderful Daryl Hall showpiece that artfully and cinematically captures and blends together a real and imaginary moment in time: a slice of post–World War II life, inspired by the diner he went to as a child. The lyrical images of dashed hopes, dreams, and love lost to time float effortlessly over a clever 1940s-style chord progression and authentic swing feel. It's all made more evocative by yet another perfectly written big-band-style arrangement by Arif. If you close your eyes, you can almost hear the clinking of glasses and plates and the hushed conversations of the regulars sitting in the vinyl booths and stools along the counter. The song represents an innocent time left behind, just as the diner itself had been left to decay and crumble like the memories of a bygone era. Looking closely at the credits you will see "Humanity Chorus," and most of Daryl's family came into the studio to sing the chanting "Month to month . . . day to day" refrain.

"Lady Rain" was an idea I came up with right after returning from Europe in 1970. A vocal group called the Moods recorded an R&B version, but Daryl and I reworked it into our live set during the ensuing years. I wanted to re-

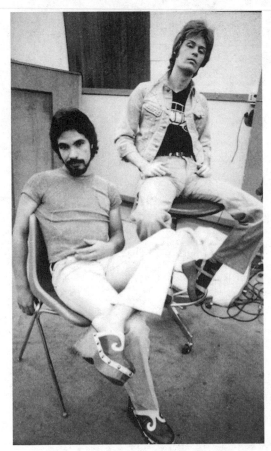

Remember clogs? In the studio during the *Abandoned Luncheonette* sessions. *(Photograph by Barbara Wilson D'Andrea)*

visit it for the album, but in a more progressive style. We talked about doing something outside the box with the arrangement, and Arif said, "I have an idea," and he told us about this avant garde musician named John Ellington Blair. Where he discovered him I'll never know, but we were all intrigued when this large bald man wearing a floor-length black cape arrived at the studio. He was enigmatic and very serious as he unpacked his secret weapon: the aforementioned blue solid-body five-string electric violin that he built himself, called a Vitar. Listen to his solo . . . its freaky, amazing, and we got exactly what we asked for. Blair, a musical genius, wound up homeless on the streets of

New York the last few years of his life, in the early 2000s. A musical genius who sadly passed in relative obscurity.

One of my favorite moments on the album is the stark and haunting "Laughing Boy"—just Daryl on grand piano accompanied by a flugelhorn. The choice of that unusual brass instrument defines Arif Mardin's sensitivity to the song— it provided a singular tonality that would enhance and not distract from the simplicity and elegance of the piano and Daryl's voice. The chord changes and melody are gorgeous, and the lyrics are somewhat biographical, but not literal.

The final track on the *B* side was a song called "Everytime I Look At You," a fun and funky jam to end the album. We all felt like we needed a final statement that would conceptually tie the record together. Here again, Arif had a personal vision for the production of this final track, saying, "I see a train speeding though the countryside, and the music of America is like a movie passing by the windows." So we set out to re-create his vision with fiddles and banjos panning and swirling about as the song fades out. It was an aural replication of a train passing through the American countryside.

And that's the album—the one I always go back to when I need to remember how things should be done. The collection that still resonates through every bone in my body. A musical moment that became such a personal benchmark, that to this day I measure everything against it.

The Cover

A bandoned *Luncheonette* sounded good.

But it *looked* good, too, thanks to the work of my friend Barbara Wilson.

As mentioned, Barbara and I met while she was attending Moore College of Art and Design in Philadelphia in 1970. She was studying fine art and photography, and soon after we met she photographed the band Valentine, which I was in, and then we met up in Europe. She had a great eye, and so I asked if she would shoot and design the album cover art for *Abandoned Luncheonette*. Remember how sacred and special album covers once were? When the artwork really mattered and had the power to forge an almost instant emotional bond with the holder? As soon as you sliced that shrink-wrap off and held it in your hands, certain sleeves just felt like they belonged in your life. You could smell the ink. Certain covers you knew you'd just carry forever. That's the kind of cover we wanted to hold the record we'd worked so hard on. Something expressive and personal that would stand the test of time. Something classic.

Outside the abandoned luncheonette. *(Photograph by Barbara Wilson D'Andrea)*

Inside the luncheonette. *(Photograph by Barbara Wilson D'Andrea)*

As a kid, Daryl used to eat at a place on High Street in Pottstown called the Rosedale Diner. After it closed down in the mid-1960s, the owner moved the diner a few miles outside of town, on Route 724, dumping it on some property he owned. Daryl was aware of the place and thought it would be the perfect image to represent the feeling and mood of the album, as well as the nostalgic title song he had written—a brilliant composition that is as timeless as its theme; a blue collar, postwar ode to broken dreams, lost innocence, and time's unforgiving march.

On a hot and muggy day in early June, Daryl and Barbara and I drove up to where the diner had been dumped so she could shoot the cover. We'd gotten permission to shoot the outside of the dilapidated structure, but once we wandered around a bit and Barbara photographed the exterior, along with many pictures of us, it only made sense to go inside and get some shots as well.

The owner was more than a little bit cranky and didn't want us to go inside, but it was too good . . . we crashed it anyway. The interior was a mess—broken glass and smashed tile everywhere. Daryl and I sat in a dusty booth, Barbara grabbed the shots, and we hightailed it out of there. That image eventually became the back cover of the album.

Next, Barbara took the black-and-white 35 mm images and, using an intensive silkscreen process that involved creating different color stencils and printing one on top of the other, did her magic. She was (and still is) a fine artist. The ethereal, evocative piece of artwork she created was exactly what we had hoped for.

Back then album-cover design truly was an art form and Barbara took the medium to a whole new level with her piece, which fully captured the sense of loss and longing in the music. Over the years it has been recognized as one of the most interesting and unique album covers of that era. When she turned it in to Atlantic Records, they loved it but felt her original slanted lettering was hard to read, so at the last minute they had her straighten the yellow neon-tube-style letters. But everything else was unchanged.

Soon after the album came out, the diner became a kind of tourist Mecca for our fans from around the world; piece by piece the little small-town structure was picked apart by souvenir hounds. It was if the diner had become a touch-stone for the endless flow of followers who had suddenly decided to make us part of their lives.

Some years later we had a gig at the Spectrum in Philadelphia. Things were much different for us by this time. We were on the top of the charts, on our way to a sold-out arena show. But for old time's sake, we had our tour-bus driver take a detour out to the old diner.

As I wrote in my journal the day of the pilgrimage:

The surroundings have changed over the years: skinny, scrawny trees grown up all around. Across the river the ominous gray towers of the new nuclear power plant in Limerick; and the diner itself ravaged by time, yes, but even more by the fans from around the world who stopped on 724 and ripped off pieces of musical memorabilia to take with them. Only two silver metal strips with the red trim still adorn the façade. We tiptoed over the broken glass and debris to pose in front, and, as if the clock were turned back, the owner lady from across the street was there in an instant, yelling for us to leave. I let her know it was us, the people who immortalized the place. That's when she flew off the handle—"I oughtta sue your asses!" she yelled, and something about a "$50,000 investment." We laughed and rode on down to Philly.

Everyone in the band piled out of the tour bus, mugging, posing, and goofing around. But for me, it was something more personal and poignant, like crossing through a time warp back to simpler life. I wandered off by myself and let my mind drift, unbridled. All of a sudden, I was back there on that gauzy, overgrown summer day in '73, capturing the final visual piece to complement the album's music, all pumped up on potential and eager to experience whatever the future had in store. Those early, desperate days of hunger and hubris apparently still rattled someplace deep in my soul, for I suddenly missed them with great force. I longed to be gently dodging the law, trespassing in the name of art, laughing all the way to the next unscripted adventure. The weeds we'd walked through were thicker now, nature reclaiming the site where a much younger and less wise me had once tramped with my partner in crime. The shiny new tour bus idling nearby seemed less a chariot at that point and more like a thief. What did you do with my old GTO? Me behind the wheel, Daryl riding shotgun, maps, bottles, and candy wrappers strewn at our feet. Chasing the sun. Running with the moon. Lost in the stars. I missed the days when there were more questions than answers. When all of life's mysteries, hopes, and desires seemed forever entombed in a disintegrating diner, set back from the road, in the woods. "Time is an illusion," said Einstein, and I think he was right. But it's also a mirror, a riddle, a fistful of sand . . . and, at least in my case, an album cover.

I heard they got rid of whatever was left of the diner by the mid-1980s. Fittingly and poetically, just as the lyrics of the title song describes, it has been scrubbed away from this earth in a controlled burn, and as all monuments of man decay in time, now trees and grass have grown in and fully reclaimed the spot. No sign. No trace. Now it's impossible to tell that anything ever existed there.

Except when you look at the album cover.

Then it all comes back.

Road Writing

began to realize how much the road had affected my psyche—shaping, bending, and coming ever-so close to breaking me. My journals became the proverbial butterfly net, allowing me to catch hordes of delicate, elusive, observational fragments I was plowing through each day. The little black books were at times confessionals, poetry pages, song starters, laundry lists, rants, raves, real-time reporting, and syntax snapshots topped with dollops of social commentary:

> *Down 90 to 71S—radar infested all the way. Randy and David in the red bug nabbed for 27 bucks at 74 mph. Beautiful Inn across from the OSU campus directly opposite the Buckeye Stadium. Sauna/whirlpool downstairs, Agora Ballroom up the block, 9:30 showtime.*
>
> *Sleep-pack-drive-play-play-sleep-pack-drive.*
> *My 24 hours allowed*
> *Are full to capacity*
> *Happy capacity*

Down South again, rumored we're doing the Boom Boom Room and pool
rooms gloom ahead for us tonight, Spartanburg, South Carolina . . . where's the
pecan pie?

Babes who want sex and dope cruisin' at the Super Boy Drive In. All
American burgers and blondes in mustangs everywhere.

There was little glamour and even less money, but it wasn't about that. It
was about growing, evolving, and learning how to survive on the road. And
like I said, these became some of my fondest memories as a musician. You never
forget the rites of passage. And no matter how big we got, I secretly sort of
longed for the fun and freedom of these days. And especially the nights.

The more we rode, the more I wrote, until the two elements started fusing
into one act of expression and reflection. I was becoming the road. And the
road was becoming me.

August 7 we opened for Sha Na Na at the Merriweather Post Pavilion in
Maryland. That was the last time we were ever billed as "Whole Oats." Another
layer shed, another booster rocket discarded as we continued to try and climb.

Abandoned Luncheonette came out in the fall of '73 and from the start got
great reviews, both critically and from fans. It wasn't selling, but that wasn't
our problem now. Our job was just to keep playing. We did a series of shows
that winter with Bruce Springsteen at Max's Kansas City in New York, and
in early 1974 headed out on the road, opening for the Bee Gees. As I recorded in
my journal after our March 4 show at New York's prestigious Avery Fisher Hall:

A good night for us, and the autographs and flashing bulbs . . . interesting
evening, even Rod Serling wandered among the backstage guests like some
fugitive in a misplaced Twilight Zone *episode. . . .*

Soon, we'd be in our own little twilight zone, also known as the *War Babies*
sessions.

War Babies

've often wondered what would have happened if there had been immediate Top 40 hits and millions of sales from *Abandoned Luncheonette*. It was musically inspired and well crafted, and yet was not a commercial success—so where was the mandate to repeat it? Of course there was none. The mandate instead became to push forward into something that, some may have a seen as a radical departure, but for us was merely the next level up the coil.

Enter the *War Babies* project.

The previous two years of touring reinforced the fact that our singer/songwriter approach, although critically well received, was not exactly kicking ass when it came to playing live. That feeling began to express itself in the songs Daryl and I began to write. Daryl in particular began to assert himself, pushing toward a more progressive approach.

Back out on the road, the yellow GTO was retired for a much larger and more practical white Chevy Suburban. But it's not like that timeworn and trusted muscle car wouldn't be missed. It had come to represent so much: an icon of wild youth, this crazy new life. And now it was about to become a speck in my life's rearview mirror. A souvenir of the heart. We all shed our toys as we grow, but I wouldn't soon forget it.

So with our new, more-functional ride crammed full of new bandmates, I continued to chew up thousands of miles of highway behind the wheel, living the no-longer new, but none-theless extraordinary, life of a touring musician. Unheralded late-afternoon arrivals in a string of small towns and big cities, methodically preparing, work-manlike guys with loud tools, worn uniforms, morph as eve-ning comes down. Then from dark

A couple of "war babies."

wings, small-gig demigods in a two-hour spotlight work hard to build believers, take what is offered up, then vanish, wraithlike, with bloodshot eyes like red tail-lights fading into an adrenaline-spiked night.

Right foot on the pedal, "Screaming Through December" to another cheap no-name motel. Stripping off the uniform and the scent of last-night's perfume, praying that sleep will make the music stop swirling round my head, but as the song went, *Can't stop the music remember the ending to the song, he played it much too long.* So it went, careening through the winter of 1974, following the seemingly random, illogical path plotted by booking agents throwing darts at a map.

The movement finally dropped us back in the cradle of New York City, and we began the search for a new record producer who might push us and the new songs to a more progressive and adventurous sonic place. We received a pleasantly surprising invitation to have lunch at the Plaza Hotel with the leg-endary producer of the Beatles, George Martin. Even though we had yet to play a live show across the pond, positive reviews for *Abandoned Luncheonette* were flowing from the normally cynical British press. Also, a sort of fervent, almost cultish kind of fan base was brewing in the British underground. It would erupt once we headed over the next year, but for now was merely the proverbial powder keg waiting for a spark. Martin, perhaps sensing the potential, wanted to know more. We joined him in the posh, stately, silver-service Edwardian Room, with its massive windows overlooking a wintry, postcard-perfect, Currier and Ives Central Park. Over a reserved and polite conversation without a lot of musical details discussed, the meeting felt more social and more an opportunity to get to know one another. Perhaps it was the style of the luncheon, held in such an imperial, somewhat stuffy venue, which put us off. There was no doubting this master's golden, elegant touch in the studio, but Daryl and I were now infused with the energy, grit, and edge of downtown New York, which I believe led us to thinking that George Martin simply was not right for us. At least in that moment. In retrospect, it was probably a musically life-changing moment that we let slip through our fingers.

But the forces at play in our creative heads brought us down to the Chelsea neighborhood of Manhattan, where Todd Rundgren would produce our next album. We didn't really know Todd. I had never met him. But we knew of him. Like us, he was a product of Philly's 1960s rock scene. He had an English-rock-influenced group called Nazz, migrated to New York, and was getting hot as a producer. The New York Dolls, Grand Funk Railroad, and others had all experienced his hand and his vision with great results. This studio was Todd Rundgren's laboratory, and for us, it was time to experiment and turn up the intensity, so we signed on with him for the next record.

His studio, called The Secret Sound, consisted of a small control room and a medium-size recording room. Once inside, on the street level (on Twenty-fourth street near Seventh Avenue), you would climb a narrow staircase up one flight and into Mark "Moogy" Klingman's ramshackle loft, which was dominated by the bulk of a grand piano and a prominent photograph of George and Ira Gershwin (Moogy claimed a distant relationship to the legendary composers). He and Todd had literally hammered and nailed their humble work space together from scratch, right down to the blue Naugahyde they had staple-gunned as a console cover.

The recording process was 180-degrees from the previous two Atlantic albums, and aggressively pushing musical boundaries was the theme. Gone was the elegant, dapper Arif Mardin, replaced by the rainbow-coiffed Todd, coming off his great and modestly titled album *A Wizard, a True Star*. He was waving his magic wand over the recording console and the entire affair. Daryl and Todd dug in like mad scientists; I felt more like a specimen in this sonic petri dish.

This was an album full of songs that were fueled by the experiences of the preceeding year. Nonstop touring begat "Is It a Star." Living in New York City inspired "70's Scenario." There was the Admiral television solo on "War Baby Son of Zorro," when we miked a TV to record game-show patter as a "solo." It was all dark and bleak and even a bit desperate. That was the mood. That was a reflection of the environment.

I didn't have a lot of song ideas going into this project. For the most part, they were random images conceived out on the ever-expanding ribbons of asphalt I was traveling each night. I just never knew where it would hit me on the road. One night, driving from Georgia to Alabama, I sensibly reduced my speed as I entered a little town that was deeply asleep. A big Suburban with New York plates and full of freaks was way too easy pickings for the local constabulary. Cruising slowly down the main drag, my eyes were drawn to an unlit marquee. The thick block letters read: JOHNNY GORE AND THE C EATERS. Intrigued by the name and not totally sure what they were advertising, I continued slowly while I conjured up an imaginary hard-core Southern rock band, part outlaw and all evil, in a parallel universe all their own. As I accelerated toward the outskirts of town, the diffuse beams of the Chevy's headlights struggled to pierce a low, eerie ground fog that stretched in all directions on either side of the empty two-lane highway. Up ahead I noticed a soft glow rising over the trees on the left. A mile later, a drive-in movie screen appeared, floating above the fog, and on that screen, going in the same direction, was an identical white Chevy Suburban. In a split second of disbelief, my foot went for the brakes, but before I could fully process the auto doppelganger, our road curved to the right and the projection was gone.

Two days later, driving back on that same highway, I slowed again as I entered the same town from the opposite direction. It was late afternoon and there on the other side of that same marquee the block letters read: JOHNNY GORE AND THE CHEATERS . . . the *H* was missing from the other side of the sign, and the idea for a song was born: "Johnny Gore and the 'C' Eaters." The road did that so many times to me—teased and seduced my radar with bits and fragments of conceptual matter. Miles melting into weird lyrical structures and inspirations. My mind became a trap for these subtle inspirations, where they would germinate long enough for me to get to my black journal when we'd eventually stop, and then I would scrawl what was being channeled. That's what I brought in to the *War Babies* sessions, those dream sequences from the road. And Todd seemed like the right guy at the right time to bring them to life.

Just being around Todd was a trippy experience, and incorporating members of our band with his collective unit, called Utopia, was a sharp departure from the studio musicans in our prior Atlantic recordings. The players, Willie Wilcox, Don York, John Siegler, Richie Cerniglia, and of course Todd, were band-oriented and intuitive. The sessions were warped and chaotic, but we did escape for air at one point to sing behind Todd in Central Park on his twenty-sixth birthday, June 22, 1974.

I was admittedly not as musically comfortable during this project, however this harder and more experimental style would become a key component in the direction and evolution of the Hall and Oates sound going forward. The album wound up reflecting that sweltering summer in New York City, and the pressure cooker it was becoming for many. Edgy, metallic, and foreboding, it cast a long shadow and became an audacious but necessary phase in our oeuvre. Along with *Whole Oats* and *Abandoned Luncheonette*, *War Babies* constituted a kind of creative triptych. Our scope of work now had a wilder and wider palette. And it was the sum total of these three albums that would become the platform from which we would discover a sound of our own.

War Babies in the Woods

After the album was finished we took the band upstate, to Woodstock, New York. The bucolic, tie-dyed enclave may not have been the exact site of the concert of the same name, but it was where the Band and Dylan laid the foundation for what would years later become known as the Americana musical genre, and where legendary manager/impresario Albert Grossman was based. He managed Todd, and through that association we were able to procure his storied Turtle Creek barn for several weeks' rehearsal. The century-old, rough-hewn barn was part of the Bearsville Studios complex, and it proved the perfect place to detox from the *War Babies* sessions and start rehearsals for our upcoming tour.

BEING UP IN the woods and taking over the barn with the band was sort of like being at a sleep away camp for the insane. Our drummer John "Willie" Wilcox, who I'd become true buddies with, roared up there on his purple Harley, and more than once during the sessions, he'd get me in wrestling holds and we'd have at it, like two kids scrapping on the lawn—which, in a way, was

The *War Babies* touring band and crew during rehearsals up in Woodstock, New York. Left to right: Randy Hoffman, Richard Reiner, Bobby Carter, Daryl, Joe (Buppa) Verga, me, John (Willie) Wilcox, Rick Laird, Don York, and Richie Cerniglia *(Courtesy John Oates)*

all we still were. Don York was on keyboards, Richie Cerniglia was on guitar, and to further reinforce the progressive-rock vibe, we managed to hire Rick Laird (formerly with Mahavishnu Orchestra) to play bass. It was a hard and edgy lineup.

We all lived together in the barn, our sleeping quarters created by hanging soft, white sheets over the rafters as dividers. The late summer air was thick at night with the croaking of frogs and katydids, and fireflies pulsated their yellow-green light. An intense and yet relaxing few weeks. Almost like a detox in the country after the mescaline-fueled city recording sessions we'd just finished.

It was sort of ironic that sequestered away in this woodsy lair we were putting together a very musically progressive and ferocious live show, in keeping with the new *War Babies* material. The stage presentation would reflect that as well. The sound-pressure levels would be off the charts, and the new songs and attitude would dominate the set list.

The band would practice long into the night, honing intricate arrangements incorporating odd time signatures and extended instrumental sections to showcase the skills of the new players. But by day, I'd soak up the outdoors, watching the rainbow trout at nearby Esopus Creek, tubing lazily in the cool, sweet mountain lakes, and tramping around Mount Tremper.

Then it was back to the barn to play deep into the night again, under both the Milky Way and thundering summer storms.

BACK IN THE city we got an offer to open a late-August show for Richie Havens in Central Park. Though the bill was a musical mismatch, it made the statement that our transition from laid-back acoustic act was now all but complete. We had officially entered into the then-current glitter-glam universe, melding Philly soul, folk, and rock with our newly created palette of knotty, synthesized excursions. Manic and at times maniacal, our show had now been transformed.

OUR NEXT GIG was back on home turf, at the Main Point coffeehouse on the tony Main Line, outside of Philadelphia. It was a gingerbread-and-herb-tea cathedral where I had seen and heard a who's who of legendary folk performers like Sonny Terry and Brownie McGhee, Doc Watson, Mississippi John Hurt, the Jim Kweskin Jug Band, Phil Ochs, and others. But on this night, the dedicated group of fans who packed the early show, waiting to be lulled and charmed with gentle, thoughtful melodies and lyrics, were about to be assaulted. With little warning, the pounding sound and fury of the *War Babies* show began. The amps were too big and the room was too small; I could sense unease and confusion from the audience as the reality of the performance washed over them. There were no sensitive ballads from the past for them to latch on to, just this totally reinvented progressive rock band . . . it was way too much for them to process.

To say it was not well received would be an understatement. When my parents came in for the second set, a fan from the early show left a scrawled note on a napkin for the next victims: "These guys SUCK!"

A letter to the editor of the *Tripod,* the Trinity College newspaper, up in Hartford, Connecticut, conveyed a similar sentiment:

> *To the editor:*
>
> *Noise can be bad for living things; the Hall/Oates concert was thus a Saturday night massacre, yielding deafness, disorientation, and headaches. Someone in authority at the concert should have demanded a decrease in volume . . . I make no value judgment on the evening's music . . . In the long, there is no excuse for blatant disregard of health.*
>
> *Yours,*
>
> *Christopher Gulick-Mooney class of '75*

Gulick-Mooney's eardrums and opinion notwithstanding, we were reinventing ourselves, and in a rare and unusually perceptive move, our booking agent landed an opening slot on the Lou Reed *Rock 'n' Roll Animal* tour that fall. Reed at that time, with his bleached, close-cropped hair and black fingernail polish, had become a magnet for fans that craved desperate, sometimes violent tales of dope, transvestism, sadomasochism, and other taboo topics from the seedy underbelly of New York City.

It seemed like a good idea at the time. The tour began and we duly hit the stage in front of thousands of rabid Lou fans who, as it turned out, were not very interested in our show or us. Drugged-out zombie faces in the dark mouthed loathing moans punctuated with tortured cries from the dark, "Bring on the fetus" . . . "Fuck you!" Meanwhile, backstage, the Lou Reed band simmered with a dismissive attitude until it was time for their headliner turn on stage. Many nights I watched from the wings as Lou would stagger out from the dressing room toward the stage swarmed over by an entourage of individuals of indeterminate sex. The band would crank up the intro to "Sweet Jane" and Lou's road manager would shove him from the dark wings into the waiting spotlight. He would stagger around in a daze as Lou's enraptured fans erupted in ecstasy, and on more than one occasion, his lead guitar player would kick him in the ass, sending him lurching toward the mic stand at the center of the stage. There he would prop himself with one arm over the stand and tie up his other arm with the black microphone cable as if he was about to shoot up . . . it was that kind of show.

We trudged from city to city playing as loud as we could and dealing with the reality of this misguided matchup. After a few shows, Rick Laird had enough. He just announced one day that he was quitting, and he disappeared. We scrambled, and fortunately found a replacement, a guy named Kenny Aaronson, to jump in, teaching him the songs in the van on the way to the show. The entire affair had a surreal quality, and I remember one late afternoon after sound check before a gig at the old Alexandria Roller Rink in Virginia, Daryl and Willie, dressed in designer Ronald Kolodzie jumpsuits decided to go roller skating and found themselves lost in the ghetto streets before narrowly avoiding getting themselves killed by the neighborhood gangs.

One late night before bed, bleary eyed in some forgotten motel room, I saw Tavares singing our song "She's Gone" on *Soul Train*. It was a reminder of the significance of having written a number one R&B hit and further reinforced the fact that this ill-conceived tour was but a temporary side trip, at least until tomorrow and another opening set before Reed's hollow-eyed acolytes.

Mick Jagger and Todd came to hang out backstage at a big show in the Felt Forum in New York, which was a sort of rock-and-roll affirmation . . . perceptions about us were changing. The buzz about us was clearly growing. In November, having survived a few insane months of touring, I returned home to New York and realized I really missed being in the city. Right away I started to re-immerse myself in the burgeoning music scene happening just a few blocks in any direction. Spawned from the legacy of the Velvet Underground and their godfather, Lou Reed, acts like Suicide, Patti Smith, and Television, still wet from the artistic shells from whence they recently hatched, were filling their lungs, testing their wings, and adjusting to the light, angry and hungry. The punk vibe of the Village in re-creation was a glittery, androgynous parade of unknown superstars, street poets, and street-smart scene makers. The folk scene had somehow morphed into an underworld Dionysian carnival, and I couldn't get my ticket punched fast enough.

The innovative, stark, and linear twin-guitar attack of Television had begun at little dive on the Bowery at Bleeker called CBGB. At the same time, Patti Smith had begun developing her poetry readings into a musical act. On November 10 I caught her now-legendary show at the Blue Hawaiian Discotheque at the Roosevelt Hotel on Forty-fifth Street. Titled "Rock 'n' Rimbaud," it was a tribute to her muse, the French poet Arthur Rimbaud. In true Patti fashion, it was an inspired, stream-of-consciousness eruption of street art. She was raw and unpredictable. I liked her.

New York was starting to seriously quake with musicians who were searching for their own brand of sonic truth. Daryl and I had veered sharply in a new direction, but we had yet to crystallize all these experiences, influences, and muses into a cohesive sound. Extreme steps and missteps are essential for growth. Running full speed toward a precipice to stand at the brink and peer over the edge is intoxicating, but the euphoria invariably wears off. Now, as would happen again and again over the course of the next forty years, the process of integrating and pooling influential elements would continue. What would happen if we took what we learned from all three albums and allowed some natural hybrid to emerge? What would that sound like?

The Silver Album

1975 may have started out like the year before, but a dramatic change was right around the corner.

Just like '74, through a bitter January and February, Daryl and I chipped our way across a frozen East Coast, playing tighter and tighter shows in new college gyms, old vaudeville houses, and everything in between. That's what my life had become for most of the year, and as rigorous as it was, it was turning us into a truly well-tuned, well-oiled live band that could hold its own in front of one hundred or ten thousand people. The band was in transition from the *War Babies* tour, and the new lineup would soon develop into something truly special. We'd softened some of the harsher edges of the previous years' show and started leaning more on our melodic sides (while still rocking pretty hard).

And in big cities a lot of big names had us on their radar. One night backstage at the Bottom Line in New York, Rod Stewart, all four members of Queen, and Robert Fripp all showed up to check us out.

With three albums under our belt, it was on to the next step. We were still signed with Atlantic records, but our experimental excursion with Todd Rundgren caused confusion and concern. It was as if we abandoned the family, and in the background, Mottola was not-so-quietly looking for a new situation.

Atlantic Records had signed the Average White Band with Arif producing, and that group filled the void we had created. Sensing an opportunity, Tommy Mottola, who would soon be immortalized in song by us as "Little Gino," started wheeling and dealing on our behalf. He began talking to other labels, from Sire to RCA to Warner. He played hardball, he played curveball, and he played knuckleball. He was a "Moneyball" star before the term existed.

Of course Daryl and I were focused on writing and touring and didn't pay much attention to what was happening on the business side. Tommy encouraged us to just keep working on the creative side and let him take care of the boring biz bullshit . . . how could we argue with a guy who had stuffed our parkas with fistfuls of cash a couple of Christmases earlier? We never wanted for anything. So we didn't ask questions.

We sat down with Clive Davis, who had the interest but not the faith to step up with the level of dough Mottola was looking for. It was RCA that seemed most motivated to sign us. At the time RCA was rebuilding their rock-and-roll roster. They did have Elvis, John Denver, Bowie, the Kinks, and Lou Reed, as well as a big country roster that included Alabama, Waylon Jennings, and Porter Wagoner, but they wanted us, too.

Over the course of a couple of tense but interesting weeks in March, Mottola and his lawyer conceived an aggressive and novel "Let's Make a Deal" strategy that they would develop and refine over the next ten years. Their first attempt to extract from the corporate coffers scored big, to the tune of more than $1.5 million as a cash advance against future royalties from our soon-to-be new record label, RCA. The way it was explained to us was, "Why wait for royalties to dribble in over a long period of time? Let's take the cash up front and let the record company wait to recoup." Sounds good, right? What could go wrong?

Before signing to a new label, however, we had to get out of the Atlantic deal. Not having been privy to the negotiations and conversations that went on behind closed doors to free us from the existing Atlantic records contract, I imagine that it very well could have gone something like this: "Why do you want to keep these guys, they're crazy, look at that last record they made with Todd Rundgren, no hits. . . . God knows what they'll do next, just let them go." (I paraphrase and imagine.) The results were that Atlantic would release Daryl and me from our obligation with the concession that they could put out a compilation of music from the first three albums plus three new songs that we would be responsible for. A year later, the warmly titled album, *No Goodbyes,* was released on the heels of our first RCA recording.

Gone were the down payments on a dream. All of a sudden we had an investment in the now. While Daryl and I made the music, Mottola worked his magic in the boardroom like a great conductor taking control of an orchestra. Except those suits weren't holding violins or trombones; they held big fat checkbooks, and our lives changed with a couple of pen strokes.

Jamaica

Maybe it was a late-night wild-hair-up-your-ass idea on tour, but somehow or another, our *War Babies* band lead guitarist, Richie Cerniglia, and I decided to take a trip to Jamaica. I hadn't traveled anywhere that wasn't work related since my return from Europe in 1970—just touring and recording, touring and recording. But leaving freezing New York City behind in the dead of winter to kick back on a tropical beach and inhale the local culture just seemed like a good idea.

It was my first trip to the Caribbean, and I watched the slender, tapered, silver wing of the jet slice over the turquoise water through the viewfinder of my Super 8 movie camera (a hobby I'd started to immerse myself in) as we approached the Montego Bay airport. A hot and sweaty hour later, I was behind the wheel, on the "wrong" side of the road, dicing with the local traffic in a clapped-out Mini Moke with no roof and no doors. Map? What map? I kind of thought I understood the sketchy-looking Rasta dude slouching outside the airport exit as he languidly provided vague directions with that distinctive local patois. I had been told that the place to be was the remote village of Negril, roughly two hours away. So with only hearsay to go on, I merged into the jostling, chaotic, Montego Bay rush hour. It was a bit of an adjustment, adapting to driving on the left side of the road for the first time while trying to get the hang of the every-man-for-himself island road rules. No turn signals; no lights; pickup trucks belching black smoke jammed with gaggles of colorfully dressed men and women hanging off the tailgate, lithely jumping on and off whenever traffic slowed down. Each curve and bend in the road was punctuated and preceded by a cacophony of horn honking and hand waving. A few miles outside of town, dusk segued into night around the same time that the asphalt ended.

The narrow dirt road, littered with potholes, was filled with tall, lanky, grown men riding tiny children's bicycles, sputtering mopeds weaving to avoid scrawny cats and dogs that appeared to be moving in slow motion as they randomly and suddenly appeared out of the darkness, barely visible in the dim yellow beams of the Mini's headlights.

Soon the jungle enveloped the tiny car as the road twisted and doubled back on itself, heading inland, alternately climbing and descending, affording occasional brief glimpses of silvery phosphorescent waves breaking below that were quickly snuffed out by the blackness of the dense foliage.

We finally arrived at the edge of Negril after surviving the nerve-wracking drive. On my right, the pure white sand of the famous six-mile beach glowed in the early evening moonlight. But sightseeing could wait . . . we were both starving. I pulled off at what appeared to be a roadside stand. The ramshackle wood hut had a rusty corrugated metal roof and a small bar with a minifridge and a handwritten sign that read: JERK CHICKEN JERK PORK. Out back, a few silent men crouched and huddled around a crude fire pit . . . the smell of roasting meat drew us in. I had no idea what jerk anything was, but my stomach said *eat*! After we ordered a couple of Red Stripe beers, the guy behind the bar handed us paper plates piled with savory, hot, smoking meat. I tore into the first succulent bite, scarfing down the jerk pork like a caveman, washing it down with swigs of ice-cold beer. For the first few bites everything was all right, but then it hit. A tingling, sharp heat began swarming through my mouth like a hundred angry wasps. It started on my lips, then sucker punched the taste buds on my tongue before violently strangling my throat on its way down to my gut. The inflamed intensity of the spices scoffed at the coolness of the beer . . . holy shit this was hot! The men sitting around the fire eyed us with knowing satisfaction, not laughing but obviously amused by our ignorance. Sweating profusely, with tears rolling down our faces, we beat it back to the car and accelerated away with a lesson about Jamaican cuisine and some parting advice to look for a place up the road called Rick's Café.

The one-lane road wound up and away from the beach back into the jungle again as I picked my way, carefully dodging mud puddles and barely visible people wandering here and there. After a few more miles we came upon some tiki-style torches, their flickering glow beckoning us down a narrow lane leading toward the ocean. Rick's Café had opened just a few months before we arrived and was a work in progress. A somewhat modern construction by Jamaican standards, yet still rustic, it was festively lit with flickering torches and strings of multicolored lights. With a carpet of stars as a backdrop, the view from the setting at the edge of a fifty-foot cliff overlooking the Caribbean was impressive. You could feel the waves crashing against the rocks below, and their rhythmic pulse blended hypnotically with the reggae bass line thumping from the jukebox.

The crowd was full-fledged maximum international hippie, and I knew we had found the right place to connect with whatever Negril had to offer. After a few more beers, the long day's journey began to wear on me, and the helpful bartender directed us to continue up the road and look for an A-frame house on the left, where we could rent a couple of rooms. We found it near the end of the jungle road that by now was barely wide enough for the Mini. A man named Joseph slouched silently in a canvas chair by the front door smoking a huge spliff. "Hey mon," he greeted us as we approached, and with little discussion he led us around back to a couple of tiny rooms. There was no talk of money or details; he merely opened the doors, turned on lights, said, "Morning soon come, mon," and left.

Morning did soon come, slow and steamy. Stepping outside into the dazzling tropical sun, we were overwhelmed by the perfume of hibiscus and the dense, verdant opulence of ferns and callaloo. The small, quirky house, dull in the monochromatic darkness of our late night arrival, was now resplendent in the sunshine, with multicolored pastel trim. On the side of the building was a funky outdoor shower built from brown wooden slats. A rusty, old-fashioned sprinkler-style showerhead with a pull chain dangled overhead.

As I wandered around to the front, there on the porch sat Joseph, in the same chair. His thick medusalike dreadlocks overflowed from a red-yellow-and-black knit Jiffy Pop-style cap. I sat down alongside him while he languidly smoked a huge, fat joint. With few words we struck a casual cash agreement for a week's rent that included room and board and a big paper grocery bag full of local herb. Home base established, it was time to dial down the city pace and get with the island lifestyle.

The Negril of 1974 was not the developed resort that it is today. There were neither Hedonism II nor couples-only Swept Away chain resorts, nor any expensive private homes overlooking the cliffs and blighting the pristine six-mile beach. From what I could see, we were at the end of a dirt road surrounded by jungle, and directly across from a dramatic set of cliffs that towered high above the calm Caribbean ocean.

Later that afternoon I decided to explore a narrow path on the other side of the road that led toward the cliffs. I wound my way through the mangrove, then carefully picked my way down to the sea. Working my way around a large boulder I emerged onto a smooth flat rock surrounded by clear tidal pools, and there, alone on a beach towel, was a cute blond girl, quietly staring out at the breaking waves. She turned when I appeared and just smiled, as though she knew I was coming. It was strange and comfortable all at once. We spent the rest of the afternoon swimming and smoking and staring at the ever-changing turquoise-and-blue-green sea. After a few hours she asked me if I could drive her down to Rick's Café for sunset. I did, and when the orange orb split the horizon, she slipped away like the last rays of light and was gone.

The days and nights blended into one long slow-motion dream sequence—no plan, no worries, soon come . . . soon come. At one point, word spread over the coconut telegraph that some locals were having a barbecue and all were welcome. As it turned out, it wasn't ribs, coleslaw, and baked beans, but instead a very pungent and frightening-looking goats head soup, eyeballs and all. I guess I wasn't on the island long enough to go in that deep. Instead Richie and I headed down the road to a party on the six-mile beach.

The serpentine dirt road was very dark and the lights of the Mini were very dim. At any moment, around any hairpin corner, the odd horse, dog, or child could wander out from the dense foliage without warning. As we swept around yet another blind bend, at the limit of the headlight beams, the figure of a man materialized. He struck a zombie pose, standing squarely in the middle of the road. I slowed and rolled closer. In seconds the details of this grisly apparition clarified, illuminated in the headlights.

He was swaying unsteadily, gesturing with one hand for me to stop while his other arm hung straight down at his side. A dark stain spread from his shoulder to his hand, and there were splatters of blood across the chest of his ripped T-shirt. I braked to a stop a short distance away while my mind tried to process the situation. As he stumbled toward the car, dreadful panic surged through my body. He growled, "Let me in mon, let me in!" There was no way. . . . "They cut me mon," he slurred more aggressively. I couldn't take my eyes off of the four-inch open gash on his shoulder. Blood oozed everywhere, and before I could react, he threw himself onto the hood of the Mini, leaning against the windshield, his blood-soaked shirt flattened against the glass. I didn't know if there was a hospital nearby, but I knew that there was a police station just a bit farther on, so I began to roll slowly forward, straining to see around his body slouched across the windshield. Eventually the glow of the police-station lights came into view, and I jerked the steering wheel to the right, pulling off the road and jamming on the brakes in front of the station house. The man on the hood must have passed out during the short drive, and my sudden stop made him slide forward, falling to the ground in front of the car. I quickly shifted into reverse, popped the clutch, and backed out onto the road while he cursed and screamed into the night. This tropical adventure was not all peace and love.

Shaken with the possibility of dealing with the strict and intimidating

Jamaican police, I floored the Mini and disappeared down the road toward the beach. Richie was reaching over the windshield and pouring out our water bottles in a desperate attempt to wash off the blood. I just wanted out of there, and we soon pulled into a secluded parking area and did our best to clean off the car.

On the other side of the trees a fat bass line beckoned us toward the beach. There on the sand, a reggae band was laying it down for a small group of blissed-out, half-naked hippie tourist beach bums and colorfully half-dressed Jamaicans. Bodies pulsed and the ganja groove was flowing like a one-love organism. Colored lights were casually strung over a low makeshift stage while an ancient PA system, cranked to eleven, spit out the distinctive distorted, nonstop reggae rhythm.

Still reeling from the unnerving experience on the road, I positioned myself at the edge of the party, checking out the band and trying to keep a low profile, when they suddenly kicked into a song that grabbed my attention. Though it was still the same hypnotic beat, when I focused on the catchy hook and sly innuendo of the words I realized they were a thinly disguised reference to the sex act, with the metaphorical title "Soldering." The very next day I drove over the mountain to a small town that had a record store and bought the 45 single.

But then it was time to get back to the real world and, with vivid experiences from the mystical islands etched forever in my mind, I headed home.

Silver. And Gold.

W e had written a bunch of good songs but didn't have a plan for recording them. During the year we were recording and touring behind
War Babies, our ex-guitar player and studio whiz, Chris Bond, had moved to
Los Angeles. He had started making a name for himself on the West Coast,
and he raved about the quality of the studios and session players available there.
Bond stayed in touch and made a convincing pitch for us to come to LA and to
work with him. In the mid-1970s Los Angeles was the place to be when it came
to making state-of-the-art professional-sounding records, and so with no better plan and caught up in Chris's enthusiasm, we headed West.

APRIL AND MAY became a whirlwind blitz of activity. We had a few shows to
play, now as RCA recording artists, and we also began brainstorming with the
label about the look and feel of our image.

At the time, New York City was awash in fashion flamboyance. Glam rock
was all the rage, and at the epicenter of the trend was a charismatic French
makeup artist named Pierre LaRoche. He began his career working with Eliz-

abeth Arden, but the conservative cosmetics company could not contain his wild creativity. So he hitched his star to David Bowie in 1973 and immediately made his mark by crafting the visual look for Bowie's Ziggy Stardust persona. The astral-sphere makeup on Bowie's forehead, the rainbow lightning bolt from the *Aladdin Sane* album cover—LaRoche created those. Right before we met with him, he had done all the makeup for *The Rocky Horror Picture Show* movie, and within a month or so he would begin touring with the Rolling Stones as Mick Jagger's personal makeup man.

Up until this time our faces had never appeared on the front cover of any of our albums. "You'll look like jet-set whores," Pierre hissed to us one night, over many drinks in the Village. We thought "What the hell?" and got caught up in the idea of being fashionably cutting edge. He had a visual concept for the look of the album package, and I distinctly remember him saying, "I will immortalize you!" Man, he wasn't joking.

DARYL, SANDY (AKA SARA), and I had been sharing an apartment on Eighty-second Street for almost three years, but while we were on tour, Sandy found a new apartment in a great location, on Christopher Street in Greenwich Village. When we came back, Sandy had moved into the new place in an elegant old brownstone. I took over the small extra bedroom, but it wasn't long before I felt like it was time to put some air between us. Daryl and I were always uniquely different personalities and had shared apartments together as friends out of a certain kind of convenience. But with Sandy and his relationship firmly established, it only made sense for me to move on, especially now that I finally had enough dough to afford it. Although we worked intensely and were together most of the time, ironically, individualism was always the most important trait in our partnership. And now it was time to start living that. After a few months, in early May of 1975, I found myself a great apartment in the same neighborhood, on Grove near Bleecker Street. It was a sublet on the fifth floor, with lots of windows and a fireplace.

The last week of May was insane. On a Wednesday we met with Pierre at

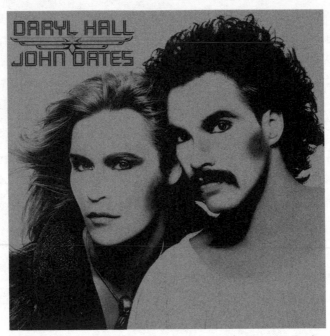

The infamous "Silver" album cover designed by Pierre LaRoche.

a studio in lower Manhattan, where the famed fashion photographer Bill King shot our album cover. From there we trekked down to a building at 200 Water Street in lower Manhattan, near Wall Street. Pierre had found a futuristic-looking neon tunnel inside the lobby where he wanted us to pose. We just went in and did it guerilla style, on the fly, no permits or anything. There were still business people wandering around the place as we shot! That image, in which I was naked, would appear on the inner sleeve of the album. It was crazy, it was glam, it was provocative and totally in sync with prevailing downtown New York fashion. The image was designed to make a statement, and to this day it's the only one of our album covers anyone ever talks about. As Daryl cracked, "He made me look like the woman I always wanted to date." Even stranger than the extreme look of the album cover was the fact that we had locked ourselves into a visual image before one note of recording had begun. The music on the record inside that album package would have virtually no artistic connection to the cover. From the beginning and going forward it would become clear that having a calculated master plan would have very little to do with the success of Daryl Hall and John Oates.

The day after that memorable shoot I moved my few belongings into the new pad, and the day after that I was on a plane to Los Angeles for the next chapter in what was becoming an increasingly interesting and intense career. We had a look, but no idea how the West Coast experience would affect the sound of the new batch of songs we were bringing into the studio. I had a vague sense that somehow all the elements of the previous three albums would coalesce and finally result in something new and cohesive. We'd soon find out.

Upon our arrival in LA, we were delivered to a modern, incredibly spacious high-rise rental apartment at 1155 La Cienega Boulevard, just off of the Sunset Strip. I dropped my bags and stood looking out over the balcony, soaking in the hazy southern California sun, when I noticed a guy in a white bathrobe who looked exactly like Marvin Hamlisch seated at a long, black grand piano across the courtyard. (I could never have imagined that thirty years later I'd be back in that exact same building writing with another great pianist named Jed Leiber, sitting and staring out of that same wall of glass.)

RCA had a limo at our disposal 24/7 and was giving us the full Hollywood star treatment. We wasted no time joining Chris Bond at Larrabee Sound Studios and getting right to work. Bond had his synth and electric guitar sounds locked down. He was prepared, full of ideas, and certainly delivered when it came to hiring top-notch session players. The first day alone we worked with drummer Jim Gordon, who had done everything from Derek and the Dominos to George Harrison's triple album, *All Things Must Pass*. (On a side note, Gordon had undiagnosed schizophrenia. Eight years later he would murder his mother and be sent to prison.) There were two other great drummers, Ed Greene and Mike Baird. The Rasputin-bearded, hot-rod maven, supercreative Lee Sklar, as well as the funky Scott Edwards, held down the bass chair. Gary Coleman played percussion, and Clarence McDonald played some keyboards. Barry Rudolph was the recording and mixing engineer. In the classic recording style of the time, the rhythm section was set up in a loose semicircle.

The sessions began every day around 11:00 A.M. and proceeded in a workmanlike fashion. The fact that we had toured and recorded with Chris Bond under Arif Mardin's tutelage made for a seamless creative flow. The sessions went very smoothly, usually tracking two songs a day. Chris had been working on his arrangement skills, and again, his experience with Arif showed. The three of us collaborated together on every aspect of the recording. The ten songs on the album were tightly crafted and much less experimental than our prior sonic excursion with Todd Rundgren. The first track was a song I had written called "Camellia," based on the unusual name of a girl called Pamellia. After he heard it, Daryl said, "Cool song John, but no one is gonna believe that Pamellia is a real name . . . why not just call her Camellia?" The second track, which would emerge as a surprise hit from left field nine months after the album's release, was Daryl's elegantly beautiful musical postcard to Sandy Allen, "Sara Smile." I pulled out the 45 single of "Soldering" that I had brought back from my Jamaican trip and we recorded a loose cover version using a primitive Roland drum machine. This was the first time we had recorded with a drum machine, and it would reappear on subsequent albums, to great effect, on some very big hit records. "Soldering" ended up as the B side of the "Sara Smile" single. It was starting to feel like we had made the right choice in coming to the West Coast.

And of course, it wasn't just the music.

Outside of the incredibly satisfying recording sessions, I was also adapting to the tempos and tightropes of the Left Coast lifestyle. Personally, my appetites never really changed when I visited someplace. I was always on a mission to taste and experience as many local offerings as possible. I worked hard in the studio, but I played just as hard at night, drifting among many star-studded galaxies up and down the coast. Often I would go to the Roxy to watch people like Emmylou Harris perform. I'll never forget seeing her with Sneaky Pete Kleinow from the Flying Burrito Brothers on the pedal steel and James Burton on the Telecaster. I went up to the Mojave Desert to watch the desert air races, spent Saturday nights watching the short-track sprint car at Ascot Park, and raced go-karts in Pomona. When I could free up a few hours I took in the nude beaches off Topanga, watching the endless parade of sexy "Malibu Barbies" as the locals called them along Zuma Beach. I even took my first trip to Disneyland. I found the pleasure dome of Southern California to be earthy and relaxed, full of glittery, amorous people that gave mid-'70s LA its special kind of magic. It was a nice counterpoint to the no-nonsense grit of New York City.

In mid-July the Rolling Stones pulled into town for a weeklong stand at the Forum out in Inglewood, so we reconnected with Pierre. In fact, one day he and photographer Annie Leibovitz (who would soon shoot our first *Rolling Stone* cover) took us out to the Wattles Mansion up in the Hollywood Hills and photographed us under the waterfalls there. I went to see the Stones one night and later caught Bob Marley at the Roxy, along with Keith Richards, Billy Preston, Buddy Miles, George Harrison, and Ronnie Wood. It seemed every time you turned your head you saw a face as familiar as one on Mount Rushmore.

Another memorable night I hung out with Frank Zappa, John Mayall, and Eric Burdon at a table in the famed Rainbow Bar and Grill. Zappa, in particular, always seemed interested in what we were doing. One night at the Roxy after he came (once again) to watch us play, he leaned over the table where we all sat and said in that deep, professorial voice of his, "You guys should have a TV show one day. I just feel it. You guys should do a TV show." Well, he certainly predicted it for Daryl, anyway, who, as of this writing, is almost nine years into his show *Live From Daryl's House*. LA was a much different scene than New York, both by day and starry night, but I got into it. I liked wrapping up the sessions and cruising up the coast in an exotic rent-a-car to Santa Barbara. Or to the Palladium for an Alice Cooper show and another nonstop party in La La Land.

BY THE THIRD week of July, we were wrapping up recording and preparing to head home to New York City. It had been an amazing experience, and I couldn't wait to hear the final mixes. We had to wait for Chris to send us tapes of the mixes, and after listening I recall numerous phone calls back and forth to make sure we were getting the exact sound we wanted. Nothing like today, when you can send music over the Internet and have an instantaneous dialog with anyone you're working with anywhere in the world. In the 1970s, it was snail mail followed by exasperating phone conversations followed by waiting some more and hoping for the best. As it turned out, being in sync with Chris Bond made a tedious process fairly easy. The album sounded great.

To go with our wildly androgynous images on the album cover, we also decided to create a logo for our band. Even though we always made it a point to use our full names on every album, the world would invariably refer to us as "Hall and Oates," which I felt had about as much panache as the name of a law firm. We needed a symbolic substitute. Looking around, we noticed that bands had started branding themselves with symbols. So we developed a stylized star flanked by a set of wings to brand our name on the album, posters, T-shirts, and everything else. Eventually we would have handmade, numbered, winged pendants made for band members to wear around their neck, and for us to present to all of the folks in our inner circle.

You never knew who would show up in L.A. after one of our shows. This is circa 1976-1977, left to right: Daryl, Frank Zappa, Eric Burdon, John Mayall, and me. *(Courtesy John Oates)*

This was a critical time. We weren't only adapting the way we sounded, but also the way we looked. And after a big cash advance and three marginally successful albums, there was more than a little pressure for us to have some commercial success—i.e., a radio hit. The album was officially titled *Daryl Hall and John Oates*, but it was destined to forever be known as the Silver album.

1975 Part II

By now there was at least one routine in my life that I could depend upon: Once an album was finished and being readied for release, hitting the road would not be far behind.

Touring was simply part of my life cycle by this point, and in the months leading up to hitting the road, I would always start mentally preparing to get behind the wheel of the Suburban and start logging all of those midnight miles.

This time would be a little different, however. Our touring band was in a transitional phase and there were some spots to fill. Earlier in the year we had brought in some new blood. The new lineup started with two friends who had grown up together in Florida: drummer Eddie Zyne and his bassist Stephen Dees (aka Slugger Blue). They had relocated to New Jersey and learned the *War Babies* album note for note before coming in and impressing us. Their pre-existing bond as friends gave them a natural chemistry as a killer rhythm section, and they gelled with us right away. (About a year later we'd benefit again from these guys when they convinced a friend of theirs from Florida, a sax player named Charlie DeChant, to come play a session in New York. Once we heard Charlie, we knew we needed him, too, but little did we know what an integral

Our terrific mid-'70s band. Left to right: Daryl, Stephen Dees (bass), Eddie Zyne (drums), me, Todd Sharp (guitar), and David Kent (keyboards). *(Courtesy John Oates)*

part of our sound he would become.) We always had great players with us up till this point, but it also always seemed as if there was a soft spot or two; now it was time to go to another level.

We held auditions in late summer before hiring an innovative keyboard player named David Kent and a wildly talented nineteen-year-old lead guitar player from Ohio named Todd Sharp. Once full rehearsals started, things started to click. This was a band that had great chemistry. Given that we now had four albums' worth of material to pull from, the show was truly going to be something that represented the full scope of our songwriting.

Even though we copped our share of the temptations that come with being on tour, there was always the voice of reason in the back of my mind saying, "You want to keep doing this for a long time, this is your life . . . don't fuck it up." I think I can speak for Daryl when I say that we both valued our creative lives enough to know when to let the circus move on.

. . .

Before getting ready to leave for our first tour of England, we did a warm-up show at the old Agora ballroom across from the Ohio State University campus in Columbus, Ohio, and the results were electric.

As I scrawled in my journal:

The lights go down, and we descend the break-a-leg wooden staircase toward the black back wall of giant amps. It all went wild before us, building applause, those crazy screaming faces pressed up against the worn edge of the stage. Howls, smiles, moving bodies, total energy from the stage jamming into every space. The response was heart-stopping. Four encores. Later, as we listen to the tape, we hear three full minutes of applause between our third and fourth encores. It was, undoubtedly, the greatest response I have ever received for any musical endeavor. At last we got the reaction we've been waiting for."

As deep as our set list was to become, that night in Columbus we actually ran out of material and had to perform "She's Gone" twice. And the crowd went even crazier the second time we played it. We felt locked and loaded for our first trip across the pond and our debut in London.

Besides knowing we had such tight band, we were also confident because we had gotten word from our record label that the buzz throughout England about our first couple of records had really started to intensify. Many British fans totally understood Philly soul, and evidently we were being touted as the real deal, a must-see. Plus, the Silver album was garnering seriously positive reviews after being released in late August. So we had high expectations about our first tour abroad.

That said, nothing could have prepared us for the reception we received.

From the moment we checked in to the elegant Athenaeum Hotel in London, I felt the buzz. We started doing press interviews literally the day we arrived, and you could tell the journalists were very into us. *New Musical Express, Crawdaddy*, and other normally critical publications were unusually positive and even celebratory about our arrival. A dedicated group of hard-core fans had seemingly devoured our first four albums, yet their hunger remained.

They couldn't get enough. The writers sat on edge as we answered their provocative, complex, and insightful questions, peering deeply into our eyes as if looking for the meaning of life. It was weird.

I was certainly happy to be back in England for the first time since my crazy postcollege trip. Todd Rundgren was touring Europe at that time with Utopia, and the night before we performed our first show we ran into him and Willie Wilcox. It was good to see my old drummer pal, and I was happy that he had a landed a gig with Todd. Things seemed to be going great for everyone.

The historic art deco New Victoria Theatre was sold out, and in attendance were not just rabid Hall and Oates fans, but some of music's elite. Pete Townshend was backstage to check out this "new American singing duo" along with Keith Moon. The guys from Steely Dan, touring Europe at that time, were also there, along with many other luminaries from our industry.

The response that night was very much like what we had experienced a couple of weeks earlier in Columbus. The reserved English response we expected was anything but. The crowd was raucous and the band was on fire. At the end of the show the audience was going crazy and wanting more. We had played everything on our set list and had run out of songs; Tommy Mottola ran out onto the stage to explain to the delirious crowd that, no, we were done, no more encores—and they booed him, so Daryl and I went out and did "When the Morning Comes," just the two of us, without the band, sweet and simple. The building shook with the applause, screaming, and stomping. It was like the second coming. The Brits were all in.

After the show, two old friends, Jules and Gabby, the couple that I crashed with on the beach in Spain back in 1970, were there to greet me backstage, where much record company champagne was flowing to celebrate our London debut. It had been five years since I'd gotten to know them, and seeing them really helped compress the time. In the jam-packed, musty, circa-1920s dressing room, I thought about all that I had squeezed into my life since I'd last seen them. It was a lot to take in. But I was happy with how things were going. On the plane to London, I had written this in my journal:

*I write now, in the air, a bit crazed, wired, and excited that all those Quince
Street dreams are now becoming a reality.*

At that point I felt no truer words had ever been scrawled in those little
black books of mine.

They got us in England. They seemed to understand all the nuances of the
lyrics and melodies. Our sparkling reception in London gave us wings. That first
show was filmed and recorded, and I would resurrect it thirty years later from an
old videotape and release audio of several songs on our 2009 box set, *Do What You
Want, Be What You Are*. Hearing those recordings for the first time was a revelation; they showcased an electrifying, energized group of young players who rose to
the occasion. Todd Sharp's solos, in particular, are jaw-dropping, especially when
you consider that he was not even twenty years old. That was one hell of a band.

We were ready now. Within days we were back on the road in America,
assuming our usual mind-blurring run of clubs, college gyms, and opening-
bill slots, this time touring with folk rocker Shawn Phillips, among others. We
were working harder than ever. But something had to give. As satisfied as
we were with the Silver album, we still needed a hit single, or the record industry would surely begin to reevaluate our place in the food chain.

With the giant backdrop behind the stage featuring a reproduction of our
now-infamous album cover, we crisscrossed the country, playing for a growing
number of fans but still missing the all-important Top 40 radio airplay that
seemed to elude us.

The year 1975 ended much the way the prior year had. We played some
big hometown shows but then quietly returned to our respective Greenwich
Village apartments to hunker down for the holidays. We were both thinking
ahead and already writing songs for the next album, which we would start recording in a few months. The cycle had really settled in. Write, record, tour,
and then do it all over again.

This was a musician's life on the upswing, but if we didn't connect on a
bigger commercial level soon, I had serious doubts if this upward trend would
continue.

1976

So arrived 1976, our nation's bicentennial. For the entire year, everywhere you looked, our country would be wrapped in red, white, and blue.
Growing up near Philadelphia, I always felt close to our nation's history, and
preparing to recording a fifth album, I began to wonder: In this remarkable
year that was unfurling before me, might this be the moment to crack into
the big time. Sure, we had a good record contract, and Tommy always made
sure there was cash on hand for us—no questions, just fistfuls of green when
you needed them. But we were ready for more than just money. We were still
playing small venues and opening up for other people. A big radio hit could
change all that.

In February Daryl and I gathered with our band at the Hit Factory in
New York City, thinking we might be able to record at home like we used to.
But the sessions soon fell apart, and we were once again headed back to Los
Angeles and once again began recording with Chris Bond and all of the usual
A-list session musicians. It was clear that's what we needed then, and we
weren't quite ready to break the pattern we had established with the Silver
album.

Just a couple of days after we arrived and got settled in to a little rented house up in the Hollywood Hills, we were invited to attend the Grammy awards at the Hollywood Palladium. They were hosted by Frank Sinatra and Gene Kelly; as legendary and amazing as both of those men were, it also certainly made a statement about where popular music was at that point in time.

And then we settled in at Cherokee Studios and began the sessions with Chris, who once again was bringing a lot of great ideas to the table along with some incredible musicians, including some guys we'd already worked with last time, like Jim Gordon and Leland Sklar. We were very excited about some songs, including one I wrote called "Back Together Again," and a song Daryl had penned called "Rich Girl," not to mention a blues-infused meditation steeped deep in the roots of Philly, "Do What You Want, Be What You Are."

On February 29, while we were recording, out of the blue we got an excited call from Tommy Mottola back in New York saying that a disc jockey, Lynn Tolliver at WIMO, a small R&B AM radio station in Cleveland, had begun spinning the song "Sara Smile" as an album cut, and was getting tremendous response. Listeners had begun calling in demanding to hear the song again and again and asking who the group was. It got to the point that the RCA promotion man for the Cleveland area called RCA headquarters in New York and advised them, somewhat urgently, to release the song as a single. So they did, and all of a sudden, it seemed like we had a little something cooking on the airwaves. Tommy was pumped. He said he thought we might be finally looking at a Top 40 song. Maybe even Top 20.

I noted in my journal:

But, let's not fire the cannons yet—we've been there before—better to maintain less lofty hopes.

John "glass half empty" Oates.

Still, it tugged at the brain. Was this the spark that might set off some bigger fireworks?

Back in the studio, the sessions were solid, as usual, and soon after the record was done, it was back on the road through America, which was gearing up more and more for the Fourth of July. As we toured, the crowds just kept getting bigger and more enthusiastic, the numbers seemingly tied into the amount of airplay that "Sara Smile" was getting. As the song pushed upward, we felt it from the stage. Audiences knew all the words and sang along. That had never happened before. A year or so later we'd finally meet Lynn Tolliver, the DJ who had set "Sara" in motion, backstage at a Cleveland-area show, where we shared some heartfelt appreciation and more than a little champagne.

In May we headed back to England, where we were welcomed with very open arms; it was bedlam wherever we went. At the BBC studios we recorded a set for the popular TV program *The Old Grey Whistle Test*, and then, right after the taping, we received a call from a now wildly excited Tommy back in the States. He told us that "Sara" was number six with a bullet; it was so hot that now "She's Gone" was going to be rereleased as a single. Which, in turn, was pushing the *Abandoned Luncheonette* album toward gold.

It was crazy. Our first Top 10 hit was actually rekindling interest in our previous work. A strange domino effect was happening whereby some of our older music was being treated as new music and finding an audience that had not been there before. It was an amazing chain of events, almost like a house of cards in reverse. "Sara Smile" would soon turn gold, which also helped push sales of the Silver album. "She's Gone" became a huge radio hit, which all perfectly set up the release of our new album, *Bigger Than Both of Us*, which would sell almost four hundred thousand copies right out of the gate.

That summer of the bicentennial, as the tall ships floated in New York harbor and red, white, and blue fireworks illuminated the city skyline, Daryl and I prepared to take off on our own rocket ride. Our days as an opening act were done. We set off on tour that fall, playing larger venues, as headliners, to sellout crowds.

In September, at the second annual, Don Kirshner-produced Rock Music Awards, Harry Chapin and Sly Stone opened the envelope for Best New Group and guess who won? Amazing. We had five albums to our credit in as many years, and we're winning an award for Best New Group? Did anything in the music business really make any sense?

As nice as the commercial acceptance was, there's always something particularly satisfying about acknowledgments from artists you respect. In October, right after we played to sold-out crowds at the Santa Monica Civic Auditorium, we went to the Forum in Los Angeles as guests of the Eagles, who were then also experiencing their first real megasuccess on the heels of their seminal *Hotel California* album. We remembered seeing those guys back at the Troubadour club a few years earlier, when we were all just coming up, when the California sound, as it would soon be called, was in its nascent phase. And so it was great to see all of those same people—Linda Ronstadt, J.D. Souther among them—backstage at the gig, helping their pals in the Eagles celebrate along with Joni Mitchell, Boz Scaggs, and others. Of course, these artists were also finding their own major successes at the time, so it was a moment for everyone to celebrate. Later that night during the show, Glenn Frey stepped up to the mic before they played one of the songs off their new album and said, "We want to dedicate this to the new kids in town, Daryl Hall and John Oates."

Tommy Mottola's Christmas celebration became even more extravagant in 1976. After we enjoyed platters of bright-red and spicy lobster fra diablo at his home in Scarsdale, out came the gifts, which included brand-new 35 mm Leica cameras, a fancy leather-bound tool kit, antique Kentucky rifles, Italian jewelry, Godiva chocolates, and a stunning gold bracelet for my girlfriend. Tommy really enjoyed playing the part of Santa Claus.

In 1977 we were back on the road, now playing arenas, stadiums, and coliseums. The new album was getting strong reviews, and one night in February, after we played a gig in Sheffield, just outside of London, Tommy called us from Paris to let us know that "Rich Girl" was becoming a huge hit back home. Within a month it would become our first number one song. The Best New Group was on fire.

Right after that we had our first cover story in *Rolling Stone* magazine, which included this:

> Hall and Oates were virtually musical nobodies until last year. After tireless roadwork as everyone's warm-up act, and after experimenting with at least three different sounds, they earned a small following in a scattering of cities, mainly because of their Top 40 single, "She's Gone," and the little gem of an album it came from, *Abandoned Luncheonette*.
>
> Then in 1975 they tried a fourth sound, switched labels, and everything fell into place. By last fall they were headlining a coast-to-coast sellout tour. During the run of it, three of their 45s and three albums went gold. Last week their single, "Rich Girl," from their soon to-be-platinum last album, *Bigger Than Both of Us*, went Number One.

We had taken that big step, and we took advantage of all the perks. The best parties, prettiest women, and whatever we felt like buying. All we had to do was ask Tommy for the money, and he would say "how much do you need?" We didn't ask to see anything: no records, no ledgers, no balance sheets. Just cash on demand. We were not paying attention to anything other than what we wanted at that moment. It seemed just perfect. Should we have been asking more questions . . . ?

In Florida we played for the biggest crowd of our lives, on a bill with Jimmy Buffet and the Eagles at the Tangerine Bowl. At the Palladium in New York City, during our show closer (a doctor routine we played out with a giant hypodermic needle for the song "Bad Habits and Infections"), Sylvester Stallone, fresh from the success of *Rocky* (and brother of my former Valentine bandmate Frank Stallone), came onstage and dragged us off the stage, to the crowd's delight.

MY WHOLE FAMILY came to our show at the Garden State Art Center in New Jersey. I wrote in my journal:

Sylvester Stallone drags us off stage in December 1977 at the end of a sold out Palladium gig in New York City. *(Courtesy John Oates)*

My grandma had cotton in her ears and my fanatical aunt Mary in the front row was rushing the stage along with a few hundred 14-year-old girls.

I'm sure that in her eyes that night, the little boy who always got the first meatball and sang in the basement for the family had "made it."

Helen Hobbs Jordan

The petite, neatly dressed woman in her early seventies perched impe-
riously on the piano bench with her back to the keyboard. The midday
Manhattan sunlight filtered softly through the translucent shades behind her,
and the muted cacophony of the city rose and fell from far below, on Fifty-
seventh Street.

She was known as the "professor to the professionals" and her name was
Helen Hobbs Jordan. Legend had it that she had played piano as a teenager
on the Transcontinental Railroad. Among her illustrious students were
Bette Midler, Paul Simon, Melissa Manchester, and most of the highest-paid
studio musicians and vocalists in New York. I'll never forget the first words she
said to me: "If you want to get a *B,* go to college. If you want to get *A*s, study
with me." Without missing a beat she continued, telling me about all the
famous people that she had rejected or, more accurately, ejected from her
classes over the years. She was a born teacher and it was a one-way conversation. I sat before her quietly, mentally questioning whether I was ready to go
down this road. Her lecture concluded with a well-rehearsed, concise description of the curriculum and what was expected of her students. When it

was my turn to speak, I told her I was a touring musician and asked if I could study when I was in New York and whether she would consider allowing me to pop in and out of her classes based on my schedule. She didn't like the idea, but I quickly added that I could carve out approximately six months of classes. She told me she'd give me a chance, and qualified that with the caveat that if my work wasn't perfect, she'd toss me out just like she did with the other rejects.

> *Journal entry:* My initial meeting with Helen Hobbs Jordan . . . my
> ignorance comes to the surface very quickly and the road to music education
> looks long, but I'm taking the first step toward something I should've done a
> long time ago. My music lessons begin. I'm nervous but do okay, with only
> enough time to cover half of what she wanted. I still have over two hours of
> homework. I am learning.

She continued by going over the class procedure, which on a weekly basis included a piano lesson, a voice lesson, a classroom session for my beginner level as well as a mandatory audit of a more advanced class, and finally, a private session with her to review everything. This was where the *A* part came in; she expected no mistakes and nothing less than perfection would be tolerated.

Why, you might be wondering, was I doing all this? Here I was, a major-label recording artist signed to a big contract—but personally, I knew there was something important missing. I felt like I needed to advance my rudimentary knowledge of music theory, because even though I could read music, I was a tyro. I was getting by on a good set of ears and a decent feel, but I knew there was so much more that I would need if I wanted to evolve as a musician. Following the completion of the *War Babies* album, the music we were making was becoming more progressive, and the players who were in the studio and on tour with us had extensive jazz chops. New songs with odd time signatures and more complex and challenging instrumental figures were pushing me to my limit as a player. It was time to go to another level.

Mrs. Jordan had written a series of textbooks, and I departed her studio that first day weighed down with assignments and anxious to get started.

Before I left she broke down her philosophy in simple terms: Every aspect of music theory would be covered, starting with basic scales, and everything would be taught and repeated four ways. The student was expected to write, sing, and play everything using traditional notation on music staff paper, repeat it with numbers one through eight (corresponding to the notes of the scale), and then repeat it again substituting "Do-Re-Me" for the letters of the notes. Each student had to write out every assignment as well as sing and play the repetitive procedure. It was very time-consuming and tedious, but the repetition solidified the lessons, and for me, the chance to see the mathematics of harmony appear on a keyboard and paper was worth the hours and hours of studying. So for the next six months I was a student again; I worked on my solfeggio (sight singing), began to play piano, and left my apartment only to attend classes. When I had some free time, I wrote a few songs.

I really worked hard and I did get As. . . . I also made sure I got on her good side early by hand delivering stacks of classical LPs by her favorite conductors, which I requisitioned from the folks at RCA. The ensuing six months were a crash course in my musical education, and to this day, the knowledge I gained in such a short period of time has been invaluable to me in every aspect of my career. Thank you, Helen, for being a stern taskmaster and a demanding teacher.

As she told me: "Rhythm is the physical, harmony is the cerebral, melody is the emotional part of music." Beautifully put.

Racing. Life Accelerated.

By the mid-to-late '70s, the novelty of smoking pot and getting high was behind me, and with a clearer mind and a bit more money, bolstered by the success of a few hits, my thoughts began to wander back to cars and racing. I fell in lust with a little Alfa Romeo Spider convertible that I saw at the New York auto show and impulsively bought one.

Black with tan top and interior, it was a lithe and lovely driving Italian sports car, but it wasn't built to survive the rough, potholed streets of New York. Then during the recording of *Beauty on a Back Street* in 1977, I was cruising by Porsche of Beverly Hills on Wilshire Boulevard in Los Angeles when my attention was drawn to an arrest-me-red 1977 Porsche 930 Turbo Carrera and I pulled into the dealership. I stepped into the showroom and gave the machine a thorough walk-around. It sat low and wide, with a whale-tail spoiler on the back large enough to double as a picnic table. Oh man oh man oh man, I wanted that car so badly. The price was $34,000 . . . more than double the cost of my parents' house. I began feeling the pangs of middle-class guilt, and I hadn't even bought it. Later that same afternoon, I casually mentioned the red Porsche to Tommy Mottola, and he didn't hesitate—we headed down to

Posing in L.A. with my new prized Porsche in 1977, the one Tommy Mottola managed to beat out Rod Stewart for. *(Courtesy John Oates)*

the dealership. In the lot was an older, beautiful, black 356 model that caught Tommy's attention, and with a let's-make-a-deal look in his eyes, we went inside and found a salesman. I pointed out the red Turbo and he responded, "Oh, Rod Stewart has a deposit on that one." I was crestfallen. Mottola put his arm around the guy's shoulders and walked into one of the sales cubicles. I have no idea what he said or did, but a few minutes later we were signing papers for two Porsches. I got the red one, he got the black one. Sorry, Rod.

A NOTE IN my journal:

> *I fought my middle-class trauma over the big bucks and it was a mental*
> *ordeal, but it is one of my few dreams and loves and I've worked hard enough*
> *to enjoy it. May 7, 1977.*

The red turbo was very flashy, with gold BBS wheels, and I had it modified for even more power with a variable boost control from legendary southern

California Porsche tuner, Andial. The car was tricky to drive and just about the fastest street-legal car available at the time. After the recording was finished I had it shipped back to New York, where it spent most of its time carving up the Long Island Expressway, back and forth from the city to beach parties in the Hamptons.

Sure, I had fun at the parties, but I had a lot more fun ripping around the winding country roads at way-more-than-sensible speeds. During one Sunday drive I happened upon a sign that read: WESTHAMPTON GO-KART RACES. Tucked away, adjacent to an old drag strip, was a tight, twisty track filled with buzzing little racing go-karts. There were little kids and adults working out of the back of pickup trucks and trailers, all in a low-key family atmosphere. Intrigued, I walked around and started asking questions about how to get involved. The bottom line was: get a kart, show up, and go racing. For those of you not familiar with motor racing, go-karts have been the traditional training ground for almost every world-class professional driver around the globe.

Later that year when Christmastime rolled around, I walked into my apartment and there, sitting in the living room, was a brand new Yamaha kart with a big red bow around it. Holy shit. . . . Mottola again, feeding my habit. The adrenaline junkie in me couldn't wait for summer to roll around. I joined the Long Island Karting Association and became a regular at the Westhampton track, learned a lot about what it takes to be competitive, eventually won a few races, and even made a trip to Florida to compete at the national championship. In 1980, after two seasons in the karts, I was ready to move up. How all of this affected my music I'm not sure, but I never did anything halfway. Just like with my music, I was fully immersing myself in racing and exploring all of its possibilities.

THAT SAME YEAR, during another tour of the UK, I had met a Londoner named Richard Lloyd. He was an avid music fan and raced in the British Saloon (Sedan) Car Championship. We quickly became friends based on our mutual interests, and with his help I signed up for a racing school following the tour. After a half-day skid-pad session at Crystal Palace, I found myself in a helmet and Nomex (fireproof) suit at the Brands Hatch circuit. I sat through a brief classroom session before being introduced to the lightweight open-wheeled Formula Fords, another of the traditional first steps up the racing ladder. Learning the racing line while strapped into the little purpose-built single-seat race car was the thrill of a lifetime. After two days of training I graduated with a provisional racing license and finished off the weekend with Richard driving me around to show me how it was really done. I had a lot to learn, but I was bound and determined to pay my dues and see where it would lead.

Where it led was to another racing school back home where I could continue to learn, and to earn an SCCA competition license. I enrolled at the Bertil Roos Racing School at Pocono Raceway, just north of where I grew up. Bertil was a stern, tight-lipped Swedish former-professional driver who ran a no-frills operation. Many successful drivers, including Michael and John Andretti, had been students there, and it was exciting to get back in the car on US soil.

Me with British race car driver (and mentor) Richard Lloyd. (*Courtesy John Oates*)

Bertil had invented a contraption he called "The Slide Car" that had a cockpit-adjustable wheeled undercarriage that when extended downward would lift the car's tires slightly off the ground and make it feel like it was driving on glare ice. He used it to demonstrate skid control on a dry surface, and it really worked. I'll never forget doing laps with him in the passenger seat while he repeated, "Where are you looking? Keep your eyes moving, look ahead . . . where are your eyes?" Those simple admonishments were perhaps the best advice that a driver could get. Staying mentally and visually ahead of a speeding race car is a technique I've never forgotten to this day, no matter where or what I'm driving.

Motor racing embraces a universal truth: When the green flag drops, the bullshit stops. It's an unwavering, clear-cut reality that appealed to my practical sense and competitive spirit. You can talk a good game, but in the final analysis, you're either quick or you're not. From the moment you climb into the race car your times are posted, and you know where you stand relative to your fellow students and, eventually, your competition. It's black and white, straightforward, no discussion. I don't know whether it was luck, raw talent, or the fact that the other guys were slow, but I always seemed to find my name at the upper end of the timing charts. Usually among the first three quickest at both the British and American race schools. So with that data as early reinforcement, I pushed forward. The time sheets confirmed what I hoped was true: I seemed to have an innate talent for driving a race car. Now it was just a matter of finding a car to drive and going racing.

I consulted Bertil Roos about renting a Formula Ford for my first race. He arranged for me to drive an older red Lola 440, and I entered it at Lime Rock Park in Connecticut for an SCCA regional race in July of 1981. I managed to finish in the top five and didn't do anything too stupid. . . . So far so good. The sanctioning organization required rookies to complete two regional races before they would issue a full amateur completion license. The next race was in August back at Pocono, where I had gone to school. This time Bertil let me drive his personal Scandia Formula Ford, which he had hand built. It was painted blue and yellow (the Swedish national colors) and had been driven the previous season by soon-to-be-world-famous Michael Andretti (Mario's son). This car handled better and was much faster than the older school cars. Having done a lot of laps at Pocono I felt a bit more confident and again finished well, earning my regional license.

The racing fraternity is a close one, and shortly after those races I met a fellow by the name of Mike Gue who ran a small Connecticut team called Essex Racing. I arranged to rent a Van Diemen Formula Ford for the rest of the summer, and the following season, in June of 1982, I won a national race at Bridgehampton, where I had been so smitten by the sport in my early teens. (Footnote: the only reason I won was that local Connecticut hot shoe and soon-to-be-internationally famous driver and good friend Drake Olson's car had mechanical problems and couldn't start.)

The relationship with Essex Racing led to the next step up the ladder: Sports 2000. A new professional series had been introduced for lightweight, sleek, fiberglass-bodied racing cars, and we made a deal with an English company called Tiga to be their official team in the United States. There were races all over the East Coast and Midwest, and, depending upon my touring schedule, I wanted to enter as many as possible. For the next two summers I would carve out as many weekends as possible and fly to various tracks, like Mid-Ohio and Elkhart Lake, Wisconsin, sometimes leaving the studio early on Fridays during recording sessions and showing up at the track at the last minute, just in time for practice and qualifying. Not the ideal situation, when many of the other drivers were relaxed and had been testing and practicing multiple times between races. The experience level of the drivers and quality of the machinery in this pro series was a distinct step up from the regional races I had been running. I ran well, for the most part, but was beginning to realize the limitations of my time commitment, since I was still recording and touring as well. I knew I could compete, but not without compromising my music career.

Road Trip

t **was springtime,** which meant, of course, it was time to repeat the now-regular pattern of heading to Los Angeles to record. One slight change in the proceedings was that for the first time in several years, we would be working with a new producer. We had moved on from our old bandmate, Chris Bond, and had found a sharp up-and-comer named David Foster.

Our previous album, *Beauty on a Back Street*, had not produced any hits, which was one more reminder of just how fleeting radio success could be. Still, we had done a massive tour that was well received, and we were excited and anxious to get back into the studio to work on what would become an album called *Along the Red Ledge*. (The title was extracted from one of my favorite novels *The Journal of Albion Moonlight*, by Kenneth Patchen).

At the end of our last tour, I had gone to Munich, Germany, for a little while to be with a girl I was dating and do some skiing. When I got home to New York City, as I started gathering my stuff together to head to California, I had an idea: Why not make it a high-speed therapeutic road trip, a clear-my-head cross-country adventure, and I had the perfect car to do it in. I had stored the red Porsche Turbo Carrera down in Jacksonville, Florida over the winter and

I enlisted one of our roadies, Glen Davis, to be my co-driver. In early March of 1978 we flew down south to pick up the car. Then, with little more than a map in hand and not much more of a plan, I settled in behind the wheel for a blitz across the country on Interstate 10.

For the next few days, I clicked on the Fuzzbuster, pointed the car west, and punched it.

Right out of the gate, the smell of skunks and diesel fuel followed us through the night, across "Flora-Bama," then on through Mississippi. As we blasted through the black of midnight, long, hypnotic stretches of highway allowed my mind to wander while my copilot caught some Zs. What a couple of years it had been. It's amazing what a series of hit records will do not just for the ego, but for the bank account, too. Well, I just assumed the bank accounts were all healthy. Not that I had ever really checked. Mottola always seemed to magically come up with the money as needed, and I was driving a Porsche Turbo . . . what was there to worry about?

We crashed the first night at a fleabag motel outside of Shreveport, Louisiana, and after just a few hours' sleep were back on the road. If I hit the brakes, it was only for a NASCAR-esque pit stop for cheap gas and greasy truck-stop grits and eggs. Near the Texas border we riffled through our pile of cassette tapes, but I couldn't find one of Janis Joplin's as we passed by her hometown of Port Arthur.

Hitting a barbecue shack for lunch one day, I grabbed my journal and started jotting down a jagged bastardized haiku impression from the trip:

> *Motor mantra*
> *Highway Zen*
> *Hypnotic home*
> *Rhythmic click*
> *Gauges flicking*
> *Low beams dip*
> *Miles of concrete slip away underneath*
> *Years of sky moving overhead*

I love how the mind opens up when you're driving down a long stretch of road. I drove nearly seven hundred miles that second day, and Texas felt like forever. Small towns slid past the window in a scrapbook blur of Middle-Americana visions. People lining up outside a small theater for the Saturday-night picture show. High-school pep rallies. Not to mention wary local lawmen, nursing their coffee on the corner and eyeing my low-slung red car as suspiciously as they would an alien invader.

Leaving the interstate we plotted a side trip through New Mexico and peeled off onto a rough, two-lane road that snaked through remote, dusty, Native American reservations. Every now and then we'd catch a fleeting glimpse of a surprised face peeking out from the scattered, ramshackle buildings, their existences sadly pushed by Manifest Destiny into this desolate corner of what was once all their own. Muddy kids, muddy dogs, and muddy cars all in dull red monochrome as if baked into the landscape. And then we wound through the hills on Route 53 until we hit the Arizona border. This was where the road really opened up. As I wrote in my journal:

140 miles an hour through Indian country! Down the empty road I coaxed the revs up in fourth gear and shut down only to crest a rise blindly. From there on it was 100/110 for 40 or 50 miles.

We stopped at the Petrified Forest and Painted Desert in Arizona, where we hit a couple of touristy gift shops for a small slab of marbleized petrified wood, and took cover as a massive, early spring monsoon soaked the ground. The word *petrichor* means the smell of rain when it hits hot, dry earth. It's a sweet and natural perfume that hung thick and heavy that day in the desert.

Although it was a bit out of the way, the Grand Canyon was on my must-see list. It was humbling to stand at the edge of the enormous wonder of the North Rim. Undulating shades of brick-red stratifications formed a backdrop as snow and rain clouds moved surreally at time-lapse speeds. I would have loved to camp and hike for a few days . . . but LA was waiting.

Back on I-40 west, we hit Flagstaff and weathered our way through ice storms, snowstorms, rainstorms, and even a bit of bright yellow sunshine. I re-member aquaplaning, with a quickened heartbeat, at ninety miles an hour coming down out of the mountains.

As we crossed the California border, as if on cue, a perfect rainbow arced over the highway . . . welcome to the Golden State. I felt energized and puri-fied after that weeklong journey in the Porsche. The cross-country trip was a rite of passage and a chance to do something that I loved arguably as much as music: Driving.

All Things Must Pass

E ven though motor racing as a sport is global in scope, the community is very much a small family. Back in the 1970s, after I'd spent time in England, my circle of friends in that world began to expand exponentially. Through my friend and mentor Richard Lloyd, I was introduced to Rupert Keegan, considered the bad boy of Formula One, who at the time was driving for ex-world-champion John Surtees's team and sponsored by Durex (condoms) and Rizla (rolling papers). This was an entree into a crazy international jet-set society, and an invitation to a world of outrageous, nonstop, high-octane parties hosted by Rupert and his fun-loving brothers, Jeremy and Rory. Attending the Formula One races around the world eventually resulted in my meeting and becoming friends with the legendary three-time world champion Sir Jackie Stewart, the "Flying Scot," who was, and still is, a fixture on the Formula One scene. His record-setting racing career followed by his innovative and controversial push for safety initiatives have made him revered and respected around the world.

And through Sir Jackie my circle of friends expanded to include former Beatle George Harrison. George, like me, was a racing fan, and he wrote a song called "Faster," inspired by Stewart. While both spending time in LA we met

I took this picture of my friend and fellow racing buff George Harrison in 1978 when we were hanging out at the Long Beach Grand Prix in California. *(Courtesy John Oates)*

at the Long Beach Grand Prix and hung out all weekend in the pits, watching the race with Jackie, his lovely wife Helen, and their two sons, Paul and Mark. We roamed around the track with the equivalent of an all-access backstage pass, and at one point I took a snapshot of George that later appeared in his book, *I, Me, Mine.*

SHORTLY AFTER THE Grand Prix, George called and invited me over to his house for a private screening of the new movie *The Rutles,* from Monty Python cast members Eric Idle and Neil Innes, which brilliantly spoofed the Beatles by creating a "Pre-Fab Four" band sensation called the Rutles. George was very good friends with Eric Idle and the rest of the comedy troupe, and when the film production ran short on money, he actually took out a loan against his home to finance and complete the movie. He even took a small role in the film. I asked Daryl if he wanted to come along, and we headed over to

George's house, just outside of Bel Air. His place was hidden deep within a eucalyptus forest, its low roofline blending appropriately with the environment. Much like the man himself, the house was unique, with an understated oriental feel in total opposition to the ostentatious megamansions erupting like wealthy blisters in the surrounding neighborhood. Highly polished dark wood and stained glass dominated the welcoming and warm interior. The impression was one of an ancient Kyoto teahouse designed by a Southern California '60s architect with refined taste and an unlimited budget. The living room was dominated by a large picture window showcasing a panoramic view of a tree-lined lake or reservoir, which reinforced the feel of monastic opulence. We spent a casual evening laughing and thoroughly enjoying the Rutles movie, and it was obvious that George was proud of his producer's role and got a real kick out of pointing out the subtle and not-so-subtle Beatles references. He asked us about the new album, *Along the Red Ledge*, that we were recording, and we invited him to come down to the studio if he felt like it. "I just want to play in the band," was his response. Which he did. No fuss, no fanfare, just a player in the band.

After the LA sessions George and I stayed in touch, mostly due to our mutual love for motor racing. The following Christmas I received a large box from him, and to my great surprise, inside was a wheel and tire from the distinctive and rare six-wheel Tyrrell Formula One racing car. The following spring, when we were on a UK tour, he invited me to visit Friar Park, his home just outside London. I celebrated the occasion by renting a quintessentially British Morgan sports car, heading out to Henley-on-Thames. Passing through the imposing rococo front gates of his property, we cruised up the winding lane to the entrance of his 120-room Victorian neo-Gothic mansion. It was a mind-blowing masterpiece of eclectic and quirky architecture with religious and occult overtones, the exterior and interior festooned with gargoyles and symbolic filigree. I recall noticing that the light panels were molded in brass to look like the faces of monks whose noses functioned as on-and-off switches!

George's wife, Olivia, joined us for tea while their young son, Dhani, played nearby in the cozy, spacious kitchen. It was a relaxed and casual atmosphere without pretense or a lot of staff hovering about. George suggested that we take a walk through his garden, and I quickly realized this was his pride and joy. Certainly the house itself was unique, but the gardens were an experience unto themselves.

This was an English garden on acid . . . meticulously tended and very extravagant in design. The casual stroll led us to a scaled-down version of the iconic Matterhorn Mountain. It was at least twenty feet in height and surrounded by what seemed to be altitude-correct alpine plants, creating the illusion that one was viewing the snow-covered peak from a distant valley. I'm positive that I was trying to keep my jaw from hitting my chest and maintain my cool, but as we continued along the winding pathways there was no hiding my astonishment over a water feature that flowed into the mouth of a stone cavern. It was immediately recognizable as the entrance to yet another incredibly realistic recreation: the world-renown landmark on Italy's Amalfi coast, the Grotta Azura (Blue Grotto). One could hop aboard a small skiff and float into the grotto on a simulated, albeit miniaturized, holiday excursion.

After we left the gardens, the next stop on our tour was his recording studio. There's no point in describing it. It was, of course, state of the art for the time, but it was the walk from the main house to the studio that sticks with me to this day. The route to the studio was through a very long corridor that was dazzlingly covered with gold and platinum albums . . . the walls and the ceiling . . . like so much billion-dollar wallpaper. Again, typical George—low key but totally aware. Interestingly, we never talked or played any music that day. I was conscious of not pushing that subject. I felt that we had a connection on a level that was more about friendship and that he may have appreciated that, so I left it there. It was a relaxing and pleasant afternoon, and one that I'll never forget.

I've met a lot of wealthy and illustrious rock stars but this was Beatle-level stuff, and what made the experience all the more impressive was George's modest and relaxed attitude. He exuded an inner calm and spirit that resonated in his music and his life. On the drive back to London I had the strong sense of have been unwittingly given a gift: The belief that someday I might discover my own personal path to true personal satisfaction and inner peace beyond the trappings of worldly success.

The Third Season

POSSESSIONS, OBSESSIONS

1980s

I Hear the Voices

"Daryl, John—why am I here?"

That's what producer David Foster asked us one night when we were sitting together at the Hit Factory recording studio in New York during the first few *X-Static* album recording sessions in early 1979. "I don't get why I'm here. You guys are making this album yourselves. You don't need me."

David's illustrious producing career was about to soar into the stratosphere (he'd eventually rack up sixteen Grammy Awards from forty-seven nominations) and quite frankly, I don't think he wanted to be sitting around in a New York studio—and we were done with recording in LA.

It was our second album with him, after with 1978's *Along the Red Ledge*. From the moment we met David, Daryl and I both realized he was an immense talent. A Canadian that started out as keyboard player for the band Skylark (that had the Top 10 hit "Wildflower" in 1973), he stayed in LA after his stint in that band and played on a lot of records, including George Harrison's *33 & ⅓*. Right after we'd started working together in the spring of '78, he brought Daryl and me to his house in LA and said, "Hey guys, wanna hear a song I just wrote with Jay Graydon and Bill Champlin? I think it's perfect for you guys." Taking a seat behind the piano, he settled into a cool chord progression. The words he sang were melancholy and bittersweet: "Something happened along the way, what used to be happy was sad . . ." At that point, we weren't that interested in songs from outside writers, so we politely passed. The song, "After the Love Has Gone," would become a smash hit for Earth, Wind & Fire a year later. Again, great song, but at that point our heads were in a much more edgy musical place. We'd been absorbing a lot of the new-wave stuff back home on the streets of New York. We had our own vibe and concept for the next album. It was more important to stay true to our own sensibilities than be driven by commerciality, so we stayed the course.

After seeing a classical-music performance in Paris the year before, I was struck by the concentration required for the high level of technique displayed by the orchestra; in a way, it reminded me of the stone-faced determination that I saw on many traditional, black-suited bluegrass musicians performing their rapid-fire, scalding, single-note runs. It inspired me to start writing a song called "Serious Music," which featured a minisymphonic homage to George Gershwin's *Rhapsody in Blue.* I enlisted the help of a blind pianist named George Bitzer, who was playing in August Darnell's band, Kid Creole and the Coconuts. I wrote the lyrics, "Manuscripted memories, Sound with no electricity, Concentration lines on the face of serious music," which seemed to sum it up. Foster's great song and soon-to-be hit just would not have worked with the other songs we were writing. We never tried to create hits. We just did what inspired us and focused on making a great album.

ALONG THE RED LEDGE was also different because it was the first time we recorded with our road band as opposed to session players. Our road band then included former members of Elton John's band who had recently become available, including guitar player Caleb Quaye, drummer Roger Pope, and bass player Kenny Passarelli. We hired them to join David Kent on keyboards and Charlie DeChant on sax. We also brought in guest guitar heroes Rick Nielsen, George Harrison, and Robert Fripp, with whom Daryl had recently recorded a

The *Voices* era. *(Courtesy John Oates)*

solo record. Todd Rundgren dropped by the sessions as well to play some beautiful parts on "Have I Been Away Too Long." The next night we joined him onstage at the Roxy to take part in a recording session for his upcoming live album, *Back to the Bars*. The show featured a lot of special guests, including Spencer Davis and Stevie Nicks, and was broadcast nationwide in real time, one of the first events of its kind like that. Daryl and I sang backup on Todd's hit "Hello It's Me" before playing "She's Gone" during the encores.

We loved *Red Ledge*, but it didn't produce any real hits, so of course the record company didn't share our enthusiasm with the effort. And in the middle of recording that album, we decided to pack it in and head back to New York to finish at the Hit Factory. Both Daryl and I had sort of had it with the LA recording scene, and this change would play a big part in the rest of our career.

Which brings us to the *X-Static* sessions. New York City in the late '70s was pulsating not just with punk and new wave, but with the four-on-the-floor hypnotic club groove of disco. On the *X-Static* album, we tried to incorporate those type of grooves with the vibe of what was happening on the streets, which involved boom boxes and early forms of hip-hop and rap. Everywhere on every downtown block kids were break dancing on sheets of cardboard, their portable radios blasting distorted heavy beats . . . we took it all in. The idea was to fuse a lot of those new sounds together and create our own hybrid. Now, again, it wasn't successful commercially. But we took a shot. People today who have this perception of us as nothing more than a couple of slick hit makers will often go back to these records and then tell us, "Hey, you guys took a lot of chances." That was us. We created the music we heard in our heads at that moment.

Anyway, as I said earlier, it was during those *X-Static* sessions that Foster came to a realization and said, "You don't need me." And that's when the light bulb went off. That's when Daryl and I looked at each other and said, "Let's take responsibility for the whole thing. Let's just start producing ourselves."

Careerwise we were at a pretty serious fork in the road. Our last couple of albums had not produced a big hit, and the explosive success that had started with "She's Gone," "Sara Smile," and "Rich Girl" seemed to have plateaued. In a desperate move, our record company (trying to cash in on the demand for live albums in the wake of monster successes by Peter Frampton and KISS) pushed us to release one, called *Livetime*. But it bombed. We'd been around long enough to know by then that you can't simply order up success. By 1979 we were no longer playing arenas and stadiums; we were relegated back to clubs. Nassau Coliseum in Uniondale Long Island a year or two before, but now it was the four-hundred-seat My Father's Place in Roslyn. On some nights we were even back to playing two sets, just like the old days. Never saw that coming! As quickly as big success had wafted in like some cloud of precious, sparkling, magic dust, it had dissipated. There was always outside pressure but never panic, somehow we both were able to look at moments like this as just another opportunity for reinvention.

My personal life had changed, too. Around this time I met a blonde Midwestern beauty after a show near her home in Minnesota. Her name was Nancy, she was a model, and within a few years we would be married. But during this period, she moved to New York and we shared my apartment. But life wasn't all touring, business, and relationships. There were a lot of new things going on in music at the end of the 1970s. Living in Greenwich Village, I was hitting the clubs every night, listening to David Johansen, Blondie, and Patti Smith, and even sitting in to play with a punky gal named Judy Nylon at downtown hole-in-the-wall music venues. Everywhere you turned, dozens of bands were also helping to carve out a new wave. I loved walking the broken sidewalks and cobblestone streets, blending into the flow of life in the Village, connected enough to have all access to the back door of Studio 54 and Max's Kansas City, yet not so famous that I couldn't move about and still be inconspicuous. It was a very creatively stimulating time, and the city provided a deep well of inspiration on many levels. Gathering ideas and writing separately, as Daryl and I usually did in the early stages of preparing to record, it would be just a matter of getting in to the studio and letting the songs dictate the direction the album would take.

It all just flowed naturally. There were no big discussions with the record company or huge press announcements. Mottola was really good at keeping the record company off our backs so when the time came, we just rolled with the unspoken understanding that we were ready to make this record. By this time Daryl and I had made so many decisions together that there was no need for long, involved conversations.

As much as casual fans would later identify us as an '80s band, based on the ubiquity of our big Top 40 hits and the pervasive repetition of MTV videos, we had both been working in recording studios since 1967, and had observed and worked side by side with many talented producers. Looking back, Arif Mardin, in particular, set the standard. His style was to surround us with a highly skilled and talented team and preside over a casual, but efficient, studio environment, where the only rules were based on musicality and appropriateness for the song. If there was a formula, it was simple: No need to preconceive . . . just write good songs, let the musicians make the music, and have skilled technical people capture it.

We began recording at the Hit Factory in midtown Manhattan with Neil Kernon, a young engineer from London. We recorded a few tracks with our touring band without a lot of overdubs or extra parts, and as a result, the album began to take shape in a lean, minimalistic style. Consciously and unconsciously the zeitgeist of the city began to emerge and be reflected in the recordings.

One afternoon, as Daryl and I wrote together in his apartment, I noticed a copy of the *New York Post* on the coffee table. On the front page was a typical blaring tabloid headline, this one about a guy who was running around the New York subways chopping people up with a machete. What could possibly be going on in someone's head that would make them want to do something like that? And then Daryl and I started riffing on a wacky idea: What if there was one of those old '50s doo-wop songs stuck in his head, relentlessly repeating over and over, driving his deranged mind to an unthinkably dark place? Conversations like this can often serve as a songwriter's device to warp reality enough to get a jump-start on a song idea.

Then we started to draw references from other famous killers to flesh out the song lyrics. "Charlie liked the Beatles, Sam he liked 'Rich Girl.'" Those lyrics referred to Charles Manson and the fact that David Berkowitz, aka Son of Sam, once said in an interview that he was a fan of the song "Rich Girl." And then of course we had our "diddy doo wop" lyrics, so we could musically justify putting some actual acapella-style street-corner singing into the song— the fictitious song that we imagined was driving the subway killer crazy.

There was no way that writing a straight-down-the-pike doo-wop song would have worked in 1980 because we would've done it so authentically it would've sounded like a relic. But by integrating our love of doo-wop, by tapping into our roots, we were able to use it as a pathway to the whacked-out theme of the song, "Diddy Doo Wop (I Hear the Voices)." Those were the voices he heard inside his head. And from that lyric, *Voices* became the title of the album.

. . .

AROUND THIS TIME, Sara Allen's younger sister Janna was living in New York and was a budding guitarist and songwriter. She and Daryl wrote a song together, and he wanted to make a quick piano-and-vocal demo recording for her. One night after we finished recording, he sat down at the piano with the Roland CR-78 CompuRhythm, a crude little brown box that we used mostly to find tempos while working out arrangements prior to recording with the band. Before Daryl hit the switch to trigger the simple preset beat, Neil, our engineer, suggested, "Let's record at 15 ips (inches per second) . . . why waste tape?"

Normally, we would record at 30 ips, (faster tape speed equals higher quality recording), but again, because it was just a quick demo and to save tape we used the slower speed, even though the audio quality might suffer slightly. Daryl sang and played the song in one take and that was it.

A few days later he played the song for Mottola at the Champion Entertainment office on Fifty-seventh Street, and Tommy went nuts. "This is a fucking smash!" he yelled. "You guys have to record this." Daryl had nailed the performance already, so it was just a matter of adding a bass and a guy named Jeff Southworth, who played a cool melodic solo on the song. The only thing he ever really played for us and it was brilliant. And that became the hit song "Kiss On My List." That little drum machine would make its sonic presence felt again to great effect on the next few albums. And it's so funny when you hear the record today—the 15 ips recording does give it a slight tape flutter, a perceivable audio thickness due to the slower tape speed. It's so subtle that only audiophiles might hear it, but it does have a unique quality to it. That casual little demo for Janna went on to become a number one record.

The album began to take on an edgy, stripped-down sound, right for the songs and right for the times. It was taut, angular, and modern, but still connected into the urban side of our roots.

But then something else happened that helped hone the sound of the album. We went on the road to do a few shows and came back early in 1980 to resume work on the record. While we were away, Mottola found us a better deal from Electric Lady Studios, closer to where both Daryl and I lived in the Village. Electric Lady was the studio built by Jimi Hendrix in 1970, and it became the perfect little haven for us. The air was just thick with history and vibe. Called the Village Barn nightclub from the 1930s through the 1960s, it was remodeled by Hendrix, but he only spent four weeks recording there before his death in 1970. His presence, however, was still palpable. Entry was through a nondescript doorway tucked between the trendy shoe stores on Eighth Street, the studio was a subterranean windowless lair dominated by a large psychedelic mural that ran from the lobby, around the curved wall, to the control room. Further down the hallway was a small room with a hole in the floor where a branch of Minetta Creek still flowed underground and occasionally flooded the back of the studio.

Now I could walk to work. Every aspect of New York street life, the cacophony of sounds, smells, sights, and characters all blended into the creative stew that would somehow manifest itself in the music.

Oftentimes when music gets created today it's focus grouped, scrutinized, analyzed, and pretested to figure out whether or not it's going to be a hit. It wasn't like that back then. Even though we were producing ourselves, there was nobody in the studio looking over our shoulders—in fact, there never really was. Our attitude from the beginning was that we were always going to make the record that we wanted to make. Period. And so we always insulated ourselves from record company and business guys. No one ever heard what we were doing until we were finished.

When we did finish recording, we would traditionally hold a listening party, inviting family and friends, the band, management, record company, and occasionally some influential radio folks to hear the album. That early summer night at Electric Lady when we cranked the album through the big speakers, it was a sonic lovefest. Everyone involved was proud of the record, and first-time listeners provided a good way for us to gauge the reaction from the outside world. But as strong as it sounded, Daryl and I walked out into the dusk of Eighth Street with a sense that there was something missing. We couldn't put our finger on it or even really verbalize what it was. It just needed something more.

With a few friends in tow we walked up the block to a pizza joint. As we were settling down in a booth, all of a sudden crackling out of the jukebox came the distinctive, bombast of the Phil Spector-produced Righteous Brothers classic, "You've Lost That Lovin' Feeling." It is one of the greatest rock-and-roll songs of all time, written by Barry Mann and Cynthia Weil. As we were eating our pizza, Daryl and I just looked at each other, and I think we both knew. We had only ever cut one cover song, and that was the obscure reggae number "Soldering" on the Silver album. But the song filling the air seemed like the missing piece that we needed for the *Voices* album.

The next morning, we went back in the studio with the band and quickly worked out an arrangement for the song that meshed with the style of the rest of the record: punchy and sleek. We cut the track with the band, sang it, and in a few hours, that was it.

THE MUSIC FOR *Voices* was officially done, but an album cover was needed. In the same do-it-yourself spirit, we came up with a stark black-and-white package spiced with a subtle embossed element. The front cover photo was a mirror image of the back cover. It looked like the album sounded: sharp and cool. After a few months, with the first pressing of the album selling well, RCA records became enamored with a more colorful photo that we had taken in Japan. The Japanese record company had rejected our original artwork as "too weird" and just released the album with their own cover. With the second pressing of this now-successful album, RCA in the United States followed suit and without telling us, switched from the black-and-white version to the Japanese color version. That's why you might see two different album covers for the *Voices* record. One can only control so much, try as we might. . . . I'm regrettably wearing lavender pants, pointy white boots, and a Pitts Go Kart Racing T-shirt, and Daryl looks like he's trying to escape from his sport coat.

We'd worked hard producing ourselves the first time, and although we loved the music, we had no idea what the rest of the world would think. The first single, "How Does It Feel To Be Back," reached Top 30 on the charts, and a few months later "You've Lost That Lovin' Feeling" made it to number twelve. In January 1981, that little demo of Janna's was released and went to number one. Following that, "You Make My Dreams" went to number five. With four songs in the Top 40, the album spent one hundred weeks on the *Billboard* chart. Time to strap in once more for an even wilder ride than the first wave several years earlier. We were not done yet.

The momentum and success of *Voices* ushered in the next wild chapter of our career. We had done it. We had produced ourselves and in doing so, tapped in to the core of who we were as writers, artists, and producers. We'd once again found a sound. There was no turning back, but we had no idea what lay ahead. As it turned out, this new phase was, for many fans, the beginning of Hall and Oates. That was like our debut album for them. But I knew better. I knew where we had been.

And as we prepared for the big-time ride that the 1980s were about to become, I already sort of missed the '70s. The fun, freedom, and independence were about to morph into a whirlwind blur of high stakes music and life.

T-Bone

t was early 1981 and we were in the market for a new bass player. We were holding auditions at SIR studios in midtown Manhattan, and a bunch of hopefuls queued up to try out and play a few songs with me; Daryl; our guitar player, G.E. Smith; and our new drummer, Mickey Curry.

One of the guys was Tommy Wolk, a quiet, gangly guy from Yonkers whose big credit at the time was having played bass on the breakout Kurtis Blow rap single, "The Breaks." He had a quirky mystique to him, cap pulled down over his prematurely bald head, confidently letting his Fender Precision bass do the talking. I didn't know much about him other than the fact that he was really good.

Finally it came down to him and one other guy, a hotshot dude from Long Island with killer chops and an even better haircut. When you're building a band, it's hard to ignore the fact that looks do come into play. So we had a decision to make: The ready-to-go rock star versus the balding, down-home, flannel-shirt dude who could play his ass off.

. . .

The man known as the "And" in "Hall and Oates"—the late, great Tom "T-Bone" Wolk. *(Courtesy John Oates)*

WE WERE TORN.

The day of the final audition, Wolk came in with his beat-up bass in one hand and an old weatherworn accordion case in the other.

"What's the deal with that?" I asked him. As it turned out, at around the age of twelve, he had become the New York State accordion champion, and was a squeeze box virtuoso. He had a session booked after meeting with us and that's why he had the instrument with him. We asked him to play a little bit, and our collective jaws dropped. It may not have been right for us at the time, but we could all appreciate the authentic, exotic, zydeco music that flowed from his fingers dancing across the keyboard and buttons. He also modestly mentioned in passing that he played some keyboards and guitar as well . . . downplaying everything, which, we'd soon learn, was just his style. He was brilliant at all those things. But he'd never be the one to tell you that.

So Tommy Wolk, who we like a lot, packs up his accordion case, and departs. A few minutes later, enter the other guy.

He and his coiffure saunter into the rehearsal room and we begin to go through a few of the prepared numbers. We play "Rich Girl"; check . . . he's on his game. Then "Kiss On My List." Yeah, he's got it down. Plays great, looks great. The gig began to tilt his way. After a few songs we sat around talking, to feel out his vibe; musicianship is one thing, but chemistry also matters. Before you let a guy into your house, into the family, it's important that you get along. Was he the missing piece of our future rhythm section?

A few minutes into our post-rehearsal conversation he casually turns and says, "So Daryl, when I'm in the band, I think I should sing 'Kiss on my List.'"

NEEDLE SCRATCH.

Just like in one of those old-time Westerns, when the saloon grows deadly quiet, before the shots ring out and the bodies drop to the floor, silence envelops the room. The pause is deafening.

He wanted to sing "Kiss on my List"?

Dead. Cold. Silence.

Daryl finally breaks the sonic void like only he can. Sitting right next to me, he sharply turns his head toward me. "John, let's go get the bald guy."

And that was it.

The greatest decision we ever made.

OVER THE YEARS, Tommy Wolk would tour the world with us as well as play with everyone from Elvis Costello to Billy Joel to Carly Simon, filling in the gaps in our schedule as a member of the *Saturday Night Live* house band for six years. But first and foremost, he was our musical soul mate. Not long after he joined the band, we were getting ready to go out on the *Private Eyes* tour. Literally the night we were to leave, with the band bus idling outside Studio Instrument Rentals, an MTV video-production crew came in to shoot a simple video for the title track of the album. The band stood costumed with trench coats and fedora hats in front of a black backdrop right before the cameras rolled when a shy and clearly nervous Wolk asked me, "What should I do?" Making videos was new to all of us, but he was way out of his element. "Don't do anything," I told him. "Just stand there perfectly still like a statue, and then occasionally move your head from side to side. That will be cool. That will look good." And so that's what he did.

SO BEGAN OUR magical musical partnership with Tommy Wolk, who eventually had the nickname "T-Bone" bestowed upon him after he burned a killer solo with his bass behind his head, just like the legendary blues guitar player T-Bone Walker (who originated the move long before Hendrix ever did it).

Years later, when I was about to do my first solo album in Nashville, I asked T-Bone if he would come with me. I knew that with him by my side everything would just work out fine. I assembled some of Music City's best session players for that project, and one by one they all naturally deferred to T-Bone. After word got out that we were recording, all these musicians started dropping by the studio . . . they wanted to meet him and hang out. He had that kind of effect on everyone he met.

In early 2010, Daryl and I and the band were playing a private show down in Miami in a truly dazzling location. We were set up in front of an ornate art museum, our backs to the Intracoastal Waterway. This was a very high-end, full-bore, South Florida-fabulous gig, replete with well-heeled, bejeweled socialites, extravagant decorations, and acrobats from Cirque du Soleil twirling in the air while pouring champagne into the guests' crystal flutes.

We would be playing on a special barge that had been dragged in up against the dock, a floating stage set against the turquoise-and-gold Miami skyline. But just as we hit the stage and started to play, the weather began morphing dramatically. The pastel-colored clouds had shifted hues to pewter, and ominous, hot gusts had started to blow. Massive, gunmetal-gray thunderheads were furiously gathering on the horizon. From the wings of the stage I could see concerned looks on the faces of our crew.

Before taking the stage we were warned that should lightning begin striking the sea anywhere nearby, we'd get a signal to stop the show. And with that, we kicked into our opening song, "Maneater." By the second song, "Out of Touch," the weather quickly turned ugly and the winds began raging. It was clear that we weren't going to make it through this set.

As we approached the solo near the end of the song, something odd happened. I was playing guitar, standing as usual on Daryl's left while off his right shoulder stood Tom "T-Bone" Wolk, who, after thirty years had become the musical director and, in a way, the ampersand in Hall & Oates. Prior to this moment, T-Bone would have begun playing this solo. But for some reason I happened to glance over to my right and we locked eyes. He had taken one step back, and with a crooked smile and a nod of his famous hat, he gestured to me with the neck of his guitar. With nothing more than that subtle, unspoken cue—the kind of thing that can only happen after years of playing together—he threw me the solo.

It didn't seem like anything special at the time, but then again, it didn't really matter. We had all developed such telepathy over the decades that it was just another live-band moment . . . or so I thought. We just managed to finish the song and, heeding the waving hands and panicky looks on the faces of our production crew, we rushed off the stage into a small tent that they had provided as a dressing room. The show was over. Bolts of lightning began to fork against the sea as the tropical storm began pounding the coast; it was every man for himself and we all we dispersed with a variety of quick adieus, headed in our separate directions. I jumped into a car with my wife, Aimee, and sped back to the hotel.

That was the last time I ever saw T-bone alive. Several weeks after that show I got a call at my home in Colorado that he'd died that evening, at home on the East Coast, a victim of heart failure. I couldn't process the reality of what I was hearing. How could it be? He was omnipresent in both Daryl's and my life, personally, professionally, and most of all, musically. Once the shock of his passing settled in, I began to reflect on so many aspects of his all-too-brief time on Earth. It was sobering to think about how close we all came to not having the opportunity to bask in his presence, talent, and friendship and how an accordion and a slip of the lip might have changed the course of both Daryl and my life.

To this day, all over the world, both fans and musicians come up and ask me about him. People understood that he was unique and gifted. I know for a fact that I've never played with anyone who possessed his level of musicianship and sensitivity to a song. He could draw from an encyclopedic knowledge of all styles of music from any era and made every person he played with sound better. His musical choices were always right, and to this day when I'm writing or recording, I often think to myself, *how would T-Bone have played this?*

"The bald guy." His funeral was filled with his extended musical family and, like his personality, was simple, down to earth, and deeply emotional for everyone in attendance.

We had gigs scheduled shortly after his death, and so we did the best that we could. Paul Pesco did a very good job stepping in to get us through the existing shows, but the band was playing as if T-Bone were still there. The arrangements, of which he was such an integral part, were missing something elemental. There was no other way to describe it. The hole was just so huge, and neither Daryl nor I were ready to accept his absence. The audience might never have known it. But we did.

As time went on and we started to heal, something really beautiful happened. We used his absence to put together a band that for me has evolved into one as good as any we've ever had. As of this writing, thanks to Eliott Lewis, Shane Theriot, Klyde Jones, Brian Dunne, Porter Carroll Jr., and our other longtime musical soul mate, Charlie DeChant, Daryl and I get still get inspired every night. This band does subtle things within the music that excite us and keep us hungry to push things further. As a unit, I think they do collectively what T-Bone always did individually. They motivate, feel, and react to the music in unique ways each night, never growing too comfortable or complacent. Our bands have always breathed their life into the songs that Daryl and I have written.

And to this day, I still play the solo at the end of "Out of Touch."

Just like T-Bone wanted.

Pop Artists

When a band is at the top of the charts, the glitterati and beautiful people of the moment are always close at hand. This was true for us both where we lived in New York City and all over the world. Swirling in and around our personal universe were many of the hot actors, musicians, and models of the moment. But among all these famous personalities, Andy Warhol's star seemed to have a more distinctive glow. He and his inner circle of downtown movers and shakers would always come to see our shows when we played the city. In fact, he and I were introduced through our mutual friends Trev Huxley and Alan Finkelstein. One day, Andy gave me a personal tour of his famous Factory near Union Square. Scattered around the floor and stacked up in corners were various finished pieces of his, as well as works in progress, many of which are now treasured collectables and valued in the millions. While casually hanging out he would snap candid pictures of me with his ever-present Polaroid camera. One of these snapshots of me wearing an Auburn University War Damn Eagle T-shirt is on display in the Auburn art museum . . . I didn't even know it existed until recently. Every once in a while, Warhol's agent would casually remark, "Let me know if you want something." I never took him up on it. That was only one among the many potentially lucrative opportunities that I stupidly let slip through the cracks over the years. (Oh yeah, let's add cell phones and scrunchies to that list of missed opportunities. But those are other stories for another time.)

But back to Andy. He was such an elusive shadow; you never knew where he'd pop up. I remember one winter around Christmas in the mid '80s, my wife and I were flying to Aspen when a snowstorm grounded our flight at the old Stapleton airport in Denver. While waiting around in the baggage area, we bumped into Warhol and his entourage—a group of nervous, fragile, artsy New Yorkers struggling to deal with a rugged and real Colorado blizzard. Andy was wearing one of those big furry Russian *ushanka* hats with Dumbo-like earflaps. For these die-hard New Yorkers, this trip to toney Aspen, Colorado, might as well have been to the Siberian Tundra.

"John," he kept repeating in that faint, flat, and frail voice of his. "Are we going to die . . . are we going to die?"

"No, Andy. You're not going to die. It's just a snowstorm."

This was not part of the fifteen minutes we'd all eventually be famous for.

Once everyone calmed down, Warhol commanded one of his minions to charter a private plane. Spending the night in the Denver airport was not going to be a reality in his holiday itinerary. They graciously invited me and my wife along for the ride. We all jumped on the tiny jet and for the next couple of weeks, party-hopped in big '80s-Aspen style. Of course, Andy knew everyone in town from the Kennedys to Diana Ross to you name it . . . it was just a big, dazzling, fabulous white out.

Throughout the decade it was just like this, all the time—a blur of jaded privilege all along the jet-set juggernaut. There was music, of course, but it wasn't like before. For over ten years my career had gone up and down, but the scale of the '80s was off the charts. What many people don't realize is that popularity and success, while appearing from the outside as glamorous and exciting, take their toll with time. I didn't know how to truly slow down and enjoy so many of the extraordinary people and things that seemed to be happening at warp speed. I never stopped running, but my feet never seemed to touch the ground. You think you want that bubble of fame and fortune. But once inside, it gets a little hard to breathe. And you start thinking about how to pop that bubble.

The '80s Sessions

f, in the 1970s, I felt like an actor cast in some magnificent, mysterious, cinematic extravaganza, by the early-to-mid '80s, the role had sharply shifted. I was no longer in the film. It was as though I was sitting in a dark theater watching a film, detached and observing. And it was being projected in mind-numbing fast motion to boot. Given the forces of gravity and nature that now propelled Daryl and me though a stupefying series of hit records and MTV videos, I'd begun to feel a strange disconnection. Life was moving at warp speed. A kinetic, seamless blur of nameless faces, pliant bodies, the stale air and tire highway hum of swaying tour buses, private jets, cavernous arenas, and hotels and hotels and hotels. Another effect also took hold, one akin to living a dual existence. The dichotomy could not be denied. One man operating in an alter-nate universe of my own design, where conventional codes of morality and even law itself seemed not to apply; the other man attempting to hang on to the middle-class values of my upbringing and seeking normalcy for brief moments amid the chaos wherever and with whomever I could find it, straining to se-cure a link to the reality of the world beyond the nonstop demands of pop star-dom. It was all held together by a tenuous thread. A sea of faces from the stage, followed by after-show hotel-suite debauchery but then inevitable escape to the sanctuary of the tour bus and the comforting familiarity of the jacked-up family that was our band: Tom "T-Bone" Wolk, Mickey Curry, G.E. Smith, Charlie "Mr. Casual" DeChant.

I'm often asked about the 1980s. Now you know why it's often hard to answer the questions. Trying to wrap my head around that mercurial era, at times simply doesn't seem possible.

Yet the brain still tries to map and resolve.

Those hyper-kinetic years had a well-worn pattern that defined my life. Rhythmically unrelenting . . . write, record, and tour. Repeat. Again. Nonstop, that routine only broken by the additional demands of doing press and making music videos to accompany and promote whichever anointed track, ordained by radio and record label, would become our next hit single. No time to think . . . just keep doing it.

The money was certainly rolling in, but not in a predictable way or with any time to really sit and analyze how our finances were being set up. It was still about cash on demand and big, showy checks from Tommy. We should have been more engaged, but we were too busy and too focused on the music. Thankfully Daryl and I had finally reached the point of having total confidence with this band lineup. We were on a creative roll, the band was precisely what we needed and so all the recording sessions during this period of time went very smoothly.

As much as the band's input was critical to the sound of the records, one song in particular stands out due to the unique way it happened.

It all came back to music; that was the escape. And sometimes, especially in the middle of all the mayhem, magic revealed itself.

The great Irish poet W.B. Yeats said, "The world is full of magic things, patiently waiting for our senses to grow sharper." Yeats could have been in the studio with us on this particular night.

We were about halfway through cutting tracks for the *Private Eyes* album and all the musicians had gone home for the day. Only Daryl, our engineer, Neil Kernon, and I remained. In the midst of casual conversation about plans for the next few days, Daryl slipped out from behind the recording console. Through the control-room glass, I could see him entering the recording studio. He sat down at his keyboard and, with his head bent low, began to play. After a few minutes I walked out and stood next to him. Sitting on top of the keyboard was the good old Roland CompuRhythm beat box. It was the same machine that he had used for "Kiss On My List." The little white button that was labeled ROCK 1 was depressed, and the stiff, simple drum groove was cycling its hypnotic two-bar pattern. With his left hand Daryl repeated a cool, vibey bass line that worked like magic against the machine's beat. Daryl's natural feel transformed the mechanical groove coming from the Roland. I don't know whether it was an idea that had been simmering in his mind or if he tapped into the muse of that moment, but whatever it was, it was *funky*. I stood there listening, and he looked up at me with this knowing smile, that said it all . . . I knew there was something very special happening. Then from the fingers of his right hand splashes of arpeggiated chords danced over and around the hypnotic bass-line groove. He said, "John, get your guitar." I knew he was on a roll and I quickly grabbed my old '58 Strat from the nearby guitar stand. As I approached, he sang a melodic counterpoint to what he was playing on the keys. "Try this," he said, and I picked up on the figure, translating it into a palm-muted single-note part on my guitar. At that moment he began singing a cool melody of nonsense words, vowel sounds that rolled off the tongue, and the magic of that circular groove overwhelmed the silence of the dimly lit empty studio. "I Can't Go For That (No Can Do)" was born.

It was Daryl Hall at his best, channeling the sum total of his influences beyond conscious thought and flowing with pure inspiration. I'd experienced this river before. Best to let it just carry you. A few days later we sat in his apartment with Sara and began to write lyrics that evolved as a metaphoric reaction to the personal and professional pressures that were coming at us from every angle. Back in the studio Daryl finished his lead vocal and we did the background parts in one day. The final touch was a classic, shimmering Charlie DeChant sax solo and some sparkly synth flourishes. It was an elegantly simple, perfect recording. A year later, after one of our shows in LA, I recall hanging out backstage with Michael Jackson and he told us how much he loved to dance to "I Can't Go For That" in front of his bedroom mirror. Listen to "Billie Jean." You'll understand.

"I Can't Go For That (No Can Do)" went on to hit number one on *Billboard*'s pop chart, the R&B charts, and the dance chart. Over the years it has endured to become one of the most sampled songs in pop-music history.

Those creative oases, where the muse meets its master, were the salvation of this period. Satisfying, creative ports in the storm, away from the madness.

But of course, after moments like that were realized, it was always back on the runaway rock-and-soul train of the 1980s, screaming onward with gold and platinum albums and number one records in its wake. It was hard not to miss the looseness and freedom of the 1970s. Busy as we were then, it still felt like we had some control over our lives. By now, it felt like every second of every day was accounted for.

VOICES, PRIVATE EYES and *H$_2$0* helped us become something we'd never really considered: bigger than life and even more famous and recognizable. Video stars, yes, but that was just image. We cared about music. And just as in the beginning, it was never about resting on our laurels for us; it was always about forging ahead. And so in the spring of 1984, bolstered by the power and commercial clout of our excess and success, we were again ready to push the envelope.

Once more, we checked into Electric Lady Studios in the Village, this time with Bob Clearmountain behind the recording console. Our touring band of T-Bone Wolk on bass, Mickey Curry on drums, G.E. Smith on lead guitar, and Charlie DeChant on sax was locked down and tight. The album would be titled *Big Bam Boom*, and making it would mark a unique and important moment in our recording history.

Here She Comes

After surviving the decadent uprooted mid-'70s circus of constant touring the globe and recording in Los Angeles, returning to New York City was a homecoming party hosted by friends, lovers, and charismatic characters who opened doors with open arms. The Manhattan universe was accelerating at light speed, fueled by the greed-is-good, winner-takes-all burgeoning energy of the early 1980s. I fully and willingly let myself be pulled inexorably into its vortex. For those of you fascinated with the era, the mood of excess reverberates for posterity in films like *The Wolf of Wall Street* and others. Up-tempo, linear, eighth-note synth and drum-machine-driven music, garish colorful clothing, cartoonish hairstyles, and absurdist MTV videos dominated radio, TV, and fashion. From my perspective, the world beyond the Hudson and East Rivers was nonexistent. Very much like the classic 1976 New Yorker illustration, *View of the World from 9th Avenue* by Saul Steinberg, where nothing of significance exists beyond the Hudson River. For me, the white-hot center of this hyperspeed, swirling collection of social and ethnic solar systems was still Greenwich Village. It felt like home, and I couldn't imagine living anyplace else. The colonial-era tree-lined streets and alleys outlined by broken sidewalks and populated by ghosts of the past alongside future supernovas yet undiscovered was everything for me. Those black-and-white memories of driving through the Village as a kid during the Beat Generation's birth had evolved into a glorious immersion, where all parts of this world were my proverbial oysters. I'd watched (and listened) how the music in the early '70s had begun changing the chemistry of the Village, and now Daryl and I were firmly a part of that culture. For me, the memories all remain vivid and vibrant. Electrifying.

Rummaging through the antique clothing store racks of quirky Technicolor bowling shirts, musty record stores with row upon row of vinyl inspiration, vintage guitar shops, seeing beautiful young girls writing their own fashionable rule books, druggie burnouts huddled on broken stoops, and all this wrapped together under a thick aroma blanket of freshly baked pizza and Italian bread . . . the Village offered up multiple sensory orgasms of possibilities around every corner.

During these years, my wife, Nancy, was a successful model with the Ford agency and was traveling around the world, and we were apart for many months. I was living a dual existence, technically married but not acting like it. There was temptation around every corner, and there was never enough to satisfy. I don't recall actually using the kitchen in our apartment, except for the odd occasion when my friends and neighbors, Alan, Trev Huxley, or Johnny C., with a retinue of wacked-out disco dolls in tow would arrive to watch the sun come up while I whipped up espressos. I ate in amazing restaurants every night for at least ten years. After dinner, early evenings flowed into art gallery openings, private loft parties in SoHo, fly-bys at the latest happening hole-in-the-wall club, at Madison Square Garden, at Studio 54. . . . Most nights, we began or ended up at the bar of a restaurant bar called Marylou's on Ninth Street between Fifth and Sixth Avenues.

Three steps down from the sidewalk, behind the heavy polished wood-and-etched-glass door lay an inner sanctum of corporeal pleasures that was the exclusive but understated night spot presided over by Tommy Baratta and named after his sister. There were no reservations or membership, entry was based on who you were, who you knew, or what you could provide to the exclusive coterie of movers, shakers, actors, models, musicians, drug dealers, and a smattering of the newly ordained would-be masters of the Wall Street universe.

One evening . . . memory claims it went like this . . . the long inner-sanctum table in the back dining room at Marylou's was shoulder to shoulder with a very attractive group of regulars. I stepped down the two shallow steps at the entrance to the room and joined the well-lubricated conversation. Spread out on the table were multiple platters of antipasti, and standing guard at intervals, deep ruby bottles of full-blooded amarone. The laughter, chatter, and buzz around the table stopped abruptly when she appeared.

Her entrance transformed the top step into a stage, the swirling and busing waiters were her choreography, the lights of passing cars refracted through the bay window behind her became a halo of backlight for her dark, casually perfect, who-cares hair. A pause, a pose . . . time stood at attention . . . a shriek from the lips that pouted from every magazine cover . . . hugs, kisses all around, she sat down across the table from me. To describe her as a devastating beauty would not be an exaggeration. Then the spell she cast was at once shattered and heightened as from the mouth of this goddess spewed forth the most foul, crude, and expletive-laced soliloquy I'd ever heard.

The contrast was shocking and it aroused, among other things, my songwriter antennae. Fully tuned in, "She would chew you up and spit you out," popped into my head, lodging somewhere deep within the right lobe of my brain. In the early morning hours that same night, the line "Oh-oh here she comes, she's a maneater," began to swirl around and around, serpentine and sinewy.

I was not able to get that germ of an idea out of my head as the hours passed and dawn's dusty light began to creep across the floor. Likely inspired by a recent trip to Jamaica, I began to strum a classic reggae guitar groove, put a tentative melody to the hook, and let the chorus evolve. I ruminated on this for quite a while as I searched for the song to go with it. I recall playing it for Edgar Winter in his uptown apartment during a writing session a few days later, but he didn't react to it. Then I played it for Daryl, and he did. I could see his mind working as I repeated the refrain, until he finally turned to the keyboard and pounded out a Motown style groove . . . he was right and I'm sure glad I agreed with him. There was an extra melody dangling off the end of the hook, and while writing the lyrics, Sandy Alan came up with the idea to drop the extraneous bit and just end with, "she's a maneater." Clean.

Many of our songs serve as commentaries on the zeitgeists surrounding us, from the streets to the most rarefied rooms in New York City. Disguised within what on the surface might seem like basic personal interactions are reflections of the cultural universe we found ourselves floating in. There was intent behind the lyrics and melodies to have more metaphoric layers than simply met the eye. To this day when I hear "Maneater," Charlie DeChant's sleek and sensuous saxophone becomes the sharp, late-day sunlight slanting off the city's steel-and-glass towers, and the song that started as an ode to a beguiling, if incongruously foul-mouthed, siren becomes a statement on life in the go-go '80s. A soundtrack to the excesses that brought many a man (myself included) to their knees. The maneater wasn't just that woman. It was New York City.

Smoking Guns,
Hot to the Touch

By 1984 analog, or tape, recording technology was at its zenith. My first recording in 1966 had been on skinny two-inch two-track tape. Now, dominating the back wall of the control room, two massive twenty-four-track tape recorders stood side by side, electronically linked together. These state-of-the-art analog machines enabled us to record forty-eight tracks simultaneously on two-inch tape. Looming on the horizon, however, was the new digital recording technology. Although the hardware was in its infancy, the binary code at its core was like the flourishing graffiti covering the New York subways—unstoppable, crude, and a bellwether of things to come.

Although we still opted to record on analog tape rather than the new digital multitrack machines, we embraced other aspects of the coming digital age. Due to our commercial success, and motivated by our creative curiosity, we were able to tap into all the latest and greatest new musical devices available—most notably, cutting-edge polyphonic synthesizers like the Synclavier and the Fairlight. We wanted to push the sonic boundaries of our records and augment the traditional rhythm section with unusual and as-yet unheard sounds. The aural palette was unlimited. We were on the cusp of a brave, bold, new era. And our

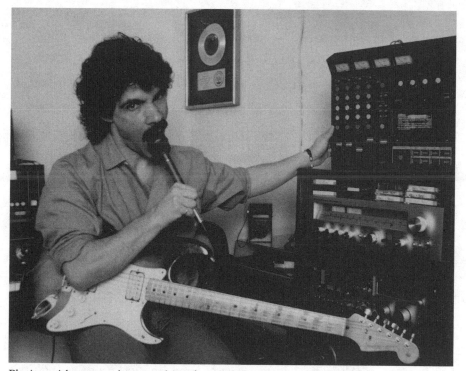

Playing with my new home multitrack recorder, on which I began composing our soon-to-be-hit song "Out of Touch." Technology was changing everything and we were right in the thick of it. *(Courtesy John Oates)*

pop-kingpin status gave us the keys to the kingdom. We were all about process and discovery. New frontiers. Breaking down walls.

But despite the technology, of course it all came down to the songs.

ON THE STREETS of New York, hip-hop was a living dance mix in real time, huge boom boxes crunching out distorted bass beats blended with taxicab horn arrangements and the ambient cacophony of city life. The walk of only a few blocks from my apartment to the studio was an auditory assault and invariably translated both subtly and overtly into the songs and recordings that followed.

In the music room of my apartment in Greenwich Village I had set up one of the latest portable multitrack cassette recorders alongside a new Roland synthesizer and began to incorporate some of this new technology into my writing process. Although my keyboard playing was rudimentary, often a new, albeit simple or quirky sound could be enough to kick off a new idea for a song.

It was 3:00 A.M. and with insomnia and creativity working in tandem, I started playing around with the new equipment. The synth had a button marked ARPEGGIO. I didn't know what it did, so I just pressed it. Out came a preprogrammed sound that is best described as a tonal percussive wood-block. By holding down one of the keys, I could make it repeat, and I could adjust the tempo by turning a knob. It was interesting and sounded cool even though it was just a randomly selected factory setting. It was a happy accident and I spent a few hours pursuing the idea. By playing around with the notes, I came up with a theme that was both percussive and melodic. I recorded it on one track of my new cassette deck and programmed a simple drumbeat to go with it. On another track I put down a quick acoustic guitar chord progression and started singing to it:

"You're out of touch, I'm out of town, and I'm out of my head when you're not around. . . ." My wife, Nancy, was away modeling in Europe at the time and the chorus just wrote itself, direct and to the point.

Now, with dawn breaking over the city below, a very hooky chorus began to take shape. I started to overdub vocal parts on the multitrack cassette deck, and the ability to bounce tracks (rerecord an original track onto a pre-existing one) gave me almost unlimited possibilities. I sang the entire chorus in octaves, and it began to take on a very classic Philly R&B vibe. I even outlined the melody with a vibes sound reminiscent of the style that Vince Montana played on many of the Gamble and Huff records.

Later that morning, with little cassette demo in my pocket, I took my familiar walk through the Village, from my apartment on West Twelfth Street to Electric Lady studios on Eighth Street, where we were working with Arthur Baker, the white-hot producer/DJ, on alternative versions of our album tracks. I knew that in addition to working with us on *Big Bam Boom*, he was also producing the Stylistics, and I thought that the demo's Philly vibe might be perfect for them.

I got to the studio before anyone else that day, and when Arthur arrived I said, "Hey, man, take a listen to this thing I came up with last night, it could be great for the Stylistics." He took one listen and said, "Are you fucking out of your mind? That's a number-one record idea for you and Daryl!"

Later that day, when Daryl came in, I played it for him. He loved the chorus, and we got together to work on the verses. He came up with a unique and cool set of chord changes for the verse, and we wrote the lyrics together. A few days later, using the demo as a starting point, we recorded the song with the band. Arthur Baker was a master dance mixer, and after we finished our album version, he took the tapes into his secret lab with some dudes he called the Latin Rascals. Their real names were Tony Moran and Albert Cabrera, and these two street-smart wizards worked in obscurity, locked away in a tiny editing room, armed with razor blades and miles of quarter-inch tape. Each strip of tape was a portion or single element of the master multitrack recording. They would reassemble various sections of the songs in a jagged, jump-cut style, often combining musical passages or individual instruments out of sequence, repeating and rearranging them in surprising ways. Their editing job on the twelve-inch vinyl club mix of "Out of Touch" is an analog tour de force and became a DJ/dance club classic. "Out of Touch" was destined to be another number one single on the Billboard Hot 100 as well as the dance charts.

The making of *Big Bam Boom* represented a fresh new musical universe for us, a truly experimental melting pot of traditional record making and state-of-the-art, for the time, technologies. Now there were no almost no limitations, anything could become a musical statement. We began to digitally sample anything and everything we could get our hands on. Using a traditional drum kit, Clearmountain and Mickey Curry spent hours recording various drum sounds, manipulating delays and reverbs, creating the huge dramatic bottom end that is now so emblematic of this album and the '80s in general. In the zeroes and ones of the new digital polyphonic synthesizers we recorded everything we could get our hands on: Boy Scout canteens, cardboard boxes, vocals, footsteps in gravel, and much more. We combined all this with the use of newer more sophisticated drum machines like the LinnDrum operated by

Jimmy Bralower and the aforementioned dance-and-club-mixing sensibility of Arthur Baker.

We were firing on all cylinders. As we did as far back as the early '70s, with the use of the primitive Mellotron and by processing natural instruments through the early synthesizers like the ARP 2600, we embraced each new device on its merits as a tool to enhance and integrate into the recording process. For us, they were instruments to be used to achieve an end: service and enrich the songs. The world of music and my personal world were all changing. In one sense I may have felt like I was watching a film about me. But when it came to making music, I was no less focused than I had been when I first wandered into Atlantic to work on Whole Oats. I was still that guy. Not watching, just creating.

And in the midst of the madness, the music saved us. Like it always did. When I think of the '80s, or when I'm asked what those years were like, I seldom think about the fame or the videos. Those seem like an insignificant blur. The writing, the recording, and the creative energy of our great '80s band are the things that resonate in my recollections. I remember the music. Because that was the only time that my life came into focus and had real meaning.

A Word from Our Sponsors...

I t was February 1985.

My Learjet touched down on the bitter-cold runway on a landing strip near Oklahoma City. The door of the sleek aircraft was hoisted opened, and I stepped out into the icy air. Following behind me were four starstruck MTV-contest winners. I looked up and down the other runways and didn't see anything. Okay, good. Had we had done it? A moment later, I saw a tiny dot in the gray sky. A jet almost identical to the one I had just arrived in was cutting through the clouds like a small white shark. Moments later it landed and taxied alongside our plane. Our little group was all smiles. We had done it.

We had beaten Daryl to Oklahoma.

This is what the mid-'80s pop insane blur had come down to. This is how excessive it had become.

Learjet racing.

MTV, RCA, and our management had concocted yet another over-the-top marketing scheme to help promote our *Big Bam Boom* album and tour. Pulling a handful of names from hundreds of thousands of entries, two small teams were created. One of them would jet with Daryl from New York, the other team with me from Los Angeles. Our destination would be an equidistant spot on the map in Oklahoma. The first plane to arrive would win. The prize was $25,000, to be split equally among the winners.

That's how we kicked off the second leg of the tour. Of course MTV was there to capture all the action, both in the skies and on the ground as Daryl and I flew over America, after making a couple of stops along the way to pick up the lucky chosen few.

In addition, by merely being chosen to fly with us, each winner was also given a brand-new 1985 Pontiac Fiero. The car company was sponsoring our megatour, and this was one of the biggest corporate sponsorship deals in music history up until that point. A fellow named Mike Joy (currently a well-known racing and automotive broadcaster) was our point person and liaison with Pontiac, and to personally sweeten the deal both Daryl and I received free cars for ourselves and for our families. In addition, a huge perk for me was an invitation to drive one of the new Fiero racing cars. More on that later.

A promo poster from the *Big Bam Boom* tour, which was sponsored (luckily for me) by Pontiac.

The Rolling Stones' 1981 American tour was widely regarded as the first major corporate-sponsored rock-and-roll endeavor. Jōvan, a major perfume manufacturer, had given the Stones several million dollars, and that really seemed to kick-start this practice of corporations underwriting rock-and-roll tours. But few people know that we actually may have been the very first group to initiate the idea of having a company underwrite a tour.

In 1980 we were approached by Carefree gum to do a tour of high schools around the United States. At first we thought it was kind of an odd deal. But the more we considered it, the more it made sense. We were in kind of a strange place that spring. We were touring a lot but still playing smaller venues, mostly clubs. We were back to grinding it out. The *Voices* album wouldn't be out for several months, and so our resurgence of popularity had not yet kicked in. But we did have a relatively new band, and so going out for a couple of months would be a great chance to break them in and work out the kinks. Twenty high schools would be chosen based on how many Carefree gum wrappers they could collect. Before long the tour throughout April and May of that year was booked.

It might have been the most fun and crazy tour we ever did. Getting our new band together in front of wildly enthusiastic, completely unjaded, scream-ing teenagers was low pressure and a blast. And of course the shows were all played in the late afternoon, which gave us a chance to carouse like lunatics all night.

Sherwood High School in Sandy Spring, Maryland. John K. Ossi Vo-Tech in Medford, New Jersey. We played 'em all, setting up in their gymnasiums just like the old days.

Carefree promoted the hell out of the "Carefree Fever" tour, as it was dubbed, and it wound up being really successful. This was before Michael Jackson made a deal with Pepsi, McCartney was underwritten by Visa, or the Rolling Stones signed on with Jōvan. Touring with corporate support was a totally new concept back then. But if we had learned nothing else, it was that the music business was highly unpredictable; you never knew what the next mo-ment might bring (or take away). Soon after that, Canada Dry would help underwrite the H_2O tour.

I HAD NO clue that a few years later these kind of corporate arrangements would involve the sort of insanity that a Learjet race represents. But back in 1980 that tour was all about the music, not wild promotions. We had no idea what would happen once the *Voices* album was released later that fall, and it didn't matter. We didn't live our lives based on what might happen. Everything was in the moment. Everything was about staying the course and doing what we had to do to keep making music. That's how we defined success: Could we keep making music?

Video Killed Some
Radio Stars

looked at Daryl and he stared back at me. It was an obtuse flashback to that fateful moment, jammed together in a cramped elevator the night we met in 1967. Only now we were trapped together inside a giant bass drum, a prop on a soundstage in a remote section of Queens, New York at 3:00 A.M. It was the fall of 1984 and our album *Big Bam Boom* was about to be released.

Other supersized props were strewn about the studio like it was some bored giant's playground. We had been shooting since early afternoon and now, twelve hours later, exhausted, we were sealed inside the drum, waiting for cameras to roll. It was hot, claustrophobic, and the air was getting thin.

We looked at each other, and I whispered, "Is this what it's all come to?"

We had jumped on board the MTV train when it was barely out of the station, becoming the first guest VJs, and our simplistic early videos swelled in scope and style along with the network's success. To us they were an adjunct to our audio recordings, and that's about it. Yet there we were in heavy rotation with Def Leppard, the Police, Duran Duran, A-Ha, Madonna, and a slew of others, an entirely new generation of up-and-coming artists, barely out of their teens, who were embracing this new medium as an integral component in their careers.

Daryl and I had twelve albums under our belt before MTV even went on the air, and although we always perceived ourselves as musicians first and foremost, we also recognized the power of music videos as a promotional tool. I remember having a bit of an argument with Madonna during a new-music seminar, and of course she took the position that her visual image was as important to her and her career as her audio recordings and she was right . . . for her. But even though Daryl and I always put the music first, we had been producing MTV-style videos for years before the network popularized the genre. In fact, we'd been part of the video vanguard throughout the 1970s. We had been experimenting with video techniques from the beginning of our career. Personally, I was always messing around with film cameras, making crude Super 8 movies during our early days on tour, and Daryl has always had a great sense of visual style.

We made our first video in 1974.

I wasn't surprised, that same year, when the group Tavares had a number one record on the R&B charts with "She's Gone." For us, having a song covered by an R&B group seemed perfectly natural. We had released the song as the leadoff single from *Abandoned Luncheonette* the year before, but it only went to Top 30 on the charts. The Tavares version sounded great, and technically, it was our first number one record as songwriters. As a result of that, and on the heels of "Sara Smile" becoming a Top 40 hit the following year, Atlantic released "She's Gone" again, and it finally made it into the top five on the charts. But back when we first released the song in 1973, we were told that we could get some television exposure down at the Jersey Shore to promote the record.

Philadelphia had a long-running teenage dance-show tradition; the most well-known was Dick Clark's *American Bandstand*. But down on the Jersey shore there was another show called *Summertime on the Pier*. It had started back in the late 1950s and was hosted by a disc jockey named Ed Hurst, who looked more like an insurance salesman than he did a purveyor of youth culture. He was kind of like Dick Clark lite, and his show was broadcast from the Steel

Pier in Atlantic City. They would bring in lots of kids from Philly to dance each week to the latest records, and showcase pop artists who would appear live to promote their latest single by lip-synching their songs.

But when our record label, Atlantic, suggested we go down there and lip-synch "She's Gone," we pushed back right away. There was no way we could envision lip-synching a song like that on television, with a bunch of kids trying to slow dance in front of us. It would have looked ridiculous. But we were in a bit of a bind. The label wanted us to promote the record, and we knew we had a do something.

So in a midnight haze we came up with an idea.

First, we made up a story that we were not available to appear live that day for the show but that we would be willing to videotape something for them to air. So we asked if it would be possible to come in and shoot something at their WPVI Philadelphia studio prior to the show. Remember, this is when there was no such thing as music videos. A band might film itself doing a straight performance of the song, but there was very little in the way of conceptual art when it came to selling a song. Of course that didn't stop us. We were always thinking about how we could push the envelope.

At the time, my sister, Diane, was a film student at Temple University and I asked her if she would direct the piece for us. Daryl and I mapped out a bizarre scenario, which would involve some unusual costumes, a few props, and some costars. In our New York apartment we loosely blocked out the skit, and my sister wrote a basic script so it would look like we knew what we were doing when we got to the television studio.

WE HAULED TWO overstuffed chairs from our Upper East Side apartment, piling them into a rented van with some other props, and drove down to Philly. The moment we walked in, all of the old union stagehands and tech guys looked at us with bewilderment, which soon turned to scorn, and finally revulsion. Here was my little sister, still a college student, directing them and making sure we got the shots we needed. This was something totally outside their conventional reality. These were cameramen and directors whose skills and sensibilities dated back to TV's earliest days, and they did not like being dictated to by a nineteen-year-old female—or anyone else, for that matter.

For my wardrobe I chose, for no logical reason, a black-and-white penguin costume that I found in a local thrift store. Daryl, then sporting an androgynous shaved-eyebrows look, appeared as a sullenly decadent, jaded English lord, swathed in a black velvet bathrobe, wearing fashionable Kork-Ease open-toed sandals and dragging on a cigarette. We forced our new road manager, Randy Hoffman, to wear a shiny red devil costume and to parade across the stage on cue, while Daryl and I (sitting with vacant, glazed expressions) tossed monopoly money into the air to represent the line, "I'd pay the devil to replace her." The "she" in the song was Daryl's girlfriend, Sara Allen, who had already been mentioned in one of my songs, "Las Vegas Turnaround," and a year later would become immortalized when Daryl added a "smile" to her name. Her job was to languidly sashay in front of us in a diaphanous gown at certain points in the song while we sat there feigning oblivious detachment.

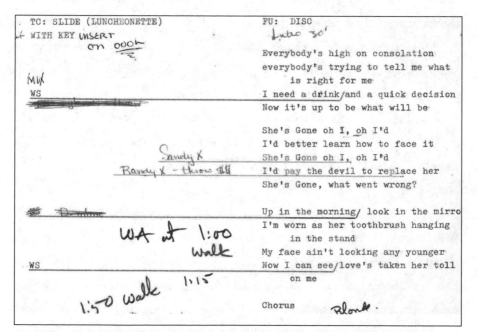

The actual "script" written by my sister, Diane, for our "legendary" "She's Gone" video in 1974. *(Courtesy Diane Oates)*

In a novelty store, Daryl discovered a new toy from Mattel called a Bath-House Brass Tooba. As the package read: "Hilarious looking horns anyone can play just by humming high or low—fast or slow. It's harmony in plumbing!" It was basically an angled bunch of replica plastic plumbing pipes that had a bell style horn at the end of it, and imbedded inside the mouthpiece was a cheap tin kazoo. Daryl wanted to use it during the saxophone solo. My penguin suit had long flippers covering the hands, so when it was time for the guitar solo, I had to keep pushing them back to be able to actually touch the strings. I finally flipped them over the neck of the guitar with no pretense of actually playing. It was totally surreal and very disturbing for the traditional TV-station production staff, who I'm sure were having their minds blown. The immediate reaction was not good. The entire TV crew got pissed off and basically kicked us out of the studio as soon as we were finished but only after enduring a brief, stoned-out interview with the hyper host.

To this day, I think it's one of the weirdest and coolest things we've ever done. A very bizarre and comical pre-MTV music video that has actually developed a cult following since we released it a few years ago. Before that, it almost never saw the light of day. I had the only copy. It was preserved on an older, professional-format videocassette and buried in a closet for many years. One day while cleaning out a bunch of junk I rediscovered it and had it transferred to DVD to share with the rest of the world. No one had ever done anything like this, and I guess the TV station thought we were mocking them and their regional teenage dance show. They were outraged and not only refused to run the piece, but called Atlantic records and told them that we were insane and would never be allowed on Philadelphia TV again. They hated the video so much, they also threatened to try and get our record banned on Philadelphia radio stations. That didn't work by the way . . . it was a visual punch in the nose that merely defined the generation gap between us and everybody else who worked there. (And, by the way, I still have the original script that my sister wrote for the production.)

If you haven't seen it, I suggest you look it up. I think it's our best video of all time. It's a timepiece that really illustrates just how experimental we could be, especially when left to our own devices. In a way it was a precursor to our next album, *War Babies*, with another Philly upstart who also liked to experiment, Todd Rundgren.

Our interest in video continued throughout the '70s, years before MTV had been even imagined.

IN 1979, MY sister, Diane, who by then was working at ABC-TV in New York, introduced us to the son of one of her coworkers. He was an NYU film student who wanted to experiment with a new technology called chroma-key or green screen. It had been popular for a couple years in TV news; they would "knock out" the green background and insert something like a weather map. But in the burgeoning music-video age, it represented a whole new way of creating off-the-wall imagery in music videos. That same year, Michael Jackson spearheaded the green screen-movement with his video for "Don't Stop 'Til You Get Enough."

And we were right there with him; we had already talked and exchanged ideas about how we could use this new technology. Our record company wanted something to promote the record in Europe, since we had no plans of touring there. In October 1979 we went to a studio in New York called Modern Telecommunications and worked all day to produce videos for several songs on our *X-Static* album: "Portable Radio," "BeBop/Drop," "Wait For Me," and "Intravino." For the latter, the idea was to have us performing inside of a gigantic boom box and then drunk dancing around a giant bottle of wine. With the crude green-screen technique, anything was possible.

We always felt that our music and look as performers was unique, so when MTV finally came along and the industry exploded, we kind of felt like we'd been there all along.

The music videos for songs from *Private Eyes* and *H_2O* seemed to fit the times perfectly because they immediately became MTV staples. Those clips for "One On One," "Family Man," "Maneater," and others became as well-known as any TV programs of the day. We worked with the best directors, from Mick Haggerty to Bob Giraldi to Jeff Stein, who was directing the "Out of Touch" video that night.

We understood why we were doing the videos, we knew the drill, but in the back of our minds, we never forgot that we were musicians first and foremost. Still, by the mid-'80s, when our career had absolutely exploded, there was no denying that big-budget videos were an integral part of the game plan. And as big as we were, no budget was too large to consider. For a song I wrote called "Possession Obsession," I got to play a NYC cabbie who, after dropping off his last fare, meets his sharkskin-suit-wearing, doo-wop-singing pals (Daryl and the band) on a dock by the river on a freezing winter night, to croon my tune.

But trapped in the bass drum that night, we started to feel like the art form we had helped nurture was now swallowing us up. It was suffocating us, both figuratively and literally. We were cast as caricatures of ourselves. The music-video industry had grown so fast and so extreme that, like many things we did in the early '80s, we were just passengers on a runaway train bound for someplace we didn't want to go. Out of touch . . . from the music.

I think we both came to the realization, inside that absurd giant drum, that soon it was going to be time to get off this train and get back to what got us here in the first place.

"Daryl, is this what it all comes down to?"

He didn't even have to answer. We both knew the answer.

Something had to give.

More Racing

I n the mid-'80s I was offered a unique opportunity, another perk to go along with the Pontiac tour sponsorship for the *Big Bam Boom* album: the chance to drive their Pontiac Fiero, campaigning in the IMSA (International Motor Sports Association) GTU (engines under two liters' displacement) category.

Joe Huffaker from California built the cars, and his driver was an experienced hot shoe by the name of Bob Earl. The IMSA races were for sports and prototype cars and were all endurance races of at least two hours or more. In preparation, I co-drove George Drolsom's Porsche 924 GTR, and we finished a credible fourth at Lime Rock. That hot summer day I nearly passed out from heat and dehydration, having never driven a closed-cockpit car in a long race. Then Richard Lloyd made the trip to America and we drove his Porsche 924 GRT at Daytona, but we retired with mechanical problems after the second hour. I'll never forget the sensation of holding that little car down low on the high banked track while the likes of Mario Andretti in the big prototypes screamed by at 200 mph, just inches from the right side of the little 180 mph Porsche. It was a blast and an eye-opening experience to be competing in big-time professional racing series. With those two events under my belt and a full FIA license in hand, I flew out to Sonoma, California, for a tryout in the Pontiac Fiero. They would give me a test and check me out before committing to allowing me to race the car.

My California test session in the Fiero went pretty well, and arrangements were made by our Pontiac liaison, Mike Joy, to run the car at Elkhart Lake, Wisconsin, in another IMSA endurance event. I had experience in the smaller cars on that challenging four-mile-long track, and although I enjoyed driving there, I never finished well. This time would be worse. Bob Earl qualified the car at the front of our class, and the decision was made for me to start and do the first couple of hours before handing it back to Bob for the finish. Sounded like a good plan and when the green flag fell I immediately lost a few places and settled into what felt like a conservatively quick pace. About one-and-a-half hours into my stint, it was time for my pit stop and handoff to my co-driver. The Elkhart Lake track had some very tricky features and fast corners. Notably the 180-degree slightly banked curve called the Karussell, named after a similarly shaped corner at the legendary Nürburgring in Germany. Exiting that long bend, you accelerate hard as the track straightens momentarily before entering a deceivingly simple shallow right called the Kink. If your car is handling well, it is taken flat out to carry momentum onto the back straightaway that follows. The Fiero had a short wheelbase and was a bit twitchy in high-speed corners, so the Kink had what racing drivers call a bit of a "pucker" factor. Translated, that means tighten your asshole . . . this could be scary. At about 120 mph, you just turn in slightly and hold your breath. Suddenly in the middle of the turn I heard a dull pop! The last thing I remember was being flung sideways, with dirt flying—pretty sure I said "shit"—then nothing more. Later I found out that a blown rear differential had locked up the rear wheels and I became a passenger in a high-speed slide into a dirt embankment before the car careened across the track, coming to a stop smashed against the Armco barrier and luckily not into the forest of trees just beyond.

My racing helmet was cracked on the right side from hitting the blue roll bar. Luckily the car didn't catch fire, since it was low on fuel as I neared my pit-stop window. That's about all I remember until I woke up in an ambulance on the way to a local hospital. When I opened my eyes I saw an EMT and another fellow in a driver's suit sitting next to me. I asked them what happened. They told me I had crashed and not to talk. In a daze, I kept going in and out of consciousness. After a few hours I woke up again in the emergency room. Surprisingly, my head soon began to clear, and they eventually released me with the diagnosis of a slight concussion and a warning to take it easy. I got a ride back to my hotel, hopped in a rent-a-car, drove myself to the airport, and flew back to New York. The next day I walked into the recording studio and went back to work. That was the last time I competed in a race car . . . sometimes it takes a good knock on the head to accept certain realities. After that, I still drove occasionally, doing a NASCAR racing school with legendary driver Buck Baker for a Canadian TV show and playing around in karts on tracks around the world when I had time. While I never raced in competition again and never will—damn, I still love to drive.

Flying

After my big crash at Elkhart Lake I made a conscious decision to stop racing. My driving had progressed to the point that I was competing in various professional racing series, but due to my recording and touring schedule, I wasn't giving it a professional effort in terms of preparation. Better to know your limits. However my need for that adrenaline rush still existed and the question was: What would replace it? Oftentimes on charter plane flights, I would sit in the jump seat, up front, behind the pilots, watching closely and asking lots of questions. Finally, the chief pilot, weary of my incessant queries, handed me a book and said, "Here, read this." It was *Stick and Rudder: An Explanation of the Art of Flying,* written in 1944 by author/journalist/aviator Wolfgang Langewiesche and one of the classic pilot primers. I read it cover to cover, absorbing every detail. The next logical step was to begin flying lessons.

One of our regular charter pilots was a guy named Jay Schley, who lived on Long Island. One spring day in 1985 he flew in to pick me up at a little airport in Danbury, Connecticut, for my first lesson. The airplane was a well-used Cessna 172, a classic trainer. I hopped in and after some brief preflight instruction, we taxied out to the runway. With one hand on the yoke and the other pushing the throttle lever forward, I accelerated the Cessna down the runway and off into the air. I was flying, and I was hooked. I began taking lessons twice a week and progressed quickly, doing my first solo flight with just ten hours under my belt. Since I wasn't comfortable flying the rented aircraft that my instructor provided, I purchased a slightly more sophisticated single-engine Piper Dakota. I worked hard and earned my private pilot license shortly afterwards. The discipline and procedural aspects of piloting were appealing, but the freedom that private aviation provided was what pushed me to advance further. I continued training and went on to earn my instrument rating. Now flying myself became a much more practical reality. Eventually I outgrew the Piper and, to accompany my advancing skill level, moved up to a Beechcraft A36 Bonanza. It was a bit larger with higher performance and better long-distance capability . . . it would also save my life.

By the late '80s I began flying that plane on tour. For safety's sake I always brought a more experienced, instructor pilot with me, but I did most of the flying, logging hours, building experience and confidence. There were nights when I would come offstage, head right to the plane, and soon Daryl and I would be cruising over a darkened stretch of Eastern Seaboard at ten thousand feet. While I looked down at the specks of light below, scattered like diamonds on black velvet, I thought back to those memorable early tours, five bandmates cramped into that '68 yellow GTO, touring the country through the same dead of night. Man, how things had changed. How many other bands were down there right now, hitting the road for the first time in pursuit of the dreams we had already fulfilled?

Still living in Connecticut and New York at the time, I would use the plane to visit many destinations in the Northeast and beyond. The beaches of Martha's Vineyard, Nantucket, and the Hamptons, as well as my folks' house in Pennsylvania, suddenly became easy regular weekend trips. Soaring above the busy highway traffic and cruising up the Hudson River with the twinkling lights of the Manhattan skyline passing below was a wonderful experience. But not every flight was good. There is one that I'll never forget, one that almost stopped both career and life in their tracks.

One of Nancy's brothers was getting married in Detroit, so we decided to fly out for the wedding. After a nice weekend, on a dreary Sunday morning we arrived at the airport to head back to the East Coast. The weather was marginal, with rain and multiple cloud layers, and the temperature aloft was cold enough for possible icing conditions to occur. Ice is a very serious go- or-no-go situation for a small, light aircraft without deicing equipment. My Beechcraft Bonanza was not fitted for nor certified to fly in icing conditions. Knowing that, I filed a flight plan that would take us, at a fairly low altitude, south from the Detroit area, over northern Ohio, then across Pennsylvania toward Connecticut.

A common cause of accidents among private pilots is something called "get home-itis," and it means just what it sounds like. That Sunday morning, I was anxious to get back home, and as I sat on the ramp with the airplane engine running, I tuned the radio to the ground-control frequency to get my clearance and departure instructions. The voice on the radio barked out a rapid-fire list of compass headings, altitudes, and radio frequencies. I jotted them down on my kneeboard and read them back, noticing that they were different from the flight plan that I had originally requested. Detroit was a busy airport, and not wanting to wait or take the time to refile a new flight plan, I accepted it. *First mistake.* A few minutes later we were airborne and climbing up into the clouds. After a few heading changes, I realized that my route was taking me straight over Lake Erie. In the clouds, over water, in possible icing conditions . . . *not good.* Ascending upwards to seven thousand feet I noticed that the windscreen was starting to ice over even though I had the defroster on full blast . . . *also not good.* Then I glanced sideways at the wings and saw a ridge of rime ice forming on the leading edges . . . *really not good.* I immediately radioed the controller and made him aware of my situation, and at the same time requested a higher altitude. He came back and told me to climb at my own discretion. I added some power and pulled back gently on the yoke. The plane began to climb; the ice began to build up.

The situation was soon approaching critical. I could feel the handling of the plane deteriorating as the ice continued to spread over the wings. A potentially deadly freezing moisture was coating the prop as well, and eventually all the windows glazed over, opaque and milky white. The cockpit felt like a frozen cocoon, but all the while I tried to remain calm and keep the plane climbing, careful not to make any sudden moves. Thankfully, Nancy had fallen asleep in the copilot seat and was not aware of the increasingly dangerous situation that was unfolding.

For a pilot, declaring an emergency is a big deal and a last resort. I was on the verge and keyed the radio asking for a PIREP (pilot report) to find out at what altitude I might reach the tops of the clouds. By this time the Bonanza was barely flying, and the controls were heavy. Passing through nine thousand feet seemed to take forever. My vertical climb rate was barely two hundred feet per minute as I alternated leveling off to gain airspeed then ever-so-gently pulling back, mentally willing the sluggish, ice-covered aircraft higher and higher. Suddenly the radio crackled with a new voice on the frequency. It was a pilot who had been monitoring my radio calls and who I'm sure picked up on the stress in my voice. Knowing I was in trouble, he reported that he was ten miles ahead and on top of the clouds at twelve thousand feet. I had to get up there. Agonizing and nerve-wracking minutes that felt like hours crept by as I continued to coax the ice-laden airplane ever higher. Then, like a glimpse of heaven above, the dark-gray ice plastering the windscreen began to lighten and glow from the brightness of the sun as we finally broke out of the clouds.

Although it was still cold at that altitude, by a phenomenon called sublimation, ice can dissipate and turn from a solid to a gas, bypassing the liquid stage. With the defroster still on high, a small area of the windscreen began to clear, and I could see the ice slowly disappearing from the wings. I let out a big sigh of relief. The engine never missed a beat, and that Beechcraft Bonanza just kept flying despite my irresponsible and potentially deadly decision to fly that route that day. I still have nightmares about it. Fortunately, I had a well-built airplane and good training . . . throughout the entire harrowing experience I could hear my flight instructor whispering in my ear, "Fly the plane . . . fly the plane."

July 13, 1985

There were ninety thousand people packing historic JFK stadium in Philadelphia on a sweltering summer day. The place that was probably most famous for hosting the Army-Navy football game was now playing host, along with Wembley Stadium in London, England, to a music event for the ages: Live Aid. Started by Boomtown Rats' singer Bob Geldof, a global mix of superstars rallied to raise awareness and money to help feed hungry and malnourished children in Africa. Our status in the rock-and-roll universe was confirmed when Daryl and I were slotted to close the show for this global event in our hometown of Philly. The concert would be beamed out to about two billion people around the planet. This would be the biggest entertainment broadcast in history.

In London, at Wembley Stadium, dozens of acts, including Queen, U2, Paul McCartney, and the Who rocked the house for close to one hundred thousand fans. Due to the six-hour time difference the UK show ended while the US show was still going on. Phil Collins, who performed a set at Wembley, had rushed to Heathrow airport to hop aboard a British Airways Concorde supersonic jet and was winging his way at Mach 2 over the Atlantic to join the American show, already in progress, to perform a set there, as well.

ON OUR SIDE of the pond, the list of superstars was impressive: Bob Dylan, the surviving members of Led Zeppelin, Crosby Stills Nash and Young, Eric Clapton, Madonna, and many others were lined up to perform. For Daryl and I, being the closing band at this event, and being right in our former-hometown backyard, was more than heady.

Daryl and I were helicoptered in during the afternoon along with Eddie Kendricks and David Ruffin from the Temptations, whom we invited to reprise our well-received Apollo Theater performance earlier that year. The backstage area was overflowing with some of the world's most popular bands as well as movie stars like Jack Nicholson, who bounced around backstage and jumped up in between sets to act as an MC. Behind the stage was a corral of white RVs, and groups had to share the cramped trailers. As soon as your performance was finished you had to clear out to make way for the next entourage of megastars . . . it was crazy. The press and the entire music industry had been buzzing about Live Aid and how it would change the world.

This was big, but then again, our entire year had been huge. We had released our album *Big Bam Boom* in the fall of 1984 and, as usual, hit the ground running—touring around the world with the biggest, most lavish stage production in our career and playing nearly one hundred shows.

The album was released and immediately produced a number one hit with "Out of Touch." It wasn't just a number one pop hit; it also charted in several other areas including the dance charts, contemporary charts, and even the R&B-singles chart. "Method of Modern Love" was another Top 10 hit. The album sold millions within a few weeks.

Earlier in the year, on January 28, we were in Los Angeles for the American Music Awards and won yet another Plexiglas plinth-style trophy, this time in the Favorite Duo or Group Pop/Rock category, besting Huey Lewis and the News and Van Halen. We also performed "Method of Modern Love" on the show. But it's what happened later that night, after the award show, that has become an event to remember.

We had been handed an exclusive invitation to attend an artists-only after-show get-together. So, ditching our manager and friends, we jumped in the limo and left the Shrine Auditorium. Our destination was the A&M Studios on La Brea to take part in a secret late-night recording session. The old studio complex had a unique charm and rich Hollywood history. Built by Charlie Chaplin in 1917, the tight maze of buildings and soundstages resembled a quaint English village, with cobblestone streets, a Tudor-mansion façade, and a series of colonial clapboard cottages. But on this night there were no movie stars, just a galaxy of rock stars. Unbeknownst to us, the recording process we were about to take part in had begun a week earlier, when a vocal guide version of the song we were about to sing had been created in LA at a studio owned by Kenny Rogers.

Gliding up to the studio entrance we were met and quickly escorted inside by a team of bodyguards. Any nonartists who did try to get in were either turned away or firmly advised to wait in the reception area. Producer Quincy Jones had posted a large sign at the door leading to the recording studio; it read: CHECK YOUR EGOS AT THE DOOR. It was a very cool and smart way of making sure that all of those who would enter that night were prepared to get with his program. No entourages or attitudes allowed. This was the night that the song "We Are the World" would be recorded, and it was an interesting experience to not only participate, but to be front and center as this once-in-a-lifetime music event came together.

THE RECORDING STUDIO had a large open floor, and tiers of narrow platforms had been constructed along the back wall in a wide half circle. Names were written in gaffer's tape on the floor so that each of the performers would know where to stand. My designated spot was in the middle of the group slightly to the left of center, smack in the middle of it all. Bob Dylan was off my right shoulder, and one row down, in front of me, was the great Ray Charles. I could have extended my arms and touched everyone from Willie Nelson and Diana Ross to Stevie Wonder and Smokey Robinson. Thinking back, it was a stroke of genius for Quincy Jones to keep the room free of handlers, managers, and agents. By doing so, he made sure all the artists naturally let down their guard, and a very open and friendly vibe began to spread among everyone . . . laughter and relaxed conversation filled the room as fluid groups of some of the world's biggest stars of the era socialized in a way that may never have happened before on this level. Someone circulated a two-page piece of sheet music, and I had the presence of mind to grab a black magic marker and walk around getting everyone to sign it. To this day it is one of my prize possessions, and it hangs in a place of honor on the wall of my studio. Finally, Michael Jackson and Lionel Richie (cowriters of the song) positioned themselves in front of the group, asking everyone to take their assigned places, and with a warm but brief "thank you and welcome," let it be known that it was time to get down to the work at hand. With a signal to the engineer in the control room, they had the prerecorded track started, and they sang together so that we all could hear the melody and the soaring, anthemlike group chorus. Soon the room was filled with the unforgettable sound of some of the greatest voices in the world singing together in unison and naturally breaking into spontaneous harmony. The effect was stirring and very moving. In an odd way it was somewhat like the ultimate high school chorus, except there were a couple too many chiefs and not enough Indians. I mean, despite Quincy's admonition to check all egos at the door, it seemed a few had snuck in anyway. After running the song down a few times, several of the big names started to take it upon themselves to get creative, offering up vocal and production suggestions. For a moment it started to feel like Michael, Lionel, and Quincy might be losing control of the situation, but then a voice boomed out and cut through the distracting chatter. "Hey y'all, shut up and listen to Michael and Lionel. It's their damn song, just sing it!" Ray Charles had heard enough, he spoke up forcefully, and that was all it took. The genius had restored order. Within minutes the big singalong chorus was in the can, and the soloists were organized into small groups around the microphones to record their individual lines. Then one by one we all drifted apart, back to the cosseting entourages anxiously waiting outside, jumped into our limos, and disappeared into the midnight darkness of the Los Angeles night.

Straight from this legendary session, we were back on the road, in Norman, Oklahoma, to kick off the second leg of the massive *Big Bam Boom* tour, playing arena after arena after sold-out arena. We wrapped up the North American part of the tour at the Nassau Coliseum on Long Island May 8, but there was one more show booked for May 23. After an extensive and long-overdue restoration, the Apollo Theater in Harlem was scheduled to reopen. Opening night was to be a benefit for the United Negro College Fund, and we were invited to perform. Anticipating this unique show, we reached out to two musical heroes from our past, Eddie Kendricks and David Ruffin from the Temptations. They had meant so much to us growing up, so we felt it would be amazing and a gesture of respect to have them join us at the Apollo.

First we reached out to Eddie Kendricks, the falsetto lead of the Temps who was gigging around in relative obscurity, playing here and there in Alabama. Then we tracked down David Ruffin, the voice of "My Girl" and "Ain't Too Proud To Beg" somewhere in the Detroit area. Neither of them was performing much at the time. A lot had changed since I met them that night at the Apollo back in '67. They were thrilled to hear from us and loved that we wanted to help resuscitate their careers. We brought them to New York City and got them rooms at the Mayflower Hotel off Columbus Circle. The Mayflower had a notorious reputation as a rock-and-roll party hotel, and our band, as well as many other assorted partners in debauchery, spent many a crazy night there doing all sorts of insane things. While Eddie was a gentle soul and quite reserved, David Ruffin jumped right in, hitting us up for extra rooms or some extra cash for his "cousins," who, like him, appeared and disappeared at all hours of the day or night. But when it came time for rehearsal at the theater, both Eddie and David were there . . . on time . . . ready to do what they do like nobody else.

The very first time we ran through the Temptations medley I knew it would be the highlight of the show: "Get Ready"/"The Way You Do The Things You Do"/"My Girl"/"Ain't Too Proud To Beg." After years of touring together our big '80s band was locked and loaded, plus we added a full horn section as well as an additional keyboard player. This would be a night to remember.

Amid all the chaos of getting everyone together one thing stands out in my mind: When it finally came time for us to start the music, David and Eddie struck their classic Temptation pose . . . ramrod straight, legs spread shoulder width apart, hands clasped behind their backs. No one asked them to do it, but the professional training and discipline drilled into them at Motown for all those years just kicked back in and they were set. We had planned on trying to re-create the crisp and precision dance steps that were one of the group's trademarks—the same choreography that I had emulated in front of my bedroom mirror when I was a kid. And now I was doing it . . . for real . . . on stage with them at the Apollo. It was a real trip to be actually realizing a teenage dream. The only thing wrong was the fact that Daryl, David, and Eddie were all tall and skinny, looking great, and I was this little guy dancing my ass off in the middle. But I couldn't have cared less, because it was a fantasy come true. On the night of the show, Eddie and David were resplendent in their slim black tuxes while Daryl and I wore our usual rock-and-soul duds. I can honestly say that for a long moment time stood still and I felt as though I was floating above my body, watching myself singing and dancing. I kept looking down at the front row, where Daryl and I had sat back in 1967, on that first night we'd ever really hung out in New York City. The night when he brought me there to see his friends the Temptations. I kept thinking to myself: *Almost twenty years ago, you were sitting right down there.*

Fortunately, we captured the performance for posterity, later releasing the album and tape cassette *Live At the Apollo*, and the Temptations medley became a Top 20 hit once again.

WHEN IT WAS OVER, sitting backstage in the midst of the after-show euphoria, Daryl and I decided to take a break from it all. There was no place to go but down at that point. Daryl Hall and John Oates had left nothing on the table. Nobody in the room could have known what was going through both our

Onstage with the Temptations at the Apollo Theater in New York, 1985. This remains one of the biggest thrills of my career. *(Courtesy John Oates)*

minds that night. An unspoken decision had been rendered. Some things are better left unsaid.

After the Apollo, we had a few loose ends to tie up. We did a quick run through Japan in June, followed by a big Fourth of July show at Liberty State Park, New Jersey, in front of about seventy thousand people. It was a benefit to restore the Lady Liberty statue, and we played with her in our view, on a perfect summer evening. We arrived by chopper from the West Side heliport. As we cruised just above the Hudson River, first we saw a crowd that looked like Lilliputians swarming around the base of the iconic symbol of liberty. Then the concert venue came into view just beyond Liberty Island, and the park was packed with fans as far as the eye could see. Once again the band, with Tom "T-Bone" Wolk, Charlie DeChant, Mickey Curry, and G.E. Smith was shit-hot, and once again we filmed and recorded the show, eventually re-leasing *The Liberty Concert* on the latest technology, called the video disc.

And then it was time for Live Aid.

Sitting backstage in that heat on a day when the world united, it hit me: None of the ninety thousand people in the stadium or the nearly two billion people watching on TV knew this was basically it for Hall and Oates . . . for now. But talk about going out in style. We were going to get up there, the last band to perform for the entire festival, play a few of our hits, and then invite Eddie and David to come up and reprise the Apollo medley. But that wasn't all. Mick Jagger had approached us about backing him up for the true finale of the show. We were happy to oblige. Similar to playing at the Apollo, this was yet another circle completing itself before my eyes. It took me back to 1974, when Mick came backstage after we had opened for Lou Reed at the Felt Forum in New York City. That was the signal to us that something was changing; Mick would not have been checking us out had we not piqued his musical interest. It was a turning point for us. You come offstage and and Mick Jagger is waiting in your dressing room. That meant something. And now, eleven years later, here he was asking us to back him up at the biggest concert in music history. So we worked up a few Stones songs and prepped a couple of duets for his surprise guest, the great Tina Turner.

Rehearsals were held at Studio Instrument Rentals on Forty-eighth Street . . . the same soundstage where we shot the "Private Eyes" video for MTV just a few years earlier. When Mick arrived he just got on with it . . . no small talk, no lollygagging about. He jumped up on the low stage and snatched the mic from the stand as we kicked into the set, which included the Stones classics "It's Only Rock 'n' Roll (But I Like It)" and "Miss You," along with a couple of Mick's new solo tunes and a cover of the Jacksons' song, "State of Shock." Even though there was no one in the room but us, Mick did his absolutely full-out arena routine. The famous chicken-wing-elbow moves, all lips and hips, as if there were thousands of screaming fans . . . it was impressive and about as real as it gets. I could tell that he really dug singing with our amazing band.

When we finally got on stage together at Live Aid his energy was exactly the same but even more jacked up, and when Tina strutted out from the wings in that black-leather miniskirt with legs up to heaven, well, the excitement level went off the scale. That is until Mick ripped her skirt off—then it was pure pandemonium. The world was watching. What a way to go out! Now this mega-event is just a few photographs and memories, but the glorious taste from the cases of Château Margaux that Mick sent to me and everyone else in the band still lingers.

And then, almost as soon as it had started, Live Aid was over. And for all intents and purposes, for the time being, so were we. A curtain had come down on Hall and Oates's first act, yet nobody knew it but us. We'd worked so hard, achieved so much, earned so much . . . it seemed like nothing could go wrong, and even though we never really kept track of it, just accepted Mottola's cash advances, we figured there had to be something big salted away for us. . . . Right?

Wall Street

Life finally slowed down a bit for me in the aftermath of all these mega-shows. The break in the action gave me a chance to spread my musical wings a bit. In 1987, I went to Australia to write songs with Iva Davies for his band, Icehouse. I'd always loved both touring and hanging out down under, so I was excited to be heading back down to Sydney. We came up with one called "Electric Blue," which actually went to number one in Australia and was a Top 10 hit in the United States. Shortly afterwards I produced an album for the Canadian band the Parachute Club, and sang on their Top 40 hit, "Love is Fire." It was a chance to reboot and step off the Hall-and-Oates freight train for a moment. Little did I know that this brief period would be the calm before the storm.

One day, out of the blue, I got a call from a guy named Sigmund Balaban. He was the accountant and financial advisor that our management company, Champion Entertainment, had used for years. Now that Tommy Mottola had moved on to greener pastures to become president of CBS and soon afterwards Sony Music, Sig and his Wall Street firm were still handling the accounting and investments of my personal finances. Although they had been representing me for many years, we rarely met in person, and I seldom spoke to the money men who kept the books and handled our taxes. Daryl and I were always isolated from all that. In a sense, the situation was not dissimilar to that of a dysfunctional family. We were the kids, encouraged to enjoy the wild, crazy, protracted-adolescence life of a rock star. You know . . . run around the world, get laid, bask in the spotlight, and buy a lot of shit. Let Daddy take care of the important stuff.

Right around the same time my wife, Nancy, and I had separated and she had moved to California to begin rebuilding her life. It was uncharted territory: no wife, no manager, no touring . . . I felt adrift and alone. It was something that I was not accustomed to.

So the surprising phone call from Sigmund Balaban certainly got my attention. He asked me if I might be available to come to a meeting at his downtown office, after business hours, as soon as possible. Considering that I had seldom talked or met with him over the years, the urgency of his request had me intrigued—and suspicious. Late in the afternoon on the appointed day I hopped in a cab and headed downtown. As I neared Wall Street an uneasy, ominous anticipation swept over me. Stepping out onto the empty sidewalk I paused for a moment before the entrance to a massive Wall Street tower of power, then reached for the oversize handle of the ornate and heavily wrought brass door. My footsteps echoed loudly on the black-marble floor as I crossed the vaulted lobby, empty now that the daytime masters of the universe had all gone home for the night. I stood alone listening to the muted hum of the rising elevator and when the door slid open, Sigmund Balaban was standing there waiting for me. He was a large man in his late sixties, swathed in a worn but well-tailored, traditionally styled pinstripe business suit. His ruddy round face, behind frameless wire-rimmed glasses presented an inscrutable countenance as he extended his hand and ushered me inside. I followed him into a wood-paneled conference room where five or six similarly dressed associates were seated silently around a long, polished, mahogany table. Balaban motioned toward an empty seat and with very little preamble got down to business. Speaking in a low monotone he began the proceedings by explaining that his firm no longer represented Tommy Mottola or Champion Entertainment. I, however, was technically still his client, and thus it was his responsibility to speak to me personally to review the status of my finances.

OK . . . now he really had my full attention.

He spoke but two words, "You're broke."

The consonants were bitter and there was no sugar on the vowels. My eyes swept the stone-faced men assembled around the table. I was dumbstruck and finally managed a feeble response. "Broke?"

That single word flashed through the synapses of my brain, then surged down into the pit of my stomach.

"In a way," he dispassionately continued. "You have lots of assets, but no money. We refer to it as 'land poor.'"

After selling eighty million records, touring the world for twenty years, one half of the biggest-selling duo in music history? *No fucking money?*

Over the next hour of this now officially catastrophic meeting, I tried my best to absorb the details and hard reality that was unfolding. Voices, numbers, dates, balances, and the irritating scrape of thickly stacked piles of papers being shuffled filled the room. I felt my brain shutting down sequentially as the grim accountants positioned around the table spat out incomprehensible sums with multiple zeroes into the thick boardroom air. I did my best to appear engaged and comprehending, but I was emotionally imploding, and by the end of the meeting it was as if my spirit had departed. I felt as though I were hovering, observing, detached and disconnected from the shell of skin and bones sitting in the chair. Physically still breathing but suffocating at the same time. How long the meeting lasted I couldn't tell you, but upon its conclusion, I managed to rise on unsteady legs and quietly make my way out of the office.

While waiting for the elevator to arrive, I felt the thick, padded arm of Sigmund Balaban fall heavily upon my shoulders. Then he solemnly spoke. "I realize that this must be quite a shock for you, but this just might very well be the best thing that's ever happened to you." I did not answer and, pardon

the mixed metaphor, but disguised within this parting slap in the face was
what I would later come to appreciate as the best kick in the ass I've ever gotten. Then the elevator door opened and I took the controlled drop down toward
the ground.

Stepping out onto the dark, deserted sidewalk, I stood for a moment, then
automatically raised my arm as a yellow cab pulled into view. "Two-ninety-
nine West Twelfth Street, please" I muttered weakly, collapsing onto the cold,
black-vinyl seat. Drained of emotion and weary of mind I surrendered to the
muted soundtrack of thumping tires over cobblestones while my half-open
eyes watched the filmic blur of city lights, streaked and distorted through the
dirty glaze of the cab window. As we rolled north on Hudson Street, suddenly,
somewhere in SoHo, I detected a tightness in my chest . . . an invisible grip
that quickly became a twisting, horrific knot. I was frozen in place and sweating. "This is it," I said to myself. "This is how it happens. . . ." Alone in the
backseat of a fucking cab. *Breathe, John, breathe!* Oh God, this fucking sucks.
While a dull thick ache radiated up into my neck and down my arms, a
strange and macabre thought raced through my mind: My dead body in the
backseat is really going to ruin this cabbie's day . . . on the bright side, I'd really
only be broke for less than an hour.

But the survival instinct is strong and I continued to concentrate on a medit-
ative breathing pattern, and within a few blocks the pain began to subside.
The cab came to a stop in front of my building. By then, considering that there
was a good probability I'd see the morning sun, I made it a point to count my
change very carefully while still leaving a karmic-ally-appropriate tip, exited
the cab, and headed up to my apartment on the fifteenth floor.

Unlocking the door and stepping inside I observed my surroundings with
a heightened awareness. I was enervated physically and emotionally. I had given
most of the furniture to my soon-to-be ex when she moved out. All that was
left was a bed and a TV. I stood in the hollow silence of the empty living room,
staring out of the south-facing windows at the World Trade Center towers. The
shifting reflections from the city lights below played like a zoetrope across the
bare white walls. Turning to my right, I found little comfort in the calm view

of the Hudson River as the reality of my situation began to clarify. I could fight, I could fold, I could say fuck it and end it. . . . The first choice so daunting, the second not in my DNA, and the third, though tempting, much too cowardly. My heart went toe-to-toe with my head. After a few long solitary moments, a serene acceptance settled over me and, as if guided by some unseen angel, I knew what I had to do.

I HAD A beautiful, old, 1830s Federal-style house with an indoor swimming pool in Connecticut, two apartments in New York City, a condo in Aspen, an airplane, a collection of antique classic cars, and maybe fifty bucks in my wallet.

I knew that I needed to start selling stuff, fast, so that I could pay my ongoing bills and keep this soon-to-be-sham of an opulent lifestyle afloat. And to make things more complicated, I was headed toward a divorce. I had amassed a lot of things, and now I was going to have to spark a big-time fire sale to generate enough money to settle with my soon-to-be ex-wife and keep up with my skyrocketing bills. This was an everything-must-go! moment. I had not seen it coming. Not even close. I was totally blindsided. I went to work.

Financial House of Cards

Oh, to have had the wisdom way back when. Back in 1972, it had been all about the sweets that followed the first holiday dinner at Tommy and Lisa Mottola's little apartment in New Rochelle, New York. Flan was on the table, but the real dessert, as you may recall, was deep inside the pockets of the green, oversized Eddie Bauer parkas. *That cash.* Unbeknownst to me then, it would become a portent of things to come. In fact, every Christmas thereafter was a clue. The gifts became more elaborate in concert with our success. To be clear, I'm not saying Tommy or his lawyer ever took anything from our share of the earnings. I just wish they'd warned us that the highlife we were living would have financial consequences. We weren't cheated; we were just seduced.

When Daryl and I escaped from Philadelphia and the tentacles of John Madara into the waiting arms of Tommy Mottola, it was agreed that this new relationship would be a three-way partnership. The concept was to "whack it up"—New York street slang for divide something evenly. There would be no commissions paid or taken.

That sounded like a righteous way of doing business to a '60s kid like me.

Right on, brother! A beautiful thing . . . a manager with every incentive to kick ass for his artist, and a couple of singer/songwriters who cared only for the music . . . and tantalized when poor palms hit pockets of cash . . . suffice it to say, appetites had been well and truly whetted.

Now before we get too deep into details, let's take a look at some word substitutions for *ignorant*: ill-informed, unfamiliar, oblivious, unaware, inexperienced . . . on and on we could continue, but why? Tomes have been written outlining the sad and calamitous dealings between the business side of music and the artists without whom there would be no business. What will follow is just another tale of the tail that wagged the dog. My own philosophical musings on personal responsibility will have to wait for another more comprehensive forum. For now, allow me to unpack a strategy that was at once brilliantly creative, ballsy, and innovative, while at the same time, at least in my opinion, ultimately disastrous from both a fiscal and moral standpoint.

But before we get to that, first a little bit of Music Business 101: The only way an artist can get instant financial gratification is to play live shows and collect the money then and there. All other potential income streams, such as royalties generated from record sales or songwriting, are paid out over a protracted period of time, and then only after various parties, such as record labels, agents, managers, and lawyers, in alliance with their faithful foot soldiers, their highly creative accounting departments, get their share off the top. (Just another reason to use the term *gross*.) But wait . . . now it's time to pay the vig. Tally up the cost of radio promotion, marketing, videos, and physical manufacturing—then whatever is left over (the net . . . named appropriately for the thing that catches you before you hit the ground) finally filters down the food chain to the artists, who reside in that stardom-infected utopia, blissfully thankful to spend their lifeblood digging deep down in the mine of creativity to discover that precious gold and platinum that funds the machine.

And thus it began. In the simplest terms, the concept was: Why wait for royalties that trickle in over the years? Get the money up front! Let the record companies and publishers wait for it. Cash in hand, right now . . . hell yeah!

A little allegory to make a point:

Imagine a hunter (manager) and his experienced guide (lawyer) heading off into the jungle (music business) preparing to bag some big game (money). They carefully plan their expedition (the pitch) and pack plenty of ammunition (hype, previous record sales, the promise of future hits). Finally, alone in the heart of the beast (the record company offices), they bravely face their quarry (the president of the label). With all their firepower cocked, locked, and loaded, they close in. The stalking technique varies based on many factors, i.e. how well they know their prey, whether they've hunted these grounds in the past, and the power of their ammunition.

Sounds like a great plan right? Well sort of . . . first of all, record companies don't just give away large lump sums without demanding some sort of collateral. It's not much different than going to the bank for a loan or a mortgage. The music business, however, unlike a conventional lending institution, bets the house on success and insures their investment by ownership in the present *and* the future. So they stack the deck in their favor before sitting down at the game, armed with a crap-table-gambler's mentality and backed by the muscle of cold, hard numbers.

So now with a Cliff's Notes knowledge of the game . . . back to our story.

The first test of Mottola's nascent concept came when he entered into negotiations with RCA records on our behalf while we were still signed to Atlantic records. Our *War Babies* album was not commercially successful, and hiring Todd Rundgren to produce the record was a bit of a snub to the Atlantic family. That was all the leverage Tommy needed. He negotiated a release from Atlantic and a rather large cash advance from our new label, RCA. It was a bold and astute business move. So once his hypothesis—get the cash up front, let them wait to get paid—had proven viable, the next deal would be at the high-stakes table. Of course, Daryl and I had to hold up our end of the deal . . . write and record hit records. Then, in 1975, enter the surprise chart-topping success of "Sara Smile," followed by "Rich Girl" and the rerelease of "She's Gone," and it was hunting season once again.

Have you ever seen a recording contract? Well, picture thick sheaves of legal paper with hundreds of pages, thousands of words defining byzantine details, much of it virtually incomprehensible to anyone but a specialized music attorney, let alone an ignorant (there's that word again) musician. All this legalese mumbo jumbo does is describe the rules of the relationship between the artist and the record label. Although many of today's more savvy and knowledgeable artists make it a point to understand what they are agreeing to, back in the day, guys like us just dutifully put pen to paper. "Sign on the line, sign on the line . . . on the line." Those words are from our '70s song "Gino (the Manager)" and speak for themselves:

> *You've got Sicilian imagination*
> *Second generation*
> *And a long way from the family crime*
> *But you've got your own way*
> *Sign on the line, sign on the line, on the line*
>
> *You're a patent leather lover*
> *With your Gucci-Pucci pointed shoes*
> *And you're swearing on your mother*
> *That, "All this could be yours"*
> *Sign on the line, sign on the line, on the line*
>
> *Gino said*
> *"Remember hard work means something*
> *Live fast, die laughing*
> *No hurt in asking*
> *Nothing for nothing"*
>
> *You've got contractual agitation*
> *Transcendental meditation works fine*
> *But now you're paying off the guru*
> *Get to heaven on time*
> *Sign on the line, sign on the line, on the line*

Remember this
Remember hard work means something
Live fast, die laughing
No hurt in asking
Nothing for nothing

You couldn't live without little Gino, no
That's what he tells me, little Gino, no
You couldn't live without little Gino, no
That's what he tells me, little Gino, no no

Gino no no no no no no no no no no
No no no no no no no no no no no no
No no no no no no no no no no no no!

So now with a few hit records for extra clout, Tommy was ready for the next big hit of his own, but this time he was going in with a sidekick: the brilliant, street-smart deal maker and coarsely charming attorney, Allen Grubman. Back in those days and even now, the offices of many of the major labels had revolving doors. Each newly installed company honcho feeling their way into their new job was like a lamb to the slaughter for Tommy and Allen. All the while Daryl and I were writing, recording, touring, and getting periodic messages about the next big advance that was just around the corner. Where was all this money coming from?

This however was not the question we should have been asking. The question should have been: Just what were we giving up to get these huge lump sums in advance? Hmm . . . didn't we just get a big check? Sure, I'd like to buy a really expensive red Porsche Turbo. One of the basic tenets that I learned very early on in the music business was to not say *no*. Let's just keep it rolling while it's rolling.

So while we were bouncing all over the country recording and touring, back in New York City, the three-way partnership had earned enough for Mottola

to move from his little office on Fifty-fifth Street over to a much more impressive suite of offices formerly occupied by Tony Orlando on Fifty-seventh Street
between Sixth and Seventh Avenues. With high ceilings and big, arched, leaded-
glass windows, the new space was christened Champion Entertainment. Tommy's personal office was decorated in an Eddie Bauer-wet-dream theme. Picture
a midtown-Manhattan hunting lodge, replete with paintings of game birds,
white-tailed deer, and, mounted high on the wall, overlooking everything with
a baleful stare, was a giant buffalo head that Daryl and I found for him somewhere in Texas.

Of course, the new office required a bigger staff. Among them the enigmatic numbers man, Al Smith. His big body was crunched into a tiny back
cubicle where he spent endless hours surrounded by a jumble of paperwork piled
on his desk and overflowing from file cabinets. When I did pop into the office
it was usually not to discuss business, and on the odd occasion when I might
have raised a question or two, the conversations were always somehow deflected
by something to do with sex or, even more importantly, what time we were
going for Italian food at Joe's Restaurant down in the Village. Big office, big
overhead . . . just keep working boys.

But let us not let the music distract us from our story. . . . To keep the home
fires burning during this late-'70s lean period, as I mentioned earlier, Mottola
found us a tour sponsorship with Carefree sugarless gum. It was a contest for
high schools around the country. The school that collected the most Carefree
gum wrappers got us to play a show in their gym. Sounds crazy? You have no
idea. It was a good payday, but I was too busy enjoying the adulation to pay
attention. At this point there must have been some wolves at the door of
the high-priced Champion Entertainment offices, and fortunately for the
partnership, Daryl and I began producing ourselves, and presto! "Kiss On My
List," You've Lost That Lovin' Feeling," and "You Make My Dreams" rocket
to the top of the charts. Just in time . . . for another big-dollar Dumpster dive
into the RCA money bin.

One scene that is telling and worth describing in detail has to do with a
particular occasion, when Mottola and Grubman came down to Daryl's apart-

ment so that we could sign yet another thick sheaf of paperwork. While the four of us sat around the living room bullshitting, cackling away in the background were Daryl's two colorful military macaws. Their names were Ralph and Alice, named after the two stars of Daryl's favorite TV show, *The Honeymooners*. Allen Grubman's attention was drawn to the big birds in the back of the living room. Out of nowhere he made an acerbic comment about one of the other big-time artists that his firm represented and said, "Yeah he used to have parrots too. Now that he ain't got no hits, he's got parakeets!" I always remember that comment when I look up on my shelf at home at a check for a million dollars that has been preserved forever, encased in Plexiglas to commemorate the occasion.

WHATEVER WE WERE agreeing to that day when we signed those papers, I'll never know. I only wish I'd paid more attention and asked more questions but I didn't. Totally on me. What we got, what we gave up . . . who knows? I never handled money, never had a checkbook, never looked at a balance sheet. If I wanted something, I just bought it. A really sweet fifteenth-floor two-bedroom corner apartment on Greenwich Village's Abington Square, with a fireplace and gorgeous views. Then I bought the one next door. A lovely restored 1830s Federal-style house in Bridgewater, Connecticut, on some beautiful land, with drystone walls and a converted barn with an indoor swimming pool? Sold.

Then came the cars:

A turquoise and white 1955 Chevy Bel Air convertible (I bought it on the way to a sound check in Toledo Ohio); a 1967 red Jaguar XKE (my midlife-crisis ride); a silver-blue 1967 Austin-Healey 3000 (a gift for my wife's birthday); a pearl-white custom-built 1984 Porsche Carrera (I special ordered it from the factory in Stuttgart while on a European tour); and a silver 1956 Porsche Speedster (the only car in the bunch I wish I still had). Then there was an industrial garage in a nearby town where I stored them. Oh, then an airplane . . . actually two. First, a Piper Dakota, eventually graduating up to a beautiful Beechcraft A36 Bonanza. The addiction to available cash was like a drug, very easy to get hooked on and not so easy to kick. In the mid-'80s I purchased a small two-bedroom condo right outside of Aspen, Colorado, which would become a sanctuary and a womb of sorts, from which I would become reborn.

Oh, I'm getting ahead of myself again . . . back to the money.

Sounds like a dream come true . . . but dreams can turn into nightmares. During our ten years at RCA, we went through four company presidents. Mottola and Grubman worked them all. Whack it up . . . whack it up . . . whack it up. . . . More, more, more. Our hits gave them the clout to support their increasingly outrageous demands. They actually had the balls and chutzpah to ask the label to sweeten one particular deal by, "throwing in a couple of red fire trucks for the boys"—a euphemism for having them buy Daryl and me two red Rolls-Royce Corniche convertibles. The automobiles never appeared but most likely the fallback position was for the label to add a few more zeroes to the next check. Just a hunch.

I learned later that back in 1983 Mottola had devised yet another plan to squeeze even more upfront cash from yet another record company. Although at that time we were still signed to RCA records, an uncomfortable, pseudo-social business dinner was arranged at a quiet little downtown Italian restaurant.

Clive Davis was the guest of honor—or more accurately the fatted calf—that evening.

Always impeccably well dressed, the urbane music-business legend sat on the other side of the table from Daryl, Tommy, and me. We didn't discuss business that night but there was a first-date feel to the conversation and not much of an effort to disguise the subtext of why we were dining together. The real deal, as usual, would be conducted without either Daryl or my participation, as we just all but ignored those aspects of our career. Shortly afterwards Tommy was excited to tell us that he had succeeded in crafting a highly unusual arrangement by which we would sign to Clive's Arista record company prior to the end of our RCA contract. Meaning that once we had satisfied our commitment to RCA we would automatically move our indentured-servantlike asses over to the Arista label.

The bottom line of this clever but seductive plan was that Arista would hand over yet another big wad of cash up front . . . the insatiable black hole of debt to the labels growing darker and deeper.

As usual I didn't pay much attention because the waves of the big '80s were rolling in like an epic North Shore swell, and it was all about the right-now ride—not the future. If only . . .

The Fourth Season

BACK TOGETHER AGAIN
THE 1990s

"Guys Like You"

'**ve seen guys** like you. I've seen lots of guys like you."

These words floated, in a professorial, calm, resonant baritone, across the comfortably furnished Upper West Side psychiatrist's office. I was back . . . this time by my own volition, settling down into a well-worn, soft-leather recliner in the very same office that just a few months earlier was the setting for weeks of couples therapy. Now it was just me and the shrink. Can't recall how she found him, but my wife, Nancy, and I had been going through the issues that led to our separation and eventual divorce. My fault . . . blame and shame on me. I should have never been married in the '80s. She was a successful model and I was running around the world like I was single. She wanted to start a family and I wasn't ready.

Meanwhile, going on in the background of my domestic life, Tommy Mottola had accepted a big-time position at CBS Records, taking over from Walter Yetnikoff, for all intents and purposes abandoning the rudderless Hall and Oates ship. . . . Oh, and then there was my Wall Street comeuppance. To describe this time as tumultuous would be an understatement.

The couples therapy sessions would not be a panacea for our marriage.

Shortly after the divorce was finalized Nancy became pregnant by a new boy-friend, and I was truly happy for her. At the same time, the meeting down on Wall Street wore heavily on me. I was mentally and emotionally adrift; it was a feeling that I was totally unaccustomed to. I needed help and at least had enough common sense to know that drugs and alcohol were not the answer. Deep down inside I knew that I had not been 100 percent forthright during the sessions with my now-former wife and with no one else to turn to, I called that very same doctor and made an appointment.

He had impressed me as a man of intelligence and experience during the sessions with Nancy, but I was back this time seeking a deeper truth. He wasted no time and pulled no punches. With a welcoming nod and a knowing expression he began, "I had a feeling you might come back. . . . I see guys like you all the time," he said. "You had all the money and everything you could ever want. You might see yourself as special, but you are not unique. There are lots of you. And guess what usually happens? You run around with young girls or hookers looking for whatever else you need to take the pain away, only it doesn't go away . . . it only increases, and time goes by, and before you know it you're mired in a miserable life of your own creation. Because guys like you often never learn the lessons about what got you there in the first place. Do you want to be one of those guys? I'm happy to take your money and we can talk in circles and generalities, or are you ready to face the truth of who you have become and who you want to be? You have a chance to reinvent yourself. But first you have to confront the truth of who you have been and what you really want the rest of your life to be like."

I'll admit, I was always one of those guys that thought therapy was for every-one else; the untogether folks who couldn't figure it out for themselves . . . bullshit and hot air. And although I've only returned to it briefly over the years, I'll never regret one moment. Because in those few months, working with him several times a week, I began to reclaim myself. I began to see that I had let too many things get away from me in life. I learned that I had very little to show for all I had worked for.

I needed to make lots of changes.

He asked me to tell him about my dreams, but I couldn't because I seldom remembered them. He suggested I begin keeping a dream journal. I was used to keeping a daily journal about my life, but nothing like this. I began keeping a small notepad by my bedside and little by little, dollops of nocturnal impressions filled the pages.

As the sessions progressed, I really began to look forward to our meetings, which over time became more and more intriguing as the revealing process unfolded. The doctor and I only looked back to move forward and that appealed to me. Soon we embarked on a set of visualization exercises whereby he guided me through techniques that would allow me to envision myself in an imaginary world of my own creation. The new-and-improved future world where I wanted to live my life. That's what he would tell me over and over. "You have to think about the kind of existence that you want. You have to imagine it and believe that it can be real. You have to put yourself in the ultimate positive setting. Build that space in your mind and then once you do, we'll talk more. We'll get to the next step."

One of the first revelations that emerged from this process was that I needed to leave New York City, both physically and psychically. Even though I was born there and my personal and professional career was intrinsically woven into the city's culture, it was time to move on, that chapter had ended. I needed to redefine myself outside of my relationship with Daryl, remove myself from the tethers of the crumbling Hall and Oates business network and all the people involved in it.

My days were spent in solitary introspection interrupted only by hours on the phone, aggressively trying to sell everything so that I could generate enough cash and, more importantly, rid myself of extraneous remnants of my soon-to-be-former lifestyle. The cars and the airplane were the first to go. (At the risk of repeating myself, damn I wish I had kept that 1956 silver Porsche Speedster—car nuts will know what I'm talking about.) The apartments in New York were next, and finally the house in Connecticut. I still had the tiny condo in Aspen, and that's where I was headed.

It was both a sad and exhilarating time. I walked the streets of New York day and night and began to see details that I had never noticed before. People looked different to me. Men's faces appeared more like masks, their clothing somehow costumelike, a failed attempt to convince the world of who or what they wanted to be. As women approached, their physical flaws stood out in grim relief. Makeup and fashion couldn't disguise their baser human qualities. Females no longer appeared as potential objects of desire, they were suddenly all too real and it made me sad, surprised, and sexually uninterested. It was as though a veil had been lifted from my eyes. With each step, emotions and memories surged through me, rising and falling like October leaves on the wind. For the first time in my life I wanted for nothing but I needed everything . . . there was no plan, no deadline, no responsibility other than tomorrow.

Even though I was alone, I craved solitude. As the visualization exercises continued, a recurring scene coalesced in my imagination. Central to the image was a solidly simple rustic log cabin with a front porch, tucked away in a beautiful, remote valley surrounded by deep-green woods and rugged, craggy mountains. As if I were floating above, I could see myself sitting quietly on that porch. By my side was a trusting and faithful dog with a thick brown-and-black coat. That was the vision. That's where I wanted to be. Sounds like a cliché right?

Back in the therapist's office, after having revealed my newly imagined physical future, he told me that I needed to begin to mentally rid myself of all the negative things that were chaining me to my old life. That it was time to take ownership of personal wrongs that I may have inflicted on the people around me and systematically begin to eliminate all of the people that had taken advantage of me, or at least had not had my back. Nameless and familiar faces from a world I would leave behind began to appear in my dreams. They would materialize in the distance, approaching in solemn procession down a narrow red-dirt path that led them to pass by, directly in front of my imaginary cabin. I'd observe them walk by silently, then watch them walk away, growing smaller in size and significance until they finally disappeared into the distance. It was a very cathartic exercise, and at times very intense. This was a start. It was getting me back on a path where I could be healthier, both mentally and physically. Small steps with a bigger purpose . . . to reinvent myself and leave behind the protracted-adolescence pop-star life that I had been living. I didn't have a lot, but if I was smart, I'd have just enough to start all over again.

Eventually, during this time, Daryl and I got back together after our self-imposed hiatus. We released an unfocused album called *Ooh Yeah!*; my head and my heart were not into it. We toured and then began crafting our next album, which would signal a true change and set a course for the future of our partnership and our music. It would be called *Change of Season*. What a perfect theme for where I was in my life. I wrote the title song with my friend, keyboard player Bob Mayo. The lyrics still resonate for me today.

Oh I need a change of season
Oh I need a little springtime in the fall
Oh I could use a change of season
Can't stop thinking about it baby
And I'm sick about it yeah

Oh I've been trying to fight this feeling
I know I know just one little brick
Gonna break the wall
Oh I might find a change of season
Will bring a freeze in summer baby
Bring a freeze in summer yeah

Seasons change people change
But you can't hold back the clock
Cause time won't stop you and me
And the world keeps spinning round
Round and round

Feels like time for a change of season
It's a crime you know that it's a crime
That I should feel this way at all

I . . . can't even find a reason
What you think about it baby
What you think about it yeah

There were other songs on the album that felt like a complete soundtrack to my life. Daryl and I covered the old Mel and Tim soul chestnut, "Starting All Over Again." It completely captured the spirit of our escape from the '80s, and for me, it was another glimpse toward my personal path out of the darkness. We toured with the album, and it was an entirely different world. We were no longer MTV pop stars, but rather veteran artists who were just beginning to start doing things on their own terms. The stage, as usual, the comfort zone. A velvet, heavily draped swag of curtain framing a hand-painted scrim of an impressionistic Maxfield Parrish-style woodland scene. The setting was acoustically cozy and warm: floor lamps, candelabras, and deep-burgundy Persian carpets. Gone was the bombast. We sat there and deconstructed both new songs and old with a great band: T-Bone Wolk on guitar, Bob Mayo on keyboards, Mike Braun on drums, Charlie DeChant on sax, Kasim Sulton on bass, as well as a small string section featuring Lisa Haney on cello and Eileen Ivers on violin. It was an early approach to what became known as unplugged concerts. Stupid name . . . who cares if you have plugs or not? Anyway, it stands out in my mind as one of our most satisfying, and musical tours.

I was growing up and we were playing our music on our own terms. That tour showed people that when we stripped down and simplified, our songs held up in ways nobody had ever imagined.

The Mustache

Our monstrous fame may have faded in the late 1980s in the United States, but we were still big stars in Japan. Like many American artists, we had always been embraced in Asia. Strangely, as our profile in the United States diminished in the late '80s, we seemed to get even bigger in Asia. That's why when Yoko Ono planned a benefit in honor of her late husband, John Lennon, in the winter of 1990; we were invited to close the two sold-out shows in Tokyo.

It was a really interesting bill of artists, including Dave Edmunds, Linda Ronstadt, a young Lenny Kravitz, and even jazz legend Miles Davis.

WE WERE FLYING back to America the day after the concerts, and there was really nothing there for me once I got back. No shows were planned, nor any recording. I would simply be picking up where I left off in terms of rebuilding my life. I was still seriously adrift, both personally and professionally. Around that same time my friend Billy Curry had begun immersing himself in various esoteric Native American practices, such as sweat lodges and vision quests, as methods of exploring philosophies and techniques that might lead to revelations about our place and purpose in the universe. All of these things piqued my interest.

I decided it was time for me to make my own personal change, but I needed a catalyst to start the reaction that might help transport me toward the next chapter of my life. It happened in my Tokyo hotel room in the middle of the night after the final show.

Gazing into the bathroom mirror, I felt like something was very wrong with my face. I stared at myself longer. Then I realized what it was:

The mustache.

That may sound silly and insignificant, but no one will ever understand how much that mustache affected my life. It was so much a part of who I had become. There were articles written about it, comedy sketches, an animated TV series, and to this day there is a Facebook page called "John Oates' Mustache." It came to represent all the swarthy and hirsute excesses of the 1980s. And it also represented me. Suddenly, I resented it.

And so, there in a Tokyo hotel room, it took but a few minutes to shed my past.

Down the drain it disappeared. With a few swipes of the blade the albatross was gone. It felt like a ritualistic cleansing.

When I arrived at the airport the following day, Daryl was the first one to notice.

"What the fuck did you do?" he blurted out, half laughing in bemused surprise.

"It's just hair, man," I replied, trying to play down the significance. For twenty-five years, that mustache and my face were one and the same. Most people who knew me had never seen me without it.

Then out of the corner of my eye I noticed Miles Davis, who was also heading home on the same flight, gliding my way. Silently, he brought his face close to mine, within about six inches. He studied me, turning his head one way and then another. After a long uncomfortable moment, never unlocking his penetrating bloodshot eyes from mine, he cocked his head curiously. Then, ever so slowly, a thin smile crept across his lips. He drew a bladelike finger across his upper lip, tracing a line where the mustache would have been. And with a mischievous smile he said in his slow-burn growl, "Now the lovin' is gonna be better!" Then he turned to Daryl and said, "When I go to the hairdresser I tell him I want my hair to look just like Daryl's . . . check it out."

That broke the tension. I cracked up and settled in for the long flight back to America.

Symbolic though it may have been, that simple gesture of shaving did mark a huge change in my life. It didn't just give me a new face. It gave me a new outlook. I had cut loose the tether of that 1980s monkey that had been riding on my back. Once I got home, little by little, a new John Oates started experiencing things differently.

How profound a moment was this for me? I think it finally hit me years later, when I was asked to write a foreword for a book by Jon Chattman and Rich Tarantino titled: *Sweet 'Stache: 50 Badass Mustaches and the Faces Who Sport Them.* When I sat down to write, I approached the mustache issue from a bittersweet, nostalgic perspective; enough time had passed and I finally understood. My fingers flew.

I couldn't wait to grow a mustache. I stopped shaving my upper lip the day I graduated from high school. By the time I was ready to enter college the following September, I had a sparse growth of dark hair sprouting due south of my nostrils. Though I cannot recall the exact date, I can never forget the deep-seated motivation for this tonsorial compulsion. On the surface, I am sure it was somewhat inspired by the desire to look older and more mature. . . . But if I had to delve, it was probably more driven by the fact that I always hated my upper lip and the way I looked when I smiled.

In fact, having a mustache and never smiling became a permanent component of my persona through the quaintly self-important decade of the '70s. Enter the big '80s and, symbolic of the zeitgeist of the era, my facial hair grew denser and more imposing, and like the supernova that was my career, the

'stache seemed to explode from my face, luminous and larger than life itself . . .
But still no smile.

Now in retrospect, I can see that my personality and my mustache had
become intrinsically linked. That dark swath of hair became my living logo.
As I begat the 'stache, the mustache became me, symbolically thrusting forward
from its prominence in the center of my countenance. A flying buttress of
follicles projecting my power and personality out to the world that fell before
it. More than a hairstyle or a beard, the mighty mustache became somehow
much more than a mere personal grooming choice. . . . Moreover, it conveyed
a subtly threatening and unyielding masculine image, complex in its message
and undeniable in its statement.

So for over two decades I bore that albatross noir through the protracted
adolescence known as pop stardom. From every angle, in every photograph,
bopping through every silly '80s MTV moment, my mustache became my
marquee, until I could not distinguish between it and me. Then I
changed. . . .

In 1990, there occurred a life-altering convergence of circumstances,
dusted with a sprinkling of fate, which led to a quantum collapse of many
close relationships, both business and personal. The resulting midlife revelation
finally shook me from my childlike stupor, and one night, bathed in the light of
where my future might lead me . . . I stared at a mustache on a stranger's face
reflected in the mirror of a Tokyo hotel room. Then, at that moment, with total
commitment and trembling hand, I knew what I must do. . . . The 'stache
had to go. The act itself, the stroke of the blade, was surprisingly simple, but as
the shaving continued, the cutting began to take on a ritualistic gravitas. . . .
For as the hair fell away, from the chrysalis emerged a man.

No longer possessed by the power of the 'stache, I was reborn, wriggled out
from under the skin of that mustachioed character, and for the first time in
so many years . . . I began to smile.

And I'm still smiling as I write this right now.

Aspen Return

And little did I know then that Aspen was the place that would someday help save my life . . . I was born in New York. But one day, I would be reborn in Colorado.

The *Change of Season* tour was a long one, about a solid year on the road, traveling all over the world, and ending November 17, 1991.

After what felt like an eternity the final show ended in Las Vegas with a band and crew party in one of our "Chez" rooms (a suite we always kept for guests and late-night after-show carousing). It was a rare occasion to have the entire entourage together in one place. I dressed up my personality with a celebratory flair, but hidden in my heart and head was a pending finality I could not reveal. My eyes scanned the faces of so many longtime musical partners and dedicated road warriors, each of them with plans for their own tomorrows and beyond. For some it was the anticipation of reuniting with loved ones, or perhaps the trepidation of lining up another gig to keep bread on the table at home. I, however, felt poised on the precipice of the unknown.

Standing on the balcony of that high-rise suite overlooking the garish casino cathedrals and dazzling lights of the Vegas Strip, I felt the urge to confess silently into the desert night. Accepting that my addiction to the road would never end, but knowing I had to kick the habit and experience life without the rush and suspended responsibility that it offered.

The following morning I flew from Vegas to Salt Lake City to take part in a celebrity ski race at Beaver Creek resort. The charity event paired Hollywood stars from film and TV with current and former Olympic and World Cup skiers by day, followed by fancy cocktail and dinner parties by night. Although the casual competition was fun, I felt very disconnected from the beautiful people and glamorous evening activities. After the event I flew straight to Aspen.

It was late November 1990, the traditional start of the ski season in the Rockies. The plan was to leave the East Coast behind and settle into my little condo just outside of town. I had bought it a few years earlier on the recommendation of my Greenwich Village neighbor Alan, and would use it here and there for brief ski trips. Prior to my buying the condo, Alan graciously offered to let me stay in his quaint log cabin at the end of a quiet mountain road a few miles west of Aspen, in the village of Woody Creek, a rural area that could be described as a bohemian enclave, a world unto itself, removed yet convenient to the world-famous resort town. Musicians like Don Henley from the Eagles; Jimmy Ibbotson from the Nitty Gritty Dirt Band; the actor Don Johnson; world-renown broadcaster and legendary Olympic ski coach Bob Beattie; and its most notorious resident superstar, gonzo journalist Hunter S. Thompson, all lived within spitting distance. In a way it felt very much like Greenwich Village did to Manhattan, and I felt right at home. Little by little I made friends and became more familiar with the Roaring Fork Valley and its mountain culture.

This time things were different; this was not just a holiday. This time I planned to settle in and check out for a while. I needed to mentally and emotionally sidestep the sad memories of life, love, and business back East. I just wanted to ski, breathe the high-altitude air, experience a different lifestyle, and let each day unfold as it would.

Shortly after I arrived in Aspen, my buddy Russ Klein, a hot-shit skier from Connecticut, had arrived in town to do a photo shoot for *Ski* magazine. To celebrate the start of the season, the magazine was throwing a party at one of the local nightspots and Russ invited me to come along. I was not in a party mood, but I reluctantly pulled it together and showed up. The folks in Aspen have a long-standing reputation for playing hard during the day and playing even harder into the night. It was especially true in the '80s and still is today. The bar was rocking; the club was packed with hot ski "Bettys" and high energy. I made my best halfhearted attempt at being social but spent most of the evening smothered in melancholy, sulking in a corner, trying to blend into the wallpaper. My friend Russ was a bit of a ladies' man and was soon holding court at the end of the bar. At one point during the evening he pointed out a petite young gal with long, dark, curly hair cascading over her shoulders. He introduced us, mentioning that she was one of the gals from the photo shoot. She was not a tall, rail-thin model type, but she was absolutely beautiful. I could tell he was more than a little bit interested in her and I could see why, as she flitted about dancing, socializing, and reveling in being the center of attention.

Clearly not in the mood to party, I left the club early. Stepping outside into the cold night, I extended my upturned hand, and from the darkness fell one exquisite snowflake of complex and unique perfection. In the years to come there would be so many millions more, but none exactly like this one.

My friend Russ left town and headed back East. The early season euphoria that accompanied the opening of the ski resort eased back into the few quiet weeks prior to the annual Christmas holiday onslaught of tourists. I didn't have a car. I took the bus and bought a mountain bike fitted with a basket, ski rack, and studded tires. Every morning I'd be one of the first on the mountain when the lifts opened. I was obsessed with improving and developing my alpine-skiing skills. Each day was a new challenge, and by late afternoon I'd revel in the exhaustion and exhilaration of the experience. I began to recognize the locals as they whooped and hollered, schussing effortlessly over the moguls and through the fresh powder snow. I tried to follow them, memorizing the hidden traverses through the pine trees that led to their secret stashes of virgin snow. I tried to tag along with world-class skiers like Andy Mill, who would kindly pause for a moment to offer advice before disappearing in a whoosh of white, cold, smoke. I quickly learned there are no friends on a powder day.

Inner Athlete

think I'm an athlete at heart, always in search of the next opportunity to challenge another competitor, whether it be man or Mother Nature herself.

IN THE 1980s, I got into tennis. Really got into it . . . and became a decent player. Because of what I had achieved as a musician, I was warmly welcomed into the whole celebrity-tennis-tournaments-and-club-playing thing. Name-drop time (ladies first): Chris Evert, Martina Navratilova, Mary Carillo, Pam Shriver, Andrea Jaeger; (guys): Matts Wilander, John McEnroe, Jimmy Connors, Björn Borg, Vitas Gerulaitis, Ivan Lendl . . . I actually got to hit and play on the courts with these legends. (Even though I always had the sense that, for them, it was like playing with a child, no matter how well I hit the ball.) I got to live every tennis fan/junkie's dream! I treated it like I did music and everything else: Study, practice, repeat. Master to the best of my own ability. (I finally regretfully gave up the game when my shoulders and wrists started hurting and it began to affect my guitar playing.)

Later in the '80s I bought my first mountain bike and rode a lot in

Next to music, another of my great passions. *(Courtesy John Oates)*

Connecticut and, later, out in Colorado. I loved climbing tight switchbacks deep in the forest and hooting and hollering through wildflower-filled meadows, flowing on board the gravity roller coaster over miles of undulating single track. Most rides were purely recreational, but one unforgettable trip involved an epic ride through the Swan Valley in Montana. In an attempt to draw attention to less-than-responsible stewardship of our national forests, I took part in an event organized by my friend Bill Curry, called the "Ride for the Wild Rockies." With TV and print journalists in tow, we pedaled for a hundred miles in an attempt to expose the damage that the lumber industry's clear-cutting practices were having on America's national forests. Gary Fisher, one of the pioneers of mountain biking, built custom titanium bikes for the Grateful Dead's Bob Weir and me for the trip. We rode by day and sat around the campfire by night engaging in serious and provocative conversations as well as some light jamming with acoustic guitars. One night after finishing a song, I recall Weir saying to me, "The trouble with you, Oates, is that you think too much." He just may have been right.

Meeting Weir on that trip led to an invitation for Daryl and me to join the Grateful Dead at Madison Square Garden for a concert to "Save the Rain Forest." That afternoon at sound check before the show, I arrived to find myself set up right next to the legendary guitarist Jerry Garcia. During a quiet moment between songs, I casually attempted to make some small talk with him. I asked, "Hey, Jerry, what songs do you think you guys will play tonight?" He looked at me blankly through those wire-rim glasses and hissed, "This is the Grateful Dead, not the fucking army."

That settled that . . . maybe I don't think enough!

As I said, I like trying to get good at things. I enjoy the discovery phase, practicing and hopefully perfecting technical skills. My personal standard of accomplishment is based on trying to keep the learning curve on an upward trajectory. Becoming a pilot and driving a racing car were both skills that I pursued with enthusiasm and dedication.

I approached skiing with that same single-minded fervor. But skiing gave me back something wholly unique: It allowed me to make a connection with nature in a way nothing ever had before. The risks, the trust, the negotiating you do with the natural world while wearing skis have their own drama and poetry.

I love tennis, so imagine what it was like to regularly play with guys like this. Left to right: Vitas Gerulaitis, me, and Bjorn Borg. *(Courtesy John Oates)*

Back in the 1960s there was a little bump in the Pennsylvania Appalachian foothills called Spring Mount. The "Mount" part was either an ill-thought-out abbreviation or an accurate description of not-quite-a-mountain. Either way, it wasn't more than a couple hundred yards of rock-strewn hard-packed snow with a rope tow that shredded more than a few pair of mittens. I tried skiing for the first time with my high school girlfriend, Lynne, and after that I was hooked. Decked out in blue jeans, wool sweater, and a nylon windbreaker, I would lace up my Garmont leather boots, strap them onto a pair of long, heavy Northland wooden skis and hit all the big-time Pocono ski areas: Big Boulder, Elk Mountain, and Camelback.

Those early few years would hardly prepare me for that spontaneous college ski trip to Aspen that had life-changing ramifications for me.

Once I finally left the East Coast and began living in Colorado, I dedicated myself to becoming a better skier. Throughout the '70s and '80s I skied all over the world: Germany, Austria, Switzerland, Canada, Argentina, and even an insane trip to Kazakhstan, the details of which are best left for another time or another book (trust me).

Playing music in front of people provides its own unique sense of thrill and abandon. I felt it at the Second Fret back in the '60s, and I feel it today at Madison Square Garden. But skiing is a different kind of performance, with its own unique set of dangers and rewards. It's in my blood and soul.

I don't really ski anymore. But I think about it. I relive it. And I dream about it. It's a fantasy, like many other fantasies, that I got to experience many times over because of my music life. But it stands alone. It represents the sum total of every sense, mood, and passion that I feel. It inspired me. Skiing let me transcend time and space. I could write a book about skiing.

Maybe someday I will.

Periodically, after relocating to Colorado, I would fly back East to continue the process of divesting myself of all the things that tied me to my former life. Everything was for sale: the cars; the airplane; the New York apartments; and, finally, the house in Connecticut. Little by little my financial situation improved to the point of knowing I wasn't going to starve, but at the same time I was cognizant of the fact that my life going forward would have to be considerably more practical and dealt with more responsibly. Let the cleansing begin.

As winter wore on and I began to really settle into living in Colorado, the reality of leaving a lifetime on the East Coast ceased to seem so daunting. The physical expansiveness of the Rocky Mountains combined with the open-minded and healthy lifestyles of the new friends I was making brought into focus the well-known Horace Greeley quote: "Go West, young man." I can do this, I can live out here and start again . . . reinvent myself . . . make the visualizations a reality.

Yes, I had been there numerous times during my rock star heyday to ski, play, and socialize. But that's not the Colorado that was summoning me. I was being called by the pure and pristine place I had first encountered on that long-ago college trip, when my buddy and I booked us a couple of student-fare airline tickets, threw caution to the wind, and embraced one of my life's first great adventures.

And it made total sense to me. Back in the late 1960s I was a twenty-year-old with few cares, fewer responsibilities, and very few material things holding me back. It was an unencumbered, stripped-down innocence and sense of adventure that first brought me to those magnificent mountains. I was wandering, eyes wide open, curious and ready to experience the world beyond the East Coast. Now here I was again, determined to redefine what had become my identity, reveling in a rediscovered freedom, and tapping into a more mature version of who I had been back in the late '60s. I felt light and limitless. Hungry once again, searching for my place in the world, and all of a sudden that little college ski trip took on far deeper implications. It was as if the Rocky Mountains had planted a seed within me in the past that was now pushing its way toward the sun. My rebirth was blossoming in a satisfying, slow motion.

The warmth of spring arrived, melting the big winter snows and ushering in the mud season. One afternoon, walking aimlessly in downtown Aspen, I saw a girl heading in my direction with what appeared to be a small red fox on a leash. It was that same pretty brunette from the *Ski* magazine party. She smiled. I stopped. In the darkness of the nightclub she was alluring, but in the late-afternoon sun her jade green eyes were mesmerizing. Then she picked up the little fox and draped him around her neck like a living fur stole. Something visceral that had been dormant awoke deep inside me.

Her name was Aimee Pommier and she called her pet Foxy. She bought him at a farm sale back home in Illinois. We walked along together, and she casually mentioned that she worked at a lingerie store close by and invited me to stop by.

A day or so later I did stop by the store and had a surprising small-world moment when I found out that the owner was a woman I had gone to school with and had lived very close to where I grew up in North Wales, Pennsylvania! Aimee sold me a pair of boxer shorts that I didn't need and I asked her out. Over the next few weeks, things moved forward slowly. She was young, had a lot of friends in town, and I was cautious. One day I stopped by her tiny second-floor apartment in the center of Aspen. It was a hodgepodge of colorful hand-painted concrete floors, a chicken-wire cage containing a duck in a corner, and an annoying cat named Willis. The charming ambience was enhanced by the periodic metallic clanging of Dumpster lids from the restaurant below. Over the weeks, we went on some hikes together. She would bring Foxy along and we'd laugh as he leapt up and down in the tall grass of the alpine meadows.

As we got to know each other she revealed that she grew up on a farm in Kankakee, Illinois, with her parents, Gary and Sharon, five brothers (Mathew, Mark, Luke, John, and Jude) and one sister (Lucy). She decided to stay in Aspen after spending the summer helping one of her brothers, who had a job as a raft guide on the Colorado River in Glenwood Springs.

One day she called me in hysterics because her pet fox had gotten away. A few days later an ad appeared in the local newspaper's lost-and-found column looking for the owner of a pet fox. Aimee went down to the town hall to claim him. Her fox was not waiting for her. Instead a very serious female deputy took her into a closed room and informed her that the sheriff's department would be charging her with animal cruelty and possession of an illegal wild animal. Turns out the laws regarding fox ownership were not the same in Illinois as in Colorado.

Aimee had no experience with the legal system, and I had no idea how to help other than the fact that I knew she needed a lawyer. I reached out to one of my skiing buddies, Gideon Kaufman, and his partner Brooke Peterson, who had a law firm in town, and they said they would represent her. When the court date arrived, I sat quietly in the back while the arresting officer made her statement. The judge seemed uncertain how to handle such an unusual case and kept referring to various statutes and arcane rulings that might apply. Aimee sat nervously up front, and our attorney ably established that it was an innocent misunderstanding and that she only wanted the best for the poor little fox. The entire proceeding had a vendetta quality to it, but in the end a compromise was reached and everyone was satisfied that the little fox would be taken to a wild-animal rescue facility near Boulder. It subsequently became a bit of a star in films and commercials.

I spent the next summer traveling back and forth to the East Coast, with a little bit of touring in between. I took Aimee with me on a trip to Panama City, Florida, and then to Trinidad and Tobago in the Caribbean. When we returned, we headed up to Connecticut to clean out what was left of my few belongings, load them into a Chevy Blazer, and head west. Our first stop was Aimee's family farm in Kankakee. There I met her family for the first time, packed up a bunch of her stuff, and then we hit the highway toward Colorado. After a long drive, I was weary and looking forward to a few hours of sleep when we reached Lincoln, Nebraska, at about 2:00 A.M.—only to find out that we had arrived on the same day as the first University of Nebraska home football game and the Nebraska State Fair! There wasn't a motel to be found within three hundred miles! I drove on through the night without sleep, straight to Aspen.

Around this time, I sold my little Aspen condo to Jack Nicholson, and we

The tiny Colorado cabin where I began to rebuild my life in the early 1990s with my soon-to-be-wife, Aimee. *(Courtesy John Oates)*

moved into an even smaller place, an old mining cabin with a tin roof on a quiet street within walking distance to the middle of Aspen. Winter was fast approaching and we settled into the honeymoon phase of what would become an idyllic and serious relationship. The rebirth had begun.

Going to the Chapel

The Aspen Chapel sits on a knoll between Maroon Creek and Castle Creek Roads, just outside of town. With its tall, slender steeple pointing to the heavens, this little interfaith country church was our Sunday source for enlightened, progressive, religious and spiritual discourse. Aimee and I enjoyed the variety of guest speakers from both the clerical and academic worlds. The pastor was a tall Minnesotan with a casual and engaging personality. His name was Gregg Anderson, and we asked him if he would perform our marriage ceremony. We met with him in his small office behind the altar and discussed the style and substance of the ceremony that we planned for November. We wanted our wedding to be simple and elegant, with a small group of family and friends in attendance. After going over some details and signing a few papers we were getting ready to leave his office when he sheepishly added, "Just in case you might have heard . . . when I married Sonny Bono to his third wife Susie I said, 'Do you Sonny take Cherie to be your' . . . then I caught myself. I just wanted to make sure you still want me to do your wedding." We laughed and appreciated that he would admit his faux pas. It didn't bother us in the least; in fact, we liked him even more.

I woke up early on November 28, 1994, to a gray, overcast sky that had dumped a foot of new snow on the mountains overnight. This was our wedding day but it was also a powder day. Russ Klein, one of my best men (I had three: Russ, Mike Mooney, and Billy Curry) called at 7:00 A.M. and wanted me to hit the slopes with him.

"Hey man, it's my wedding day!"

"So? It's a powder day too!" Russ replied.

I kissed Aimee while she was still half asleep and I was half dressed in my thermal underwear. An hour later I was on the chairlift with Russ, looking down at the acres of untracked Colorado dry-powder snow sparkling in the early morning sunlight. For three hours we pounded down the mountain, then I jumped in my truck and sped back home to Woody Creek to get dressed for the wedding. We had booked a suite at the Jerome Hotel (where years earlier I'd visited on that first trip to Colorado) and Aimee had gone into town to meet her mother, sister, and a few friends and get ready. Back home I stripped off my ski clothes, showered quickly, and put on my suit. As I pulled up to the chapel, the slightest hint of sun began to break through the dark gray sky. Inside, the pews were filled with guests, and the gentle strains of a cello and organ filled the air. Then, as if the Almighty was the director of an old Hollywood romance, right on cue, sunlight bathed the chapel hall in warm colors as its rays streamed through the tall stained-glass windows. I'll never forget the feeling I had in my chest when I first saw Aimee walking down the aisle. Her natural beauty filled me with an emotion I could hardly contain. Later that evening, as I carried Aimee across the street to the reception, soft snowflakes fell around us, as pure and perfect as the color of her gown.

Prelude to Reclamation

know it might seem strange to fans that are most familiar with us from the 1980s, but in fact, Daryl and I were always kind of outsiders when it came to the recording industry. I think it went back to when we first started as a post-Vietnam, quasi-folk act, playing coffeehouses and art galleries around Philadelphia and building a local following by playing lots of shows, honing and crafting our songs, and developing a sound before we ever had a recording deal. A couple of kids dedicated to music and navigating our way up the stream.

When you think about how today's indie acts struggle with forging their career—well, that was us. We always did things by kind of taking matters into our own hands and then just going out and doing them. We never lost that sensibility, even after we became very well known. And to that end, we also always lived and worked in our own little private solar system, revolving and evolving in a different universe from the rest of the music business. We didn't think or live by industry standards. Stubbornly, sometimes right and sometimes wrong, but that's the way we did things. Critics didn't get us, but we simply didn't care. We were truly independent, no matter what level we were at.

But by the early 1990s, the music business and its complicit sibling, commercial radio, were undergoing a seismic shift from the dominant power pop of the '80s to the emerging era of raw, antislick, grunge-band music. Melody and chords were out, high-volume angst with a don't-give-a-shit attitude was in. We didn't adapt or compromise, we just stopped.

Acutely aware of the unique confluence of circumstance surrounding me, I sensed that I needed to seize this rare moment in my life. There were no recording projects and very little touring between 1991 and 1996. Just some sporadic shows to keep some cash flow going. It was an opportunity for me to start anew. I was driven to restructure my personal life—in fact, not rebuild, but actually experience having a personal life. My separation and divorce had been finalized, and each new day brought challenges and possibilities that were both daunting and exciting. However, no matter which direction my life was taking, hovering in the background was the specter of twenty years of byzantine, mind-numbing, complex corporate contractual obligations that were not going away by themselves. It was like trying on a new set of wings and yearning to soar into the blue of a future sky with a $9 million ball and chain of debt around my ankle. To be honest, I couldn't even tell you what Daryl was up to during that time. It was just time for a new paradigm.

Chickens

By 1992, I had accepted that I would be living in Colorado full time. My old life back East was over. The house, apartments, cars, and airplane were gone, and my relationship with Aimee was in full bloom. It was time to rebuild, figuratively and literally. We had outgrown the cramped miner's cabin and I began looking to purchase a house in town. I had found a place on the banks of the Roaring Fork River, not far from Main Street, and was preparing to close the deal. I brought Aimee there to look at it with a real-estate agent, and Aimee's first question was, "Can we have chickens?"

Maybe it was the way she asked, in her ingenuous Midwestern style, that made such an impact . . . for it certainly wasn't the kind of question I would have thought to ask a real-estate agent, or anyone else for that matter. Aimee was so damn serious I thought she might be kidding. She wasn't.

A determined woman is a formidable adversary and our poor real-estate agent was not up to the contest. A few days later, Aimee asked me to meet her at the Woody Creek Tavern, just a few miles west of Aspen. On a late spring afternoon, we drove up the road toward the old mining town of Lenado. Pulling off onto a dirt lane, I observed a small, weathered, log cabin within a fenced in pasture, and a ramshackle horse barn surrounded by a broken-down split-rail corral. Something told me that this might be the answer to the chicken question—and it was. Away went the contract on the house in town, and we made a deal to become the newest residents of yet another neighborhood of artists, freaks, musicians, and freethinkers.

Our new real-estate agent, the soon to be legendary Tim "Timber" Mooney (busted for cutting trees to make his own personal ski trails on Aspen Mountain) had all the right answers. "Horses, sure! Chickens, I don't see why not!" He also mentioned in passing that some very interesting and colorful neighbors surrounded this particular piece of property. His comment was punctuated by a blast from a 12-gauge shotgun. Now for most folks, unexpected gunfire at close range during a real-estate negotiation might be considered a deal breaker. However, these are the delicate moments when a real-estate agent either earns or burns his potential commission, and Tim was up to the task. "Oh that's just the Doc. He's usually not up this time of day," he glibly ad-libbed while expertly redirecting our attention to the many other attractive qualities of the ranch, like the small herd of horses munching away in the far pasture, and the long, red 1975 Pontiac Grandville convertible parked inside the log cabin. Suddenly I got the feeling that owning the deed to this piece of land could be like purchasing a ticket to another psychic time zone.

A few days later Tim called us with answers to all our questions. The horses belonged to a guy named Zeno, the car in the cabin belonged to the guy with the shotgun, local rock star/writer Dr. Hunter S. Thompson, and the five acres were owned by an old friend of mine from London, Jeremy Keegan, who was happy to "keep it in the family." That and the knowledge that we could have chickens pretty much sealed the deal.

The fact that two strangers were keeping their horses and a car on land that belonged to some guy from England without his knowledge or permission didn't seem to faze Mooney, whose reaction was, "Welcome to Woody Creek . . . things are different here."

First we had to deal with the mystery horses. Once the word got out that there was a new owner in town, Zeno promptly showed up and graciously moved them while I pumped him for info like I was cramming for a Ranching 101 final exam. The car was another matter.

They say you can tell a lot about a man from the car he drives, and that menacing, mile-long red convertible stuffed and seemingly abandoned in our quaint little cabin should have given me some indication of the kind of guy who might be lurking in the compound across the road. Now, it's not like I had just crawled out of a hole, I had read *Fear and Loathing in Las Vegas,* but the distinct possibility of random nocturnal explosions with nothing more than a few acres of dry grass and an ancient split-rail fence between us—well, that was a reality that I was not 100 percent sure I was ready for. However, we could have chickens. . . .

Aimee and I decided we'd convert the cabin into what would someday be our guesthouse, and we would live there while we figured out how to build the rest of the house. But first we needed to move that car. By now Tim Mooney had transcended his role as real-estate agent and had become a sort of de facto consigliere between the newcomers and the neighborhood.

I called him in his office to explain that I wanted to start construction on the cabin and that we had to move the car. A day or so later he left us a message on our answering machine: "Hunter says, 'The car likes it there.'"

Well okay, this was shaping up to be a mano-a-mano situation. The next morning I walked up the lane and knocked on Thompson's door, completely oblivious to the fact that *no one* makes unannounced personal appearances before 4:00 P.M. at Hunter Thompson's house. Maybe he was just taking pity on my ignorance, but there were no gunshots and no answer. I came back again the next day and quietly pinned a note on the side door. It was polite and to the point, explaining that I too appreciate fine automobiles and would hate to see this particular example damaged at the hands of an insensitive carpenter. Again no answer.

Finally, the day came to start construction on the cabin. I plugged in my portable battery charger, hooked it to the heart of the big convertible, and waited. The fact that the keys were in the ignition was a major asset to the operation. Fingers crossed and right foot poised on the gas pedal, I cranked the starter. The engine fired with a belch of glorious blue-black smoke. Selecting reverse on the chrome column shifter, I eased the machine backward into the Colorado sunshine. It was an enjoyable short ride, as I cruised with the top down slowly up the lane, across the road into Thompson's driveway. The entrance to his rustic compound was flanked on either side by welded metal nightmare bird sculptures perched atop tall wooden posts. The car rolled to a gentle stop on the grass, its massive chrome grill facing the front door. I switched off the key with a satisfied click and walked home.

Perhaps he forgot where he parked it, or perhaps he thought it just materialized overnight in his front yard, or perhaps he just didn't give a shit, but Hunter never said a word about it.

Jasper

How many guys do you know that can say they got a jackass for their birthday . . . from their girlfriend? When I first met Aimee she was walking a pet fox on a leash down the Hyman Avenue Mall, so I was already well aware of just how unconventional she could be. That being said, I was, of course, intrigued when she phoned saying "I have a surprise for you!" and telling me to drive out and meet her at our new property in Woody Creek. It was an overcast day in April when I arrived and stepped out of the truck, sinking up to my ankles in mud. This should have been my first clue that this was to be no ordinary birthday.

Our five acres, now devoid of the neighbor's rogue horses and Hunter Thompson's red convertible, was at that time not much more than a bunch of split-rail fences in various states of disrepair; a small, ramshackle barn; and pastures full of a shitload of thistle. This was all soon to change; my future wife had a plan.

My reaction to what was to transpire this day might be better understood if I explain first that as a kid I had very bad allergies. My exposure to animals was parentally limited to a puppy that died and a parakeet that rarely sang. So imagine my surprise when Aimee greeted me in the middle of our pasture with a small gray burro with a large head. It sported a ragged red ribbon attached to its mane, directly behind its even more exaggerated ears. Believe me when I say that I did not know this creature was a burro; in fact, for all I knew, that bow could have been all that remained from a Kentucky Derby-winning garland and a mythic, heroic, race-winning past. So with that in mind, and for all of you out there who are secure enough to admit their equine ignorance, here is the definitive word on this subject:

Mule: A domesticated, hybrid animal that results from crossing a mare (female horse) and a jack (male donkey).

Ass: A four-footed, hoofed mammal related to the horse, but smaller, with longer ears and a shorter mane, shorter hair on the tail, and a dark stripe along the back.

Donkey: A domesticated ass.

So there I stood, eyeball to eyeball with my surprise birthday present, and as I stared into those big, baleful eyes I experienced a rather startling revelation . . . it was as if I could see my future in the milky brown orbs of this mysterious beast. That final definition "Donkey: A domesticated ass" suddenly took on a much more portentous meaning.

"Let's go for a ride!" These words jolted me from my daydream. When my senses returned, I saw Aimee approaching from the old barn with her arms full of worn leather straps, brass buckles dangling down and swirling around her ankles like something that would have been a big hit during the Spanish Inquisition or an X-rated cowboy video. I stood in awe as she deftly sorted through the jumbled leather and draped the burro, buckling and cinching until the antique harness magically took shape. All the while the tranquil burro stood stock still, in what appeared to be a well-practiced pose of resignation.

Almost simultaneously, the animal and I both turned our woolly heads, as the creak of the barn door opening caught our attention. I noticed his dusty back give a nervous twitch in reaction to the sight of the contraption that appeared inside. In one smooth motion, Aimee gathered up the reins and led the burro toward the barn. I followed in a trance, my thoughts alternating between a growing curiosity and a gnawing apprehension.

Inside of the stall sat a two-wheeled cart unlike anything I had ever seen. It looked like the back half of a pickup truck, with bald tires on rusted metal rims attached to a heavy rear axle and differential. The entire rig, which looked like it weighed a half-ton, could have easily passed for some bizarre farm sculpture created by a redneck with a chain saw and a welding torch. On its side were crudely painted letters that spelled out JASPER #1 ASS. Well at least now I could put a name to the beast.

Aimee deftly backed old Jasper into the space between two slender wooden poles that extended from the cart. He slowly obeyed with a bored shuffle and a subtle hint of something that in retrospect might have been hatred on his face. On went the harness while he quietly scuffed his hoofs in the dust.

"Do you want to drive?" Aimee asked, offering me the reins as she climbed onto the piece of barn siding that served as a seat.

The blank look on my face was my only answer as I nervously hoisted myself up beside her just as the cart began to move.

Ever-so slowly at first, the poor little donkey strained to pull the ponderous carriage . . . thoughts of pity and commiseration began to wash over me as I watched him struggle out of the barnyard and into the field. But these flaccid feelings began to transform into turgid terror as I observed Jasper's ears slowly folding back against his neck. His change in body language was accompanied by a distinct increase in acceleration.

Suddenly, the once-sleepy burro's entire body stiffened as though he'd just been struck in the spine by a lightning bolt. We both ducked as his rear hoofs kicked up a clod of grass straight back in our faces, and while we bounced, barely hanging on, he took us careening though the pasture. Aimee clutched the reins and I clutched her . . . she was screaming and I was quietly praying that my birthday present couldn't possibly last much longer. The speed increased . . . the fence line at the end of the pasture loomed larger . . . the screams got louder . . . my prayers went a whole lot deeper. Then, for some unknown reason, as if the hand of God reached down to snatch the reins, Jasper locked his knees and dug his hooves into the turf just as we reached the end of the field. Finally, he stopped, dipped his head toward the new spring grass, and calmly began to eat. There seemed to be no acknowledgment of what had just happened, just an insouciant flick of his tail.

That day Aimee gave me a birthday present I'll always remember and Jasper taught me a lesson I'll never forget. The next day we sold that damn wagon and never asked that burro to do anything . . . ever again.

Our little ranch in Woody Creek seemed to exist in another dimension. Here, I could work in the fields, breathe fresh air, and occupy myself with building a home on this rustic broken down property. Try as I might to disengage from the outside world, the nagging urge to uncover the secrets of the life that I wanted to put behind me lingered. A mountain of debt that had grown to over $9 million dollars, in part as a result of all the cash advances that were taken throughout the 1970s and '80s (coupled with my lack of financial awareness), was not going to go away by itself. Was there a way to find resolution?

Meanwhile, Back at the Ranch

After buying the property in Woody Creek, the first thing we did was convert the log cabin into a self-contained guest apartment where we would live for two years while we saved money and figured out how and what to build as our main house. I met a contractor named Barry Lindahl, who was originally from New York but had moved to the mountains and had just started a small remodeling business. We had a lot in common and over the years became great friends.

Although I grew up in the Pennsylvania countryside, I had lived in cities for most of my life. Now, as the owner of a small ranch, I was unprepared but eager to face what would become a very steep rural learning curve. Surveying the property, all I could see were acres of old, worn, broken fences, and pastures full of rocks and thistle.

Down at the end of the lane, my neighbor Bob Beattie's son, Zeno, had been using the vacant fields to graze his horses, so he was my first call when it came to trying to figure things out.

He was a huge help and over time, with a smile, would refer to me as "Farmer John." Luckily I had other resources as well. First there was my soon-to-be new wife, who grew up on her parents' farm in Illinois. I could always count on her father and mother, Gary and Sharon Pommier, for good advice. In addition, a bit further up the road lived a rancher named Jesse Steindler, who would later become a sheriff; and a mile further on, an older fellow named Stan Natal, the descendant of one of the original ranching families in the valley. Seemed like I was always asking someone a question, and seemed like there was always some-one to turn to for help. Boy did I need it. I had no tools, no equipment, and no experience. That would change fast.

The tools I gathered one by one, here and there, starting with picks, shovels, pry bars, posthole diggers, and fencing pliers—but what I needed most was a tractor. Over in Delta, Colorado, I found a medium-size John Deere that would become, without a doubt, my most important purchase, and one that would have significance far beyond its value as a farming implement.

As the deep winter snows melted and the days grew warmer, I would spend weeks walking around, propping up the sagging cedar split-rail fence, digging out and replacing the old ground-rotted posts. It was backbreaking work, but I got stronger and I got into it. When you work on a farm you don't need to go to the gym. The pastures, filled with rocks and dense with tough, prickly this-tle, were the hardest part; the task of clearing them seemed impossible. I would pick up rocks for hours on end, filling the upturned front bucket of the tractor, breaking the monotony by pulling and spraying the weeds with 2,4-D (one of the ingredients in Vietnam's Agent Orange) in a vain attempt to eradi-cate them. To make the job more frustrating, the adjacent fields to the west of my property were even worse. Each season the evil seeds from those unkempt acres of thistle would waft on the wind and deposit themselves in my fields, effectively wiping out all my hard work. It got so bad that I finally realized that the only solution would be to hook up the brush hog and mow my neigh-bor's fields to prevent the seeds from spreading.

Year by year . . . a little bit here, a little bit there . . . the ranch began to look a bit better. There was so much to do, but the satisfaction of seeing the improvement was worth the effort.

In between working in the fields, I continued to do shows with Daryl every

Our new home comes together in Woody Creek, Colorado, along with our new life.
(Courtesy John Oates)

once in awhile, eventually setting aside just enough cash to begin building the main house. I knew I wasn't flush enough to do the entire thing, so Aimee and I made a plan to build in stages. First we attached a small addition to the little cabin: just a simple two-story structure with a garage below and two bedrooms with bath above. While the construction was going on back on the ranch, I'd hit the road for the occasional Hall and Oates show. During those days, as I'd be playing on stage, in the back of my mind I was thinking *strum a chord . . .* this will pay for the windows *. . . strum . . .* floors *. . . strum . . .* doors *. . . strum* another chord.

ONE HOT AFTERNOON, while I was taking a break from picking another of the endless loads of rocks, Aimee walked out to meet me with a bottle of cold water and a sandwich. It was a welcome respite and we sat together, leaning up against the big tractor tire, looking around at the land that was becoming our home. We talked about the fact that I had to keep working and touring to keep afloat, there was no fallback position. She sagely said, "We have to tour together, as a family." In the past going on the road had always been a boy's club, and I had never considered taking my wife along. "It's the only way we'll stay together," she continued, wise beyond her years. I had already accepted that my life's paradigm had to change. This was just another step, and so from that day forward, we began to travel together all over the world. The family would come first, and sooner than I expected.

Build a House,
Birth a Baby

The red-dirt lane carves through the scattered pines and scraggly groves of cottonwoods and aspen trees. Clouds of dust rise and settle from construction traffic making its way in and out. Yawning, rumpled tradesmen in worn Carhartt uniforms assemble in the chill morning air, coffee cups steaming on the hoods of their old pickups. In the distance, from the main road, a rumbling truck approaches, creaking and groaning under the weight of a massive crane.

The men are gathered before a gaping, gray, concrete foundation pierced by stubby lengths of vertical rebar that horizontally describes the shape of a house to come. The crane sets its stubby support legs firmly into the ground before its steel arm rises into the cloudless sky and waits. A short time later, with military precision, three flatbed trailers roll slowly down the lane, each laden with thick, triangular stacks of logs from Montana. The kids from the Aspen Community School on the bluff across the road walk down to watch. A very pregnant Aimee and a very anxious John stand on the upper driveway as the foreman orchestrates the team of men and machines. We watch as the crane swings the long, heavy logs acrobatically through the air. The end of each log is roughly marked with black numbers. Barry and Chain Saw Dave nudge and manhandle them into position. In a surprisingly short time, the stacked logs form walls rising from the foundation, and by the end of the day, a roofless house had taken shape. It had a crude but substantial beauty, with checks in the exterior log ends facing downward so as to not catch moisture. The interior beams were highlighted by dramatic and strategically placed burn marks from lightning strikes. A true log home is a work of art, and the architect from Victor, Montana, had put a lot of care and passion into this design. But we would soon learn that the initial laying of the logs would be only a tease compared to the time-consuming, frustrating, and fascinating labor of love that would eventually result in a home for the "Circle of Three" that was to be our family.

In the years leading up to this we had spent time up in Montana with my friend Billy Curry and begun to learn a bit about the ways of the Native American Lakota Sioux culture. Back in Woody Creek, Aimee and I bought a teepee made of tan canvas that was fifteen feet in diameter and stretched over graceful hand-hewn poles. We set it up on the high ground near the cabin, and there it posed like a regal sentinel from another time, overlooking the primitive-yet-modern house that was emerging below.

Aimee and I spent many cool summer nights in that teepee, and one warm early evening, as the sky turned red in the west, our son was conceived. That same night we drove my truck up to Snowmass Village and spread out a blanket to watch and listen to James Brown perform on Fanny Hill. Before the show, lying back, rapt in the afterglow and lost in the brushstrokes of constellations across the infinite black sky, my reverie was jolted by a loud scraping and banging coming from somewhere down the mountain. On the rugged rock-strewn road that led up toward the makeshift stage, a white stretch limousine was bottoming out as it struggled haltingly upward, doing its damnedest to perform like a 4x4. Stepping out from the dusty Lincoln, James Brown hit the stage to the groove of a tight, crackling, rhythm section, his signature scream shredding the thin air. "This is a man's world . . ." felt like a benediction, and I reached over to grasp Aimee's hand, unknowing but somehow sensing that she was about to bring forth the greatest gift I never knew I wanted.

Midnight, June 19, 1996

The long well-lit halls of the Aspen Valley Hospital are empty. The emergency room, frantic and overworked during ski season, is relatively quiet. Aimee waddles along, holding her swollen belly. I hold her by the arm, knowing that from here on I would be of little help. The time has come; our baby is on the way. The nurses and midwives in the prenatal area are all friendly, familiar faces, and we are the only couple there that night. They prep Aimee and the dilation countdown begins. We had gone through the birthing classes, the breathing routines, and I am as ready as any about-to-be new father could be . . . or so I thought. Aimee tries her best to endure the pain but by 4:00 A.M. enough is enough, and she calls for the anesthesiologist. The epidural works quickly, and we wait.

Around 7:00 A.M. the doctor stops by and pronounces that she is getting close to giving birth. Perhaps to break the tension, or due to nerves, I ask if I have enough time to run back to the ranch to feed the animals. He tells me to go, and I race down the road and quickly return to the hospital. I got back just in time and I watched helplessly, in awe, as a tiny arm appeared from below the white sheets . . . then a head . . . then a baby boy.

With newborn, Tanner, one of the proudest moments of my life.
(Courtesy John Oates)

I broke down and cried. I guess I may have tried to make myself believe that I was too macho to have such an emotional and deep reaction . . . but I had never felt anything so profoundly moving. It was as if I had given myself up to a higher purpose, and everything that I had been or accomplished instantly faded in significance before this miracle of new life.

TANNER JOHN OATES was in the world and in our lives. He was a big infant, but his oxygen intake was low, a common issue with babies born at high altitude. They placed a cannula into his tiny nostrils and gave him some supplemental O_2. We spent a quiet night in the hospital, and the staff treated us like royalty. Aimee was so comfortable after a long nine months of pregnancy that she didn't want to leave. A day later, with the responsibility of parenthood weighing heavily on our shoulders, we drove back to the ranch with a newborn, a tank of oxygen, and the sober realization that a lifetime of responsibility was beginning. Fortunately, Aimee's mom and dad stayed with us for a few days then; after that, my folks arrived to help out.

Being first time parents is a big adjustment and we settled into a routine of checking little Tanner's pulse and oxygen numbers with and without the supplemental oxygen. Then a week went by, then another, then we started to really be concerned, even though the doctors assured us that his lungs would eventually open and he would be able to do without the supplemental oxygen. Another week, still no improvement. Finally our doctor told us that if we went down to sea level everything would be fine. Taking oxygen tanks on a commercial airplane is a big hassle of red tape, so I called in a favor from a guy I had met on the Carly Simon tour a few months before. His name was Dirk Ziff. He was a guitar player, successful businessman, and he had a private airplane. After I provided only a brief explanation of our situation, he graciously sent the plane to pick us up in Aspen and we flew to Fort Lauderdale, Florida. We stepped off the plane in the early evening and drove straight to the hospital. When we arrived the nurses removed the oxygen tubes, and after a few

My folks, Anna and Alfred, along with me, Tanner, and Aimee, at Christmas. *(Courtesy John Oates)*

Our little devil. *(Courtesy John Oates)*

minutes Tanner's pulse and oxygen readings were perfectly normal! Relief and
a few days in the warm Florida sun to unwind, and then it was back on tour . . .
this time as a family. Tanner was only eight weeks old; the three of us toured
together as a family for the next thirteen years!

WHEN TANNER REACHED school age we enrolled him in the Aspen Community School, right across the road from our house. Preschool then kinder-
garten followed by first and second grades. We would periodically pull him
out of classes in those early years for our concert tours, and he seemed to be

able to keep up, but by third grade things began to change. If we wanted to keep traveling together as a family, it seemed like homeschooling was the only alternative. We enrolled him in a program called Laurel Springs based in Ojai, California. They would send us books and materials and assigned a teacher to us who would review the work, which we would send to her every few weeks. At first Aimee and I tried to teach him his third-grade schoolwork, but by the end of the year we realized that parenting and teaching weren't always compatible. As embarrassing as it may sound, fourth-grade math was stretching the limits for John the musician and Aimee the farmer. We needed help fast, and Aimee found her in the Aspen public library. Casey White was a nice young elementary school teacher doing private tutoring while on pregnancy leave. We offered her a full-time tutoring job and she accepted. Casey was easygoing, and she and Tanner developed a wonderful student-teacher relationship. She taught him for six years, in the meantime also having two children of her own. It was a good arrangement for all of us;, she lived close by and got to stay home with her kids while Tanner received a very exclusive one-on-one education. By sixth grade, the math and science courses were getting the better of Casey, so she concentrated on the English and history while Tanner worked on his math with local tutors Tom Paxton and Philip Kalfas. All the while, we still traveled together as a family, taking the bookwork with us and supplementing the curriculum with real-world experiences all over the globe: Kangaroo preserves in Australia; ancient Buddhist temples in Japan; important historic sites; magnificent cathedrals and cultural touchstones throughout Europe; road trips through England and Scotland; beaches in Hawaii; scuba diving in the Caribbean, and no matter where we were, we always visited the local science museums.

When we were home Tanner volunteered at the Aspen Center for Environmental Studies, but as he matured, an innate curiosity and talent for the technical and experimental sciences blossomed along with a strong passion for engineering and physics. We'd go skiing together but he would be more interested in stopping to examine the mechanism of the big snow-blowing machines and the massive steel, braided cables that hauled the gondolas up the mountain.

I hoped that he would embrace the athletic mountain lifestyle that appealed to me, but Tanner was less interested in climbing peaks and more focused on the rock formations themselves. He tried music lessons to no avail; somehow science was in his DNA. At night before bed we would often read books on quantum physics and military history; eventually these subjects, in particular, became his métier.

Tanner's education was reminiscent of the age-old method of tutelage usually reserved for royalty. Although it could be construed as a sort of elitism, our only motivation was to be together as a family for as long as possible. Somehow we all made it work. That is, until he reached thirteen years old.

I had been invited as special guest on a Jerry Douglas Christmas tour, wryly titled "Jerry Christmas." It was an honor and a challenge for me to play with Jerry and his band of high-level musicians. But for Aimee and Tanner it was a long grind of one-nighters throughout the Northeast in December. That tour was the tipping point for Tanner and his life on the road. After it ended, he announced, "Dad, I'm done. I want to go to a real school with kids my age. The next time I go on an airplane or to a hotel, it's going to have to be a vacation."

And so our son's life as a road dog came to an end, while my life as a road dog still had no end in sight. We enrolled him at Colorado Rocky Mountain School, a local boarding school in Carbondale, for his freshman year. Not exactly an institution one would describe as offering a formal education, but certainly a very unique one. It was a small, close-knit, liberal-minded prep school with a heavy emphasis on outdoor experience. Tanner spent four years there learning, and dealing with nonconformity and how to adapt to a communal system so unlike his homeschool experience. He satisfied his scientific interests by working by himself at home on various esoteric projects. At the age of fifteen he built one of the world's smallest inertial electrostatic confinement nuclear fusion reactors, and he spent his summer vacation interning at NASA under the watchful eye of Raymond Pages, one of the chief scientists at the Goddard Space Flight Center. After graduation he was accepted into the electrical engineering program at Virginia Tech. From there he moved to Washington DC, spending six months interning in Congress. He's now a student at

George Washington University and employed part-time with an international security company. He's a hardworking, strong-willed, independent thinker, and we couldn't be prouder.

I remember when he first went off to boarding school for ninth grade, I told him, only half joking, "Don't worry about flunking out of school, there will always be a black T-shirt and a bunk for you on the tour bus." His response was, "Thanks Dad . . . but I'll be going to college."

Hawk

In addition to building a family and building a house, Aimee began building a growing menagerie of animals to populate our little ranch. This is a story about a dog named Hawk, but this is also a story about trust.

We found him when we needed him. Living in the Colorado high country, we share the land with bears, mountain lions, unpredictable neighbors, the occasional suspicious drifter, and other predators. My wife and I would sometimes wake up in the middle of the night with eyes wide and hearts pounding to various strange and frightening sounds. Too many sleepless nights finally convinced us that we should implement a canine security system. Now at the time we did have a tough little Shar-Pei named Jolene, who was the queen of the castle. Though she had a big heart, she wasn't going to keep the demons from the door—what we needed was a big dog.

Although I've never felt comfortable with the idea of owning a trained guard dog, I will admit that we did visit some breeders; they were, for the most part, scarier than the animals they were selling. Their dog compounds resembled prison camps, with yards of chain-link fence and an unrelenting cacophony of howling. The trainers, all of whom seem to affect a paramilitary bearing, enthusiastically gave creepy demonstrations of their testosterone-engorged beasts, who only responded to commands in German and carried out their orders with a soulless, mechanical precision. Weighing our nocturnal fears against our concerns with liability, our situation still did not seem to warrant this type of canine commitment. No, what we wanted was intimidation without a hair trigger; a warm-blooded deterrent that could keep the uninvited cowering inside their cars or outside of our fence line. Of course, we still needed the basics like propane and UPS deliveries. So how would we ever find a dog who could discern between the threatening strangers and the good guys, between innocent children and pesky varmints? What we were looking for was a very special animal, and in this department I always defer to the expert . . . my wife.

You want a Transylvanian naked neck chicken? Done deal. In the market for an Angora goat? Or perhaps you fancy a brace of Lady Amherst's pheasants . . . easy as pie. Her resources are endless, her perseverance withering, and her results unfailing. Watching her slipping on her boots with cell phone and checkbook in one hand and a *Bargain Hunter* newspaper in the other is like watching a big-game hunter locked and loaded with a nostril full of big-game dung.

I was working out in the pasture one day when I heard my truck squeal out of the driveway. As Aimee raced by, she shouted that she was on her way to Denver to pick up a hairless Chinese crested, which I assumed had to be the answer to our security dilemma. Surely something this exotic had to be fierce and intelligent beyond my comprehension.

When she finally returned with a quivering, moist, bulgy-eyed creature that resembled a cross between an alien and a Chihuahua, I began to have my doubts. When she said that it couldn't go outside without freezing to death, I thought she was losing her touch. I had envisioned Lassie with balls, but instead I got Topo Gigio with a head cold. Not to worry, she assured me. All we had to do was to sic Little Chico on the bad guys and then I could easily subdue them while they were doubled up and incapacitated with laughter.

It wasn't long before we accepted the bittersweet realization that Little Chico was not going to cut it on the ranch. So we gave him away to a very nice retired lady who needed a warm-bodied sofa companion and resumed our search for the perfect guard dog.

Within a few days we received a call from our friend Seth, who runs the Aspen Animal Shelter. He had a dog that he thought might fit the bill. When we arrived at the shelter, Seth began with this disclaimer: "A lady wanted a protective dog . . ." he paused, gauging our reaction ". . . but it attacked a Rottweiler downtown in front of Boogie's Diner so she brought him here."

Our response was instantaneous, "We'll take him!"

His name was Hawk, and Seth thought he was about one year old. He was big, with long thick rust-and-brown fur. His nose was long and he carried his bushy tail low and tight between his legs. He looked roughly like a collie, but his wary yellow eyes and the way he walked reminded me of a wolf. Seth said he came from a ranch out near Rifle, Colorado, and that his back was covered with scars. We opened the tailgate of our truck and without hesitation he effortlessly leaped inside, lay down, and curled into a ball. As we drove home he remained motionless while we were both silently feeling a bit unsure about this impetuous adoption.

As any dog owner knows, there are only two kinds of canines: the alpha and the rest. Dog owners also know that introducing unfamiliar adult dogs is always a crapshoot. The submissive ones just roll over, give up their belly, and it is done—order established. They then proceed to get on with their playful doggy lives. However, throwing two strange, dominant, male and female dogs together is a guaranteed recipe for confrontation. We just didn't realize how alpha our little Shar-Pei was until Hawk jumped out of the pickup.

Sparring is for humans in a ring with gloves. What we witnessed at that moment was all-out war—primal, fang and claw. The attack was instantaneous and vicious. There was no taunting or sizing each other up, just a fluid, rolling, gruesome battle. Aimee was screaming and I instinctively and stupidly tried to insert myself into the brawl. In desperation, I tried to kick them apart. The Shar-Pei, being the smaller of the two, seemed like my best option, and I somehow managed to connect my boot to her midsection, causing her to tumble down the hillside into the aspens. Now I found myself standing between them, but neither of the dogs seemed to have any regard for my role as human referee. They circled each other, and I noticed small patches of blood appearing on little Jolene's head. From the open door Aimee threw me a broom screaming, *"Make them stop!"*

Luckily I didn't have to. Hawk held the high ground, his huge teeth bared, while Jolene paced back and forth, keeping a respectful distance. It wasn't as if she was ready to relinquish her crown, but she certainly was not ready for a rematch either. I had never seen teeth on a dog like the ones that Hawk now so defiantly displayed. They were a jagged row of yellow daggers glistening with saliva. But the two long fangs shooting up from his bottom jaw were what really caught my attention. They were unnaturally large and rose up over his shiny black upper lip like scimitars. Unsure of what I should do, I held my position between the two animals, alternating my attention to avoid getting caught in the middle of a surprise attack. Fortunately, this didn't happen. The little Shar-Pei finally retreated and disappeared around the back of the house. Hawk closed his mouth and dropped into the grass, resting his head on his front legs as if nothing had happened.

His nonchalance was impressive and unnerving at the same time. He lay there with the air of a warrior who had won the battle before it had started— he'd done this before. I wanted to approach him to pay my respects, to place my hand on the head of victory and perhaps understand a little more about him. But something in his eyes made me drop to one knee and wait. Now was not the time; I was yet not his friend and certainly not his master.

Time passed and little by little he opened up to us. Little by little, more and more often, he would approach us and sit at our feet while we cautiously petted him and gently pulled burrs from his thick fur. There was no playing, just a tacit acceptance of his new owners and his new home.

By day he mostly slept, unless a visitor or passing car required his attention. By night he roamed the ranch, patrolling the boundaries and barking away any nocturnal aggressor that might be contemplating making a meal of our livestock. Aimee and I slept well.

That is until one night when the sound of the barking modulated.

I snapped from my sleep with the feeling that something was not right out there in the darkness. It wasn't winter but I recall that it was cold when I opened the back door and peered outside, raking the flashlight beam out across the field. Closing the door behind me, I followed the sound and focused the light on a horrific tableau. There atop a fence post perched the biggest raccoon I had ever seen. A few feet below, both dogs circled, snarling and jumping up at the cornered invader. In case you don't know, raccoons have powerful claws that are strong enough to open clamshells and sharp enough to tear the eyes out of a dog. That is exactly what was about to happen—the dogs would jump up and the coon would swipe down at their faces, slashing and hissing. Even half asleep I realized that this was going to end up very badly.

I ran to the barn and frantically grabbed the first thing I could get my hands on. Brandishing a rusty shovel, I sprinted back out to the dark battle. I dropped the light and held the weapon with both hands. Could I drive off the dogs? Could I kill the coon? There was no time. I saw blood fly in the dim moonlight. I saw missing eyes. I saw midnight rides to the animal hospital. I saw vet bills. I swung!

Perhaps now might be a good time to recall that I never made it past Little League. In fact, when I was a kid, my team would charitably let me play a few innings in left field, if they were winning by at least six runs. But that night I was Barry Bonds—pure instinct and reaction. The shovel whipped through the strike zone and the ball was nothing but flesh and bone. It was like watching a slow-motion replay, as the raccoon rose from the top of the post and seemed to hang in the air. Then the action snapped back into real time as a furry blur flashed up. I jumped back and felt the muffled thud of bodies hitting the ground. It was over in an instant. Hawk's jaws crushed deep into the neck of the motionless raccoon, and all I could see were his yellow eyes through the matted fur of the dead animal. I took a cautious step toward them and heard a low, menacing growl. I stepped back quickly and watched as Hawk struggled to his feet and dragged the coon off toward the pasture, until he was absorbed into the darkness. He didn't need me. I had served my purpose that night and now it was better if I went back inside—back to the place where the humans sleep and dream.

Hawk lived with us for ten faithful years. I don't think we ever became friends in the sense that most dogs and their owners do—we just were. He never let danger darken our door and we fed him. One summer afternoon, he died of a heart attack in the shade of the pickup truck that brought him here, and here he will stay forever in our heart and memories.

Finally Meeting Hunter

A few weeks after moving in to our place in Woody Creek we met Hunter S. Thompson face-to-face at the Woody Creek Tavern, where he often held court. He was in full dress uniform: floppy hat, classic aviator shades, complete with the ironically effete long, slender cigarette holder.

I introduced myself. "Hunter, I'm John Oates, your new neighbor."

"What the fuck are those birds about?" he grunted.

"Those are our guinea fowl, sorry if they're a nuisance," I explained.

"Hell they're fucking weird. . . . I thought I was trippin'. They look fucking prehistoric. I love birds. But I hate dogs. I see you've got dogs. And if they come over to my property, I'll shoot them."

Then just like that, as if I weren't there, he turned back to the bar and resumed an intense conversation with some cowgirl that he had cornered. Heeding his warning about our dogs, I wasted no time putting up an invisible fence around our property. Who needs a dog with a butt full of buckshot?

The birds he was referring to were guinea fowl. In addition to the real-estate-approved chickens, Aimee wasted no time collecting about a dozen of these plump speckled little African birds. She said they eat bugs, and when aroused, their loud cackling served as a kind of barnyard security system. How she found them I'll never know, she just has a knack for locating unusual critters. Every so often we'd go out to the fenced-in pen with a long-handled fishing net. I'd run around and snare one in the net, then hold the bird while Aimee trimmed feathers from the ends of their wings so they couldn't fly. But every now and again we'd miss one, and for some reason they always flew straight over to Thompson's property. I think they liked to hang out with his peacocks.

Bringing up a small child and working on our property was a full-time job in those days, so we didn't socialize with our neighbors very much. One of the few gatherings that Thompson hosted was his annual Kentucky Derby party. Hailing from the Bluegrass State, he seemed to really enjoy pouring endless mint juleps for his coterie of eclectic friends that included the sheriff, artists, ranchers, and longtime locals, all mingling in various states of inebriation. We'd walk up the lane, cross the road carrying our little boy, and spend a few late-afternoon hours, until the race was over and the sun was setting. That's when the real party started, and we'd slip out the kitchen door before the invariable explosions and gunshots split the night.

Aimee also loved peacocks; we'd drive all over western Colorado picking up these magnificent birds to add to our growing menagerie. In fact, our peacocks would also fly across the road and visit Hunter's peacocks. I think our peacocks fully won him over because soon after we got those birds, I started getting invited over to his fortified compound to watch sports. Officially called Owl Farm, his place was a dense, cluttered, rustic crib. Books and paperwork were strewn about everywhere, skeletons and skulls from local and exotic species resided alongside taxidermy and telescopes. But the beating heart of Hunter's home was his kitchen. Walking in from the side door, you'd enter a sunken area filled with overstuffed chairs arranged in a comfortable shamble in front of his big-screen TV and vintage sound system. The legendary writer held court behind a long, wooden countertop covered with piles of paper, books, baskets of pencils, pens, and the dominating centerpiece: his trusty IBM Selectric typewriter. Hunter had a penchant for shooting typewriters. It could have been his way of dealing with writer's block, or perhaps a celebratory ritual fueled by the ecstasy that comes from crafting a perfect phrase . . . who knows? He just liked to blow the shit out of typewriters with a high-powered handgun from close range. What's so strange about that?

Perched on high at his kitchen command post, with his collection of colorful cronies below, he presided over a kind of Rocky Mountain salon. A stoned-out Algonquin Round Table of sorts, although I doubt whether the elite gathering of New York intelligentsia at the famous hotel would have ever imagined that their host might suddenly brandish a .45 Magnum or toss a cherry bomb into their beer without warning. Hunter house rules were simple: You had to bet on whatever sporting event was being broadcast, and you could only talk during the commercials, during which time he muted the TV and encouraged provocative discourse. Dare to be boring at your own risk . . . the consequences could be fatal.

Thompson was addicted to sports. But he was also addicted to cigarettes, cocaine, guns, and whiskey, among other things, which made every visit more than a little interesting and highly unpredictable.

After I had lived in Woody Creek for about ten years, Jason Binn, owner of *Aspen Peak* magazine, asked if I would write an occasional column about my life in the valley. It gave me the opportunity to dust off some of my college journalism chops, and it inspired me to write about my adventures as a newbie rancher.

For my first column I decided to write about my entrée into Woody Creek, along with my neighborly relationship with Hunter S. Thompson. However, I was wary and hesitant to submit it to the magazine without giving the world-famous author next door the chance to read it first. After all, he had fired his shotgun in our direction when we were first looking at our property. God only knew what he would do if I wrote an article that pissed him off.

So I called him up. "Hunter, I've written this magazine article that talks a little bit about you and I'd really like you to read it." "Great!" he growled. "Bring it over during *Monday Night Football*." Then *click* . . . he hung up the phone.

For Thompson, *Monday Night Football* was akin to a weekly religious service. A sacrosanct ritual with a congregation of intoxicated acolytes, fueled by a seemingly endless flow of whiskey, weed, and minimountains of cocaine. I mean, he drank his whiskey not by the shot or in a small tumbler, but in a tall, old-fashioned milk glass, filled to the brim.

Anticipating the situation I'd be facing, I decided to bring my wife and young son in the event that I might need an excuse for an early exit. I also brought along my good friend Jed Leiber, who was writing songs with me, staying at our house, and could hang with the best of them when it came to an all-night bourbon bender. My thinking was to make it a social visit—just drop off the article and bug out. But once we got there, it was clear that a quick-and-clean getaway was not in the cards.

"Okay, ante up!" Thompson shouted as we walked in the door. I tossed a twenty-dollar bill into the pot and quietly said to my wife, "Aimee, why don't you take Tanner home and I'll be back as soon as I can. This may take a while."

Doc was already well into his cups and the game was on, so I stood off to the side, trying to be patient but dying to find out if my writing would pass his muster. After a commercial or two I took my opportunity to ask my wired host, "Would you like to read the article?"

"*You'll* read it aloud for everyone. But wait for the next commercial!" he answered.

Okay, I got this . . . don't interrupt the game, but recite for Hunter S. Thompson . . . right.

I'd sung in front of millions of people, performed since I was a little kid, was totally comfortable on stage. It rarely ever fazed me. But all of a sudden, I was nervous. The air in the room felt volatile, as if the mood could ignite in any number of ways, not many of them good.

At last a commercial break hit, and Thompson killed the sound. "Get up and read it," he ordered. This was the moment. I felt caught in an imaginary spotlight. I cleared my throat. All the loaded eyes in the room locked in on me.

Unsure of myself, in an unsteady voice, I tentatively broke the silence with the title of the piece:

"Can We Have Chickens?"

"*Louder!*" Thompson barked.

I started to sweat, then I restarted, this time with a little more energy.

"*Can We Have Chickens?*"

"*LOUDER!*" Thompson blasted. "*BRING IT, GODDAMN IT! OWN IT!*"

I did not want him going for the .45 Magnum that was sitting on the countertop in full view. So I stepped it up and did my best to deliver the words with feeling, emotion, and animation.

"I was born in New York City but grew up in a small town in Pennsylvania. My life has always been a challenge to balance my rural desire with my professional need to be urban. Within days of graduating high school I moved to Philadelphia, and not to just any random neighborhood but the late-'60s hippie enclave of Center City. It was a gathering of artists, freaks, musicians, freethinkers, the franchised, and disenfranchised . . . blah, blah, blah, blah . . ."

I was feeling good. But just as I started to get into a serious groove, the commercial break ended, the game came back on, and Thompson's focus shifted back to the TV.

"*Okay, shut up!*" he commanded. Recitation over.

At the next commercial break, Thompson quickly muted the TV and ordered me to resume. I got through another chunk of the article then *bam*, the game was back on and he snapped, "*Quiet!*"

A timeout was called, then another commercial, then again I picked up right where I left off.

"Living extra-large in the '80s took its toll on my life and cut deep into my heart, mind, and pocketbook. All that, in combination with a profound midlife revelation, led me to my next move . . . here to Aspen Colorado and a wholesale life change. . . ."

Thompson, who was sitting right next to me, all of a sudden started stabbing me sharply in the ribs with a giant bowie knife as I finished each paragraph, shouting, "TOP NOTCH! TOP NOTCH! THIS IS GOOD STUFF! TOP NOTCH!" Each poke of the blade an exclamation point. Of all the audience reactions I've received around the world, I don't think anything ever gave me more pleasure or relief than those rave-review knife jabs in the ribs.

It was just one of many unforgettable moments with the good Doctor Thompson.

Like the day when I was leaving my driveway and saw him sitting out on his lawn. Or at least I *thought* it was him. When I rolled down my window to say hey, I realized that it wasn't Thompson at all. Turns out, it was Johnny Depp, dressed exactly like Thompson and mimicking his voice and behavior to a T. Depp lived there on and off while boning up for the film adaptation of Thompson's, *Fear and Loathing in Las Vegas*. The actor was preparing to *become* Hunter S. Thompson.

Another time, one of the local characters was keeping his horse in the big pasture across the road from Owl Farm, and on the other side of the lane we had our miniature-donkey stud, named Tornado. The cowboys who sold him to us had drugged him up because he was as calm as a summer breeze when we handed over the money, but once we got him home he turned into an aptly named cyclone of a beast. Well, once Tornado realized there was a hot-to-trot mare just on the other side of the fence, he went wild with desire. Pacing back and forth along the fence line, braying and hee-hawing all night and day. It was a racket you could hear for miles, and Hunter's house was right in the middle of the action. Finally, I got a call from Bob Braudis, the sheriff, acting as an emissary for my neighbor, telling me that Hunter thought it would be a good idea to let them go at it. He said that Hunter thought those two "needed to make a love connection" and he was willing to facilitate it . . . whatever the hell that would entail was beyond my ken.

On one dark February night Aimee, Tanner, and I were driving up the lane toward the main road. I noticed a Pitkin County sheriff's car parked at the end of the lane, and another one blocking the entrance to Thompson's compound. I rolled down the window and asked the officer, "What's going on?"

"Just a situation. . . ." He trailed off, evasive in his response. We drove on and headed into town for dinner. At the restaurant, we were sitting next to a friend who was a local EMT and fireman. Suddenly his beeper went off, and he abruptly got up and left.

A few minutes later, Aimee got a call from our neighbor Jeanne, who was an emergency-room nurse. She told us that Hunter S. Thompson had just been brought into the emergency room, dead from a self-inflicted gunshot to the head.

I was shocked but not surprised. He was just so mercurial. He'd had recently gone through a series of surgeries on his hips and legs resulting in serious complications and pain. He had spent months bound in a cast up to his hip. I'll never know what made him decide to end his life, but from what I did observe, he seemed to revel in his role as Hunter S. Thompson "Gonzo Journalist." At sixty-seven he could no longer live the don't-give-a-shit, motorcycle-machismo, wild-man character of his own creation. His writing and lifestyle, along with his trademark hat and shades, became a brand recognized and revered around the world. To me he always seemed supremely self-aware, but then there were moments when the image wavered and the soul of a true Southern gentleman surfaced. His was one of the most original and powerful journalistic voices of the mid-twentieth century. His literary legacy will live forever. One thing I do know is that Hunter saved his best story for last. It's one of the wildest and most impressive exits in modern history. One for the ages, as they say.

Ashes in the Sky

A flatbed truck carrying a long, shining, silver cylinder stopped by the side of the road in front of the quaint Woody Creek post office. I was walking toward my pickup truck, holding my mail, when the driver of the semi leaned out the window and called to me. "I'm looking for Owl Farm," he shouted over the wheezing and clacking of the diesel engine. "Follow me," I answered, and I got in my truck and pulled out slowly in front of the big rig. I noticed the California license plates in my rearview mirror as we proceeded up toward my place and neighboring Owl Farm.

For a few weeks prior to this, earth-moving machines had begun arriving, gouging out a rough dirt road through the field just to the right of the late writer's house. A fleet of dump trucks loaded down with road base and gravel were followed by pickup trucks filled with construction workers. From across the road I could hear the sounds of earth compactors pounding incessantly as the mysterious work continued for days on end. Rumors circulated among the locals down at the Woody Creek Tavern. Hunter this, Hunter that . . . even in death he continued to be the topic of conversation and controversy. It was common knowledge among the locals that there was going to be a funeral and, in

The "cannon" that would deliver Hunter S. Thompson's ashes into the stratosphere, as it looked from our back door. *(Courtesy John Oates)*

the spirit and legend of the guest of honor, everyone knew it would be unconventional and over the top.

Occasionally I'd walk up the lane to sneak a peek, but all I could see was a low, wide mound being formed in a clearing far behind the house. Then one day we had a knock at the door. Standing there was an attractive group of fashionably hip kids in their midtwenties.

"Sorry to intrude," they began politely. "We're here to relocate your animals."

Aimee and I were taken aback at this unexpected statement, for it wasn't presented as a request. "There are going to be pyrotechnics," they continued, explaining that they were part of the "funeral production staff" from Los Angeles. Of course they were. Hunter's great friend and fan Johnny Depp had mobilized a full Hollywood production team to realize and stage his idol's funeral. Holy shit! After the absurdity of the animal-relocation request had sunk in, we patiently explained to them that the reality of Hollywood movie wranglers rounding up a mob of six-foot emus and a herd of llamas and alpacas might not be quite that simple. We told them that we'd take our chances with the fireworks. They left, but now we were really intrigued. Just exactly what was Depp planning?

ABOUT A MILE up the road the crew from LA had secured a house to serve as their command post. I decided to stop by and check things out. The rented house had been converted into a fully staffed on-location office humming with laptops, cell phones, and a frantic urgency. I introduced myself to the man in charge, an engaging dude named Jon Equis. He in turn led me upstairs and introduced me to a wiry, intense, young man named Foster Timms, who was casually strumming a guitar. I assumed he was a friend of a friend of Depp. We talked for a bit, and he played me some very quirky but cool original songs and told me he was going to play at the funeral. Then Jon Equis asked me if I'd like to play. Hell yeah! He went on to describe in vague terms how the ceremony was going to go down. Words won't do it justice . . . but I'll try my best.

From the back door of our house I watched the gleaming silver, tubelike tower rise above the trees, growing taller each day. The cylinders were hoisted into the air by a crane, and workmen dangling from rigging bolted it all together. This would be the cannon from which Hunter Thompson's ashes would be shot into the atmosphere. The base spanned twelve feet in diameter, and when completed, the cannon would be as high as a five-story building. When it had reached its full height workmen draped it in a blue scrim-style sheath. The final touch was a huge, red, double-thumbed fist with a green peyote button in the center of its palm. It was Hunter's Gonzo logo rendered in metal. After it was attached to the silver tower the workmen draped it in a blood-red shroud.

The buzz around town and around the world was insane. Network-news helicopters circled incessantly, photographers with telephoto lenses tramped through the scrub oak on the bluffs behind our house to get a better angle and exclusive shots of the towering funeral cannon. The FAA had to declare a temporary airspace restriction over our valley . . . it was getting weird and wacky, just the way Hunter would have liked it! In the days leading up to what was quickly becoming a historic event, Gonzo fans from all over the world began to descend on the Roaring Fork Valley. The local newspaper's headlines and editorial pages were filled with humorous and fond recollections of Thompson's legendary escapades, offset by more than a few grumpy opinions related to the general public's exclusion from the invitation-only affair.

In the late afternoon cars and buses began to arrive. Soon Woody Creek Road was bumper to bumper. The sheriff's department was doing its best, but the situation was getting out of control. There was nowhere to park, people were stopping and abandoning their cars on the roadside, many others were hiking through the surrounding fields and lining up on the high ridges surrounding Owl Farm, hoping to get a glimpse of whatever was about to happen. Aimee and I walked up our lane with our neighbors Bob and Marcie Beattie and Mark and Jeanne Bedell, crossed the road, and approached the large, canvas, rectangular tent that was erected to the right and slightly behind Hunter's house. We climbed a set of wooden steps and entered the tent. It was dark and quiet inside, with small groups of people gathered in hushed conversation. The interior was draped in black, illuminated with candles and soft lighting. The mood was reverential but void of any religious overtones. Former Senator George McGovern, Ed Bradley from *60 Minutes, Rolling Stone*'s Jann Wenner, Hunter's son Juan and his widow Anita, each in turn, stepped up to a small wooden lectern and spoke. It was respectful and brief. As soon as the eulogies ended the back of the tent was rolled up and the guests were ushered outside. The canvas curtain dropped down behind us. The mingling crowd was a mixed bag of longtime Aspen locals and many of Thompson's famous friends: Jack Nicholson, Charlie Rose, Bill Murray, Benicio del Toro, John Cusack, Sean Penn, Josh Hartnett, and at the center of it all, Johnny Depp, who blended into the star-studded crowd in an unassuming way, circulating on the periphery of the guests. It was understood that Depp had spent $2 million to realize Hunter's final exit. A video of Hunter and his longtime pal Ralph Steadman appeared on a large suspended screen. Excerpted from a 1978 BBC documentary, the film showed Thompson describing his own funeral and sketching the giant cannon that would blast his ashes into the sky over the land behind his house. "It's in the will . . . ," he narrated in his grumbly, mumbled style. Now, there in the middle of his beloved field, bathed in floodlights, stood the grandiose, shrouded, very manifestation of his dream departure, courtesy of Johnny Depp's respect and generosity. This was going to be historic, no doubt.

Suddenly, from behind the crowd, the back curtain of the tent rolled up and the somber black interior had been theatrically transformed into a raging bacchanal: red drapery; colored lights; multiple bartenders pouring any and every liquor drink known to man; waitresses circulating with trays of THC-infused cookies and brownies . . . it was on, Gonzo style! On a stage behind the tent a bunch of us starting jamming: Lyle Lovett, Johnny Depp, and David Amram, with my buddies John Michel and Michael Jude holding it down on drums and bass. But the live music was just an opening act for the real headliner about to take center stage.

When the live music ended, the signature distorted guitar riff from Norman Greenbaum's 1969 psychedelic classic, "Spirit in the Sky," blared from the PA system, coordinated with colorful theatrical lights slashing through the darkness. As the hypnotic, afterlife lyrics echoed overhead, there was an audible gasp from the assembled drunken and stoned as the long shrouds covering the tower suddenly dropped away. Then, on cue, klieg lights illuminated the shining 154-foot towering cannon, a gleaming silver superstar brandishing its throbbing double-thumbed red fist with a pulsing green peyote button. That had been the graphic Hunter had originally used in his failed 1970 campaign to be elected mayor of Aspen. But on this night, the colorful pulsing Gonzo logo seemed more like a passport to the great beyond. With Roman candles and exploding fireworks bursting from the base of the cannon, the moment for the iconic journalist's final chapter had arrived. There would be no postscript, just a big ending. *BOOM!* Hunter S. Thompson's ashes exploded, incandescent and glorious, into the blackness of the Colorado night. Just the way he wanted it.

A month or so later, the note Thompson left behind was discovered. It read in part: "No Fun—for anybody. 67. You are getting Greedy. Act your old age. Relax—This won't hurt."

It was titled, "Football Season Is Over." And in a way, at Owl Farm, it was.

Money, Money, Money

I t would be safe to say the early 1990s were lean years. There were no new recordings, and I was more focused on rebuilding my life in Colorado. Sure there
were the occasional shows, but the Hall and Oates heat was on a low simmer. I
was skiing every day, and my life was idyllic, therapeutic, and a welcome respite
from what I'd gone through in the prior few years. I left the mountains only on
occasion, one of which was to attend the Rock & Roll Hall of Fame ceremony,
then held in the ballroom of the Waldorf Astoria hotel in New York. There I happened to be seated at a table next to the CEO of Bertelsmann Music Group
(BMG), Michael Dornemann. Almost oblivious to the musical festivities, we
spent most of the night talking and bonding over our passion for skiing. Having
spent most of his winter adventures in the Alps of Europe, he was interested and
excited to come to Colorado. We made plans to meet there.

Over the course of the next few years we became friends, and he eventually
bought a house in Aspen. Later that winter he invited me to come along on a
private-helicopter trip to ski some remote peaks out beyond the boundaries of
the resorts. Heli-skiing is the holy grail of the sport. With an exclusive group

Me and my friend (and skiing partner) Michael Dornemann. *(Courtesy John Oates)*

of friends, we explored vast, pristine snowfields with no lift lines and crowds. It was wonderful, challenging, and exhilarating.

As I got to know Michael, my respect for his intelligence grew, and I thoroughly enjoyed his company. He was a fascinating, inquisitive conversationalist, knowledgeable on many subjects, and had a worldview that was broad and thought provoking. Eventually it occurred to me that in all the years of my involvement in the music business, I had never really had a personal relationship with anyone on the other side; by that I mean anyone who worked for the record labels or publishing companies that I was involved with or contracted to. They were always portrayed as the adversaries from whom I should remain at a long arm's length. A smile for the camera during a platinum-record presentation, a handshake at an awards ceremony or business event would be the extent of those relationships. Around this time, Dornemann was transitioning toward his retirement, and my self-imposed hiatus found us relating on a neutral field, neither of us with any agenda other than schussing the slopes and enjoying each other's company over après-ski dinners.

As we got to know each other better, some of those conversations on long chairlift rides eventually turned to subjects related to our careers in the music business. His insight and perspective were interesting to me for many reasons. One, he was German, and two, his company, BMG, had purchased the American labels RCA and Arista, Clive Davis's company. (Daryl and I were signed to RCA for most of our career, and then to Arista in the late '80s.)

Michael spoke humorously about his encounters with the colorful, quirky personalities who worked for the record labels, and about having to adjust to their unorthodox, American style of doing business. For him, the US music business was like the Wild West. Rules could bend, break, and often be determined by who brought the biggest six-shooter to the fight. Over the years he was involved in numerous meetings with our manager and lawyer, and he admitted to being surprised about certain demands that were presented on Daryl's and my behalf. He expressed to me that he felt uncomfortable with the fact that the artists were not directly and meaningfully involved in the negotiations. As time went by, my curiosity was piqued with regard to the negotiations that had gone on (again, this is on us) without our personal participation.

The more we talked the more I began to feel the nagging urge to uncover the secrets of the past that I wanted to put behind me but just couldn't ignore. Was there a way to find resolution?

Show Us the Money

Over the years, Daryl and I have always tried to keep our extended musical family together. Whether it be band members, techs, or roadies, loyalty has always played a big part in our lives. Back in 1978, a college kid on a path to become a teacher got a summer job selling T-shirts at a Marshall Tucker Band concert in Maryland. His name was Brian Doyle. He liked music and travel, had a developing sense for business, and within a year was working for us, handling merchandise sales at shows. His amiable and ambitious personality eventually landed him a promotion as our assistant tour manager. As the '80s exploded he progressed to become our tour manager and had a ringside seat for the crazy Hall and Oates pop-star circus.

Once Daryl and I had made the decision to cut back in the late '80s, and Mottola departed for greener corporate pastures, we hired Doyle as our manager. We had become close, and with our predilection to promote from within, Brian became the natural choice. But little did we know that in addition to managing us, he would also become an important asset in helping to uncover some of the deep, dark secrets of our twenty-year financial fiasco. He worked hard on our careers all through the '90s, but then he got involved on a whole new level. He began chasing down those suspicions that Michael Dornemann had opened my eyes to.

Doyle, along with his brother-in-law Richard Flynn and a small, dedicated group of lawyers, had begun working quietly in a small office in New York City. They had received some startling information from a fellow named Bob Donnelly. Donnelly was a sharp lawyer representing a number of big-name artists. He had begun investigating the accounting practices of some of the major record companies. His probe uncovered something called "suspense accounts." Over the years, record labels had been stashing away millions of dollars in unpaid royalties, rightfully due artists, while collecting interest on the sums for years. Donnelly explained to Doyle about these unpaid royalties accounts, and that working with current New York State Attorney General Eliot Spitzer, he had devised a creative strategy to apply New York State's Abandoned Property laws to these unpaid royalties and thus put pressure on the record companies to release this money to the rightful owners: the songwriters and artists.

When You Start to See the Light at the End of the Tunnel

With that information as a starting point, our team basically became music-business detectives and launched a forensic investigation of our former record labels going back to the early 1970s and '80s. What we discovered was staggering. Evidently this practice of withholding millions of dollars in artist royalties in these so-called suspense accounts was pervasive. The excuse, as I learned during the course of the investigation, was that the companies were withholding the funds because they did not know how to reach the individual artists in order to pay them!

Now I'm sure if you want to go back to the early years of rock-and-roll there were many obscure and perhaps deceased artists who actually were difficult to track down. But when it came to folks such as David Bowie, Dolly Parton, James Taylor, and Hall and Oates, it was laughable that record companies would even try to make that argument. An exhaustive May 2004 *Billboard* magazine feature detailed exactly what had happened, and the scope of corruption was breathtaking. The record companies knew what they had: tens of millions of dollars generating enormous amounts of interest every year. It's not hard to understand why they weren't going out of their way to distribute these funds.

But this was our money. We were entitled to it. Imagine working for a company for twenty years, having money placed in a 401K or some other holding account for you, only to have it mysteriously disappear because they could not track you down—even though they never really tried.

Once we realized all that was at stake we began multiple audits and negotiations to recover these funds. Not only was there little-to-no pushback, but after a few arduous months we began seeing checks in the hundreds of thousands of dollars. All told, we were able to recoup several million dollars' worth of royalties that had never been paid to us (and that nobody had ever fought for). Thanks to Donnelly, Spitzer, and our team's dogged persistence, we finally began to see some of what was rightfully ours, as did many other artists.

But this was far from the end of the financial reclamation process. Even though the suspense-account situation was in the process of being resolved, I was still haunted by the unsettled black hole of debt that had been amassed on our behalf over the years. The actual amount varied according to which side of the corporate fence one stood on. Estimates ranged from somewhere in the $8 to $9 million range. How did this happen? Well, recall the concept of taking large lump sums of cash advances against future royalties?

Each time an advance was made to us we had to give up a portion of our future rights as collateral. The more money we got, the more rights we had to give away. Of course Daryl and I had no idea of exactly to what extent this was happening, and when the dough was rolling in we didn't really care or think about it. Our royalties as songwriters, artists, and producers, and even the rights to our master recordings, were all cross collateralized against each other, so even though our music continued to generate income over the years, the debt never went away. It was a depressing and daunting task to try to uncover and untangle the huge files of byzantine, complex contracts and paperwork so that we might be able to continue reclaiming what was rightfully ours. Once that process was started more and more startling and shocking information came to light. Even though this multimillion-dollar debt remained, royalties from our income streams continued to flow into the record labels' bank accounts, and after many more expensive and tedious audits, we were able to determine that the constant flow of royalties that were generated every year had actually paid off the debt many times over! Yet the red balance still remained on the corporate books.

At this point I reached out to Michael Dornemann and asked if he could intercede on our behalf before he finally retired from his executive position at BMG. He did, and little by little we made headway toward recovering some of the rights to our intellectual properties. Songwriter royalties and publishing rights began to trickle back to Daryl and me. However the rights to all our master recordings were sold away to the record companies in perpetuity (that means forever)!

In a karmic twist of fate, the recovery of these royalties just so happened to coincide with a fiscal feeding frenzy on Wall Street for the acquisition of music and songwriting rights and catalogs. Suddenly, numerous financial entities were competing to buy up anything and everything. At last, kismet and timing crossed paths. So now, after having reacquired our rights, we took a chunk of our catalog and put it up for bid among three competing publishing companies. The bidding war was intense. Offers of large multiples based on the value of our newly acquired catalog were flying back and forth, validating all the hard work that we had put in over the decades. For all we had been through over the years, finally we were in control of our own destiny. A thirty-year musical legacy finally secure in the palm of our hands. But true to form, once we reclaimed what was ours, rather than rest on any kind of laurels, rather than take any victory laps, we did what we always did: buckled down, hit the road, and worked as hard as we ever had. In that sense it was no different than the very beginning. We committed ourselves to the music first and approached it with unending curiosity and interest. I guess some things never go out of season.

Peak Perspective

Moving through the dark, moist, wooded gully, a line of humpbacked shadows, breathing rhythmic and measured, trudging head down with deliberately efficient steps, lugging loaded packs with slender skis in inverted *V*s. Less than an hour ago, the light show of spring snow microcrystals vanished when the headlights faded and the heavy, lugged tires of my truck squeezed to a stop. It's late April, but at nine thousand feet and at 5:00 A.M., winter still rules the darkness. For me the preparation reverberated like the early 1970s, alive with the anticipation and excitement of doing something for the first time. Geared up, energized by the unknown ahead, a goal in mind but not yet in sight, just like long ago.

I take a final glance back as the silhouette of my truck is enveloped by the darkness. Now is not the time to dwell on distance or failures or achievements, only purpose marked by the metronome of one step at a time. Familiar territory, yet I've never set foot here before. A new mountain. In this moment, this world exists only in the four solitary headlamp beams of my climbing partners, each illuminating their chosen point of view, each carrying a weight. That's why we're here, that's what we signed on for. Dipping down through leafless anorexic branches, armored in cocoons of wool and Gore-Tex, I feel impenetrable.

Until I face a frozen log that crosses an icy stream. My mind whispers a reminder to proceed with caution, repeating, "You're only one slip away, one slip away."

A gig, a record deal, an encore . . . just first steps; best not to focus too far ahead. I follow the guide as he forges deftly forward into the woods. Surrounded and safe within the sweet scent of the pines, I can't and don't want to forget but move inexorably on . . . toward the beckoning pink threads of dawn. There is always that creep of doubt . . . there is always a chance to turn back . . . I didn't then and won't today. When you see the light at the end of the tunnel, remember, you're still in the fucking tunnel. That's my mantra. It stokes the furnace inside and pushes me onward. Then in the soft mauve of the eastern sunrise, Hayden Peak appears majestically through a break in the treetops. With head down, committed, I follow the route as it angles through a gully, then up into the light.

Shed layers of clothing, affix the climbing skins, and begin kicking and gliding upward. On this day, what lies ahead for me will be an unspoiled achievement, but in truth, I know, I'm just following in the path of those who came before me. At best I might leave a sign, an impression of my passing for others who will pass this way another day.

When the flush of beginning ebbs and the grind sets in, that is the signal to reach deep inside and wrestle with demons and doubts. In the high-rise offices back East, there is an entirely different mountain of paperwork to conquer. What once seemed insurmountable is poised to finally crumble. The $9 million black hole of debt is about to disappear up its own asshole. I raise my eyes, above and ahead the sky is clear and deep blue.

Passing ten thousand feet, the wind at my back kicks up a notch. Yeah, now's the time to keep it going, going, going, don't stop to think, just keep going. I know how to do that. The sun casts a distorted MTV-video shadow walking beside me on the snow. That's not me, that's just a remnant of what I was. The shadow fades and like the snow will melt away someday. Another step ahead is stepping out of the past, and the ascent is purity in joy and direction. Now there is no turning back, nor reason to want to. My gaze follows the undulations along the windswept ridge as the peak ahead appears, disappears, and reappears through the vaporous air.

What do you get when you really get there? There are mountains that have a false peak but you can climb them and claim them. I stand quietly in the dazzling sunlight and close my eyes. Time turned back in imaginary 3-D.

Thursday night.

May 23, 1985.

The air was sweet outside the Apollo Theater. It was a warm spring night in Harlem out on 125th Street, which still pulsed with light at this late hour, long after our shows with the Temps. I'd just started to accept what had happened inside. Not the concerts themselves, which will forever rank as some of my favorites. Rather, my thoughts returned to what Daryl and I had covertly decided: to walk away from our partnership . . . for a while.

To explore. To create. To be free.

If Spring was all about rebirth, then freedom was now more important than ever.

But little did I know how free I would be become.

Free to clean up tangled webs. Free to fall down. Free to grow up. Free to discover what really matters in life.

Free to shed the mustache. Free to reclaim what I earned. Free to rebuild, recover in Colorado, find true love, and start a family.

Free to take responsibility. Free to follow whatever way lies ahead.

Free to musically rekindle a smoldering ember of a passion left behind but not forgotten and recapture a creative spirit overshadowed by the pop music and stardom of the 1980s.

Free to change, just as the seasons do.

Back on the mountain, standing at thirteen thousand feet, I turn slowly to appreciate and embrace the 360 degrees of possibilities that lie before me. Down in the valley below, a winding road works its way toward the horizon. It looks like a good road to follow, and it's headed south.

To be continued. . . .

Afterword
Whole Oates
by Chris Epting

When **John and** I first began working on this collection, we crafted the guidelines and ground rules right up front.

First and foremost, we were not setting out to write a Hall and Oates book. The most obvious reason for this, of course, is the fact that Daryl Hall and John Oates are two distinctly different artists and men. Always have been and always will be. Of course, their creative union has produced some of the most beloved music of their generation, and a lot of that music would certainly need to be represented in a book like this. That's a given. But thankfully, neither of these men has ever tried to speak for the other, and so it would be beyond presumptuous for one of them to try and represent the group on his own. Their perspectives, angles, and experiences are wholly unique and separate.

Might they sit down one day together and collaborate to document what they have been through as a unit? Anything's possible.

But that was not this book.

So just what were some of the other guidelines and ground rules that we laid out? Pretty simple stuff, actually. First, keep things moving. Literally. The concept of movement has been such a central theme to John's life that he knew right away how integral it would have to be in his memoir. The movements of his life resulted in the sparkling journey you just experienced, just as I'm sure movement and travel have affected your own life. I hope you'll relate to why this concept is so important, and perhaps after reading this you'll even be reflecting about how your own travels have sculpted your life's experience.

John has also always been acutely aware of how the timing of his life has paralleled the evolution of so much vital American music. And so that became another running theme throughout his narrative. John grew up with the music, the music grew up with him, and along the parallel coils he had the opportunity to learn at the feet of many masters. Those voices and spirits live in this book, which is as much a celebration of the American music experience as it is the memoir of one man.

This is a history book, it's a travel book, it's a confessional, it's a diary, it's a fairy tale, and it's a love letter. You may think you know John from the music, the videos, and even the mustache. And on a certain level, you do know him thanks to those things. But those façades belie a knowledge, passion, insight, and intimacy which all burn deep in this artist.

Researching and writing about the early days was a challenge, but a fun one. Same for the period in the 1970s and '80s. You think you know the story, but you don't really know it until the curtain gets pulled back and the demons are confronted. It's amazing how many myths and clichés perpetrated by the heat of the MTV generation are simply smoke and mirrors.

One thing that never wavered was the work ethic. As John told me one day in Nashville while eating barbecue, "One thing we learned over the years was that there was never any guarantee of success. All you could do is do what you do and hope for the best. Work as hard as you can and hopefully good things will come from it. Just the basic blue-collar, American way. That was me and Daryl. From day one, that was always me and Daryl." He was fiercely dedicated to this project, rewriting over and over while constantly unlocking memories and observations. He joked that the process had become like "regressive therapy," but he took it just that seriously. One got a sense that this is simply how he is with everything, be it music, or driving, or flying, or skiing—he obsesses over craft.

A true revelation for me was understanding the reemergence of Hall and Oates in the 1990s, once the arena-packed glory days were seemingly done. Both as a solo artist and as a partner to Daryl, John wondered, as the first decade of the new century got underway, if anybody would be there to hear them. Radio as they had known it had all but dried up, as had the record business. But they still toured on a pretty regular basis, and the old fans still seemed to enjoy the songs. And if it all ended there, I think John would've been fine.

But then something started to happen. Hall and Oates stopped being a Reagan-era punchline and started being a hip, pop-culture touchstone. It was nothing they pushed. It just sort of happened.

It probably started when their music began getting used in movies. "You Make My Dreams" in particular became one of those go-to songs. In 1998 it was featured in *The Wedding Singer.* In 2008 it was in the Will Ferrell movie, *Step Brothers,* and the next year it was featured in *(500) Days of Summer,* which brought the song to a younger, fresh audience that probably wasn't very aware of Hall and Oates's music.

On television, both *Saturday Night Live* and *The Office* used "You Make My Dreams" to great effect, which also helped secure the song's place in the American psyche.

Hall and Oates were being embraced in a whole new way. There was even an animated TV series made about John's mustache!

Rap artists also had a lot to do with reestablishing Hall and Oates in the public consciousness. Everyone from Kanye to the Wu-Tang Clan to Heavy D to Method Man, along with dozens of other artists, sampled their music. That gave them some seriously strong street credibility. When Daryl started his show, *Live from Daryl's House,* in 2007, he began collaborating with a wide array of artists who weren't even born when Hall and Oates started out, but who loved their music. Chromeo and Gym Class Heroes are but a couple of examples. Talk about dedication—the front man for Gym Class Heroes, Travie McCoy, even had Daryl and John's faces tattooed on his hands.

These were great reminders of some of the influences that Hall and Oates have had on other artists. As John related to me in a Vegas hotel room, "I remember one night when the lead singer from Guns N' Roses, Axl Rose, came backstage to see Daryl and me. He was at the top of his game then, and what did he want to talk about? How much our music meant to him. 'Your first album, *Whole Oats*,' he said, 'is my favorite. The song 'Waterwheel' is still one of the most beautiful things I've ever heard, and I sing it all the time to myself to this day.' A pastoral, introspective ballad embraced by a hard-rock god. Go figure."

More recently, after appearing on a bill with John, Zeppelin drummer John Bonham's son, Jason, who performs a beautiful tribute show to his dad's music, told John that his father had been a huge fan of *Abandoned Luncheonette,* and that Jason remembered hearing it around the house as a child.

The *New York Times*, never a huge fan, in 2009 published an article titled "In Defense of Hall and Oates." Not that John and Daryl felt they ever needed any defending or cared about critics, but still, it was interesting to watch former critics turn the corner and make a case for their music.

And there were plenty of other journalistic props being paid to them.

"But Hall & Oates never garnered critical respect. In their 35 years of recording, the two have never taken home a Grammy. Yet their influence—the strong R&B inflections in unabashedly slick pop arrangements—can be heard in the platinum music of such contemporary acts as Robin Thicke, Justin Timberlake and Gym Class Heroes. Ben Gibbard of Death Cab for Cutie and Brandon Flowers of the Killers have name-checked Hall & Oates in interviews. Hip-hop stars such as Kanye West and Wyclef Jean have sampled their grooves and lyrics."—*Baltimore Sun*

"Prominent rockers like Brandon Flowers of the Killers and Patrick Stump of Fall Out Boy have outed themselves as vociferous fans. Last summer the Hall & Oates hit 'You Make My Dreams' played a

pivotal role in the beloved indie breakout film *(500) Days of Summer.*—
Los Angeles Times

What really did matter to John was being inducted (along with Daryl) in 2004 to the Songwriters Hall of Fame. It was a big deal to fans a number of years later when they were inducted into the Rock & Roll Hall of Fame, but that was more political. The Songwriters Hall of Fame was something special. It's a very serious organization that over the years has honored those who helped create and craft the great American songbook, and John was deeply moved by this honor.

And together, Daryl and John also made some new music. In 2003 they released an album called *Do It For Love.* They covered a bunch of their favorite soul songs in 2004 with the album *Our Kind of Soul,* and in 2006 they released a Christmas album—all on their own label. They were in control of their music, and of their lives. In 2015 they even played at the White House, invited by the first couple. Amazing. Those two college kids that randomly met in a service elevator, playing for the leader of the free world.

Why is their music ubiquitous today? John has a few theories. "First, there is diversity. No two of our hits sound remotely the same. We also tapped into many diverse influences. Also, thanks to the writing contributions of Sara and Janna Allen, often we had a female point of view represented. But I think the bottom line is simply that we wrote and recorded well-crafted songs with some of the best musicians on the planet. We cared about our music. Looking out at the crowds today, which continue to be huge and passionate, it's amazing to see such a broad cross section of people. All ages, all nationalities. Just like it was back at the Philly coffeehouses in the late '60s. We played for everyone then, and very little has changed except the size of the venues."

Because they cared about their music, their music took care of them, through thick and thin. Which then allowed John the freedom to move ahead to even greener pastures in Nashville, where he discovered a solo voice that had been brewing and steeping for years. His acceptance in the Nashville community seems to have stoked and inspired John in ways that will affect him deeply the rest of his life. In a sense, New York and Philly routes notwithstanding, I get the feeling this is where he was born to be. Somewhere, Jerry Ricks must be smiling. Doc Watson, too.

We didn't set out to write a Hall and Oates book. We wrote a book about John. But hopefully you also learned a lot about this magical duo, the amount of work it took to establish themselves, and their perseverance as they did.

But beyond that, we hope you enjoyed the story of an American kid who simply fell in love with American music and never looked back.

Thank you, John, for the music, and for the privilege of being allowed to help tell your story.

Acknowledgments

A full life is a like a gem with countless facets, each one absorbing, reflecting, and refracting the light that touches it.

To my parents, who never asked me what I wanted to be when I grew up. For that alone, I dedicate this book to Anna and Alfred Oates, along with more than sixty years of respect and appreciation for their ethnic values, good genes, and exemplary relationship. To my sister, Diane Oates Lopez, who endured being forced to wear her prom dress while being pressed into the role of teenage background singer, and who has gone on to become a highly respected, Emmy-winning television producer.

To my loving wife, Aimee, who has stood by me every step of the way and whose inner resolve should never be underestimated. She taught me how to be a farmer, shared her solid Midwestern values, and set me on the road to a new way of thinking about life and relationships. To our son, Tanner—his high ideals, moral compass, and independent thinking fill me with pride. Thank you for being your own man and for not following in your father's footsteps. To Gary and Sharon Pommier along with Aimee's five brothers and her sister, who over the past twenty years have given me a second home on their Illinois farm.

Great teachers, some of whom you have read about in these pages, have blessed my life. There have been many more, and although not mentioned by name, their lessons live on in my thoughts, heart, and writing.

Music has defined my life and taken me on unimagined journeys. So I thank all the gifted fellow musicians, songwriters, producers, and engineers who have had a hand in molding and shaping that experience along the way. To all of you, my deepest gratitude. To have spent a lifetime surrounded by talented, creative people is a gift that goes beyond any measurable value.

I sincerely hope you know that the lack of a personal acknowledgment is not in any way representative of the high regard that I hold each and every one of you, and of how much I cherish our friendships.

Thank you to my editor, Marc Resnick, and the supportive, creative St. Martin's Press team in the Flatiron Building for showing me the view and taking a chance with a first-time author.

As this book approached four hundred pages, I purposely and reluctantly made the decision to conclude this story at the beginning of my solo career. The unexpected musical experience that has unfolded over the last sixteen years is deserving of more than a footnote at the end of this volume. It is a tale of profound personal rediscovery, and the long list of deep friendships that have accompanied me on this journey are deserving of a detailed and respectful retelling. So to all of my wonderful friends, fellow musicians, and business associates in Nashville and around the world that have supported my solo efforts . . . I didn't forget you. Your dedication and belief in me is something I hope to express in the depth that it deserves. To the current Hall and Oates band and team who soldier on into the new millennium, and to the millions of fans whose love has continued to support me for the last forty plus years . . . a heartfelt thank you!

Thanks to my agent, Peter McGuigan, and my team of Jonathan Wolfson, Judith Ricci, Terry Mathley, and Kate Richardson for keeping the wheels greased, and lastly, to Chris Epting for the guidance, stewardship, dogged research, and positive spirit of collaboration that he brought to this project. Were it not for his encouragement and a series of insightful interviews this book would not exist. Thank you, Chris.

Chris Epting

As always, to my wife, Jean, son Charlie, and daughter Claire—thank you for your constant support and patience. To John's many friends, bandmates, etc., who allowed me to interview them for this book, I am deeply grateful for your time and stories. Barbara Wilson D'Andrea, your classic photos are priceless for a project like this; thank you for your generosity. To my agent, Peter McGuigan, thank you for being as excited about this book as I was, and to everyone at St. Martin's Press, in particular our editor, Marc Resnick, thank you for giving this project the home it deserved with such passion and enthusiasm. Lastly, thank you to John Oates. It's one thing to, for decades, admire an artist's gifts from afar, but to have the opportunity to help tell their story is a rare privilege. And as much as a musical craftsman as John is, watching him spread his wings as an author has truly been a delight.

Index